COOKING WITH
Bon Appétit

COOKING WITH
Bon Appétit

Recipe Yearbook 1989

Editors' Choice of Recipes from 1988

THE KNAPP PRESS
Publishers
Los Angeles

Copyright © 1989 by Knapp Communications Corporation

Published by The Knapp Press
5900 Wilshire Boulevard, Los Angeles, California 90036

Library of Congress Catalog Number: 83-643303

ISBN: 0-89535-217-6

Bon Appétit Books offers cookbook stands. For details on ordering please write:
  Bon Appétit Books
  Premium Department
  Sherman Turnpike
  Danbury, CT 06816

On the Cover: *Deep-Dish Cranberry Apple Raisin Pie. Photographed by Irwin Horowitz.*

Printed and bound in the United States of America
10   9   8   7   6   5   4   3   2   1

❧ Contents

❧ *Foreword*

Here in our third annual collection of recipes from *Bon Appétit* magazine, you'll find an exciting diversity of delicious and memorable dishes. From the spicy surprise of a chili and cheese dip to the all-American Rocky Road Fudge on the last page, we offer terrific recipes and inspiration for preparing an elegant dinner party or a casual family meal. Some of the country's most talented cooks and finest restaurants have contributed to the 200-plus recipes here, chosen by the editors to represent the year's best and to reflect important trends.

One of the outstanding features this year is a trend toward assertive spicing—there is an emphasis on good-quality ingredients with strong fresh flavors. We're no longer shying away from dishes with a bit more zip—along with fresh herbs, you'll find spices such as cumin and cayenne used creatively to add kick to everything from Tomato and Cucumber Soup with Cayenne Pepper Croutons to Spicy Indian Beef Stew.

But the most important spice that you'll find throughout this book is variety. In addition to the boldly flavored international dishes like Thai Cilantro Beef and Potatoes, Grilled Swordfish with Japanese Eggplant and Sesame Sauce and Mediterranean Fish and Orzo Soup, there are plenty of good old-fashioned comfort foods, things like roast turkey with corn bread dressing, and Black Bottom Devil's Food Cake.

The American regional cooking that has been so popular during the past few years is still going strong in dishes such as Traditional New England Clam Chowder with Fried Leeks, Barbecued Spareribs with Red-Hot Sauce and Spicy Fried Chicken. You'll see a lot of these favorites updated—for instance, the all-American hamburger is here, but now it's better than ever—our jazzed-up version is topped with a zippy, creamy blue cheese sauce.

A sense of fun in cooking and eating comes shining through in many of the recipes. You'll find inventive, creative dishes that put together ingredients in a new way, with perfectly delicious results. Among these twist-on-tradition dishes is Cheese Quesadillas with Black-Eyed-Pea Salsa—Mexico meets Mississippi in this terrific appetizer that substitutes that Southern staple, black-eyed peas, for the traditional tomatoes in a zesty salsa.

The recipes in this collection come from all areas of the magazine, from departments like "The Weekday Cook," "Too Busy to Cook?" and "R.S.V.P." to cooking class, restaurant, entertaining and travel features. The "Cooking Healthy" column, initiated last year, has become one of the most popular in the magazine, and you'll find some of those great-tasting, light and healthy recipes here. The new year brought a new look to an old *Bon Appétit* favorite—the "Food Processor" column became "Shortcuts with Style," and was expanded to include innovative micro-wave tips, timesaving cooking techniques and more inspiration for the busy cook.

The new design of *Bon Appétit*, which had its debut in the October issue, gave the magazine a fresh, updated look. We added more lively features and recipes. And many of those recipes are now shorter, recognizing that we don't have as much time to cook as we'd sometimes like. All in all, the new look means more food and entertaining for today's lifestyle, more of what *Bon Appétit* is all about.

To round out our review of trends, we've included at the back of the book a section called "News '88—The Year of Food and Entertaining in Review." Consisting of brief notes on new food products and services, restaurants and people, cookbooks, travel tips and diet news, "News '88" tracks some of the most interesting developments of the year. All prices, addresses and other information have been updated as of this yearbook's publication date.

Enjoy the best of 1988!

1 ❧ Appetizers

This year's best appetizers are exciting, colorful and diverse—the international array that we present here includes Italian, Mexican, French, Oriental and Middle Eastern specialties that go perfectly with any kind of meal, from casual to elegant. Minted Chick-Pea Dip, a lively version of hummus, the popular Middle Eastern spread, is a natural with pita bread and crisp vegetables. Another terrific partner to fresh vegetables is Ginger Peanut Dip—it gets its intriguing Oriental flavor from a blend of creamy peanut butter, garlic, cilantro and ginger. For the Italian Salami and Cheese Crostini, toasted bread slices are topped with garlic, olive oil, salami and provolone cheese for a simple yet satisfying appetizer—a zesty beginning to a casual Italian meal.

For a sophisticated starter, you might try Caviar in Potato Baskets, baked in miniature muffin tins and filled with red, golden and black caviars for a pretty presentation, or Shrimp-filled Dumplings in Basil Cream Sauce, made in a snap with purchased won ton wrappers.

Tamari Mixed Nuts

You can prepare these nuts up to one week ahead. Use one type of nut or a mixture of your favorites.

Makes about 4 cups

1 pound assorted shelled nuts, such as walnuts, almonds, pecans and cashews
4½ tablespoons tamari soy sauce* or regular soy sauce

1½ tablespoons vegetable oil
2¼ teaspoons chili oil** or ¾ teaspoon cayenne pepper mixed with 2 teaspoons vegetable oil
¾ teaspoon salt, preferably coarse

Preheat oven to 350°F. Place nuts in large roasting pan. Sprinkle with soy sauce, vegetable oil, chili oil and salt; toss well. Bake until nuts are toasted, stirring twice, about 10 minutes.

Cool nuts completely. *(Can be prepared 1 week ahead. Store in airtight container at room temperature.)*

*Tamari soy sauce is available at specialty and natural foods stores.

**Chili oil is available at oriental markets and some supermarkets.

Marinated Cauliflower with Orange and Thyme

This dish is best prepared one day ahead. Serve with party picks or small forks. Present as an accompaniment to a purchased country-style pâté.

20 servings

2 heads cauliflower (about 2 pounds each), cored and separated into florets
¼ cup fresh lemon juice

1 cup olive oil
½ cup white wine vinegar
¼ cup water
2 tablespoons slivered orange peel
2 garlic cloves, crushed

1½ teaspoons salt
1 teaspoon fresh thyme leaves or ¼ teaspoon dried, crumbled
1 cup diced onion
1 cup diced red bell pepper
¼ cup fresh orange juice
¼ teaspoon freshly ground pepper

2 tablespoons minced fresh parsley
Fresh thyme sprigs (optional)

Bring large pot of salted water to boil. Add cauliflower and lemon juice and cook until cauliflower is crisp-tender, about 3 minutes. Drain. Refresh under cold water and drain. Place cauliflower in large bowl.

Bring oil, vinegar, ¼ cup water, orange peel, garlic, salt and 1 teaspoon thyme to boil in heavy large skillet over high heat. Remove from heat. Mix in onion, red bell pepper, orange juice and pepper. Pour marinade over cauliflower. Cool. Cover and refrigerate overnight, stirring once or twice.

Drain cauliflower; mound on platter. Sprinkle with parsley. Garnish with thyme sprigs and serve.

Minted Chick-Pea Dip

This is a version of hummus, *a popular Middle Eastern spread usually eaten with pita bread.*

Makes about 3 cups

2 15½-ounce cans chick-peas (garbanzo beans), drained
⅓ cup fresh lemon juice
1 tablespoon coarsely chopped garlic
½ teaspoon salt
⅓ cup olive oil

1 tablespoon chopped fresh mint leaves
1 tablespoon chopped fresh parsley
2 tablespoons olive oil
Pita chips*
½ pound large carrots, peeled and cut into ⅛-inch-thick rounds

Coarsely puree chick-peas with lemon juice, garlic and salt in processor. Gradually add ⅓ cup oil in thin steady stream and blend to smooth puree. Spoon dip into shallow bowl. Cover and chill. *(Can be prepared 2 days ahead.)*

Sprinkle mint and parsley over dip. Drizzle with 2 tablespoons oil. Place bowl with dip on platter. Surround with pita chips and carrots.

*Available at some specialty foods stores. If unavailable, cut pita bread into wedges and cook on baking sheet in 325°F oven until dry and crisp.

Ginger Peanut Dip with Raw Vegetables

10 servings

1¾ cups creamy peanut butter
2 medium onions, chopped
6 garlic cloves, minced
6 tablespoons fresh lemon juice
¼ cup chopped fresh cilantro
4 teaspoons grated fresh ginger
4 teaspoons soy sauce
2 teaspoons dried red pepper flakes
2 teaspoons turmeric
Vegetables, such as blanched Chinese long beans, snow peas, peeled jicama and water chestnuts, carrots and celery

Combine all ingredients except vegetables in blender or processor and puree until smooth. Add water to thin if necessary. Transfer to bowl. Serve peanut dip with an assortment of vegetables.

Chili Con Queso Dip

Serve with frosty Margaritas and/or Mexican beer to get the party going.

Makes 4 cups

2 bacon slices, cut into strips
3 tablespoons chopped green onion
1 large tomato, peeled and chopped
½ cup chopped canned green chilies
½ teaspoon ground cumin
½ teaspoon salt
½ teaspoon dried oregano, crumbled
8 ounces sharp cheddar cheese, grated (2 cups)
8 ounces American cheese, grated (2 cups)
3 tablespoons tomato juice (optional)
Minced fresh cilantro
Tortilla Chips*

Fry bacon in flameproof serving dish over medium heat until crisp. Add onion and tomato and cook until onion softens, stirring occasionally, about 5 minutes. Stir in next 4 ingredients. Reduce heat to low. Gradually add cheeses, stirring until melted and bubbling. Thin with tomato juice if desired. Garnish with cilantro. Serve immediately with Tortilla Chips.

*Tortilla Chips

6 servings

Vegetable oil (for deep frying)
1½ dozen 6-inch corn tortillas, cut into 6 wedges each

Line bottom of brown paper bag with several layers of paper towels. Heat oil in deep fryer or heavy large saucepan to 375°F. Add tortilla wedges in batches of 12 and fry until crisp, turning with spoon, about 1½ minutes. Using slotted spoon, transfer to prepared bag. Serve chips in basket.

Spicy Cheddar Cheese Spread

This rich and spicy cheese mixture can be shaped into a ball or log or packed into a crock. Accompany the spread with assorted crackers, celery sticks, apple slices and salami-wrapped breadsticks.

Makes about 3½ cups

8 ounces chilled sharp cheddar cheese, shredded
8 ounces chilled Monterey Jack cheese, shredded
1 medium onion, quartered and shredded
½ cup (1 stick) unsalted butter, cut into small pieces

2 teaspoons hot pepper sauce (such as Tabasco)

Assorted crackers
Celery sticks
Apple slices
Salami-wrapped breadsticks

Combine first 5 ingredients in large bowl. Cover and let stand until cheeses soften, about 1 hour.

Using electric mixer, beat cheese mixture until fluffy, stopping occasionally to scrape down sides of bowl. Spoon cheese into crock. *(Can be prepared 3 days ahead. Cover and refrigerate. Bring to room temperature before serving.)* Serve cheese spread with crackers, celery, apple slices and salami-wrapped breadsticks.

Goat Cheese Marinated in Rosemary and Lemon

Goat cheese is available in a variety of shapes, sizes and flavors. For this recipe, be sure to select a plain one, without an ash or an herb coating, but feel free to vary the shape by choosing discs, pyramids and/or logs. Begin preparation at least two and up to five days ahead.

20 servings

1 pound goat cheese
1 tablespoon fresh rosemary leaves, minced or 1 teaspoon dried, crumbled
1 tablespoon chopped fresh lemon peel
1 garlic clove, flattened
¼ teaspoon freshly ground pepper

1 cup olive oil

2 heads Belgian endive, cored and separated into leaves
2 pounds plum tomatoes, quartered or cherry tomatoes
Fresh rosemary sprigs (optional)
French bread slices

Place cheese in dish just large enough to accommodate in single layer. Add 1 tablespoon rosemary, lemon peel, garlic and pepper. Drizzle oil over. Cover and let stand 4 hours at room temperature. Refrigerate cheese at least 2 days and up to 5 days, occasionally spooning marinade over.

Let cheese stand 30 minutes at room temperature. Transfer to platter using slotted spoon. Drizzle marinade over. Arrange endive around cheese in spoke pattern. Garnish with tomatoes and rosemary sprigs. Serve with bread.

Cheese-filled Figs with Prosciutto

Any remaining filling is delicious on toast.

Makes 24

24 large or 48 small dried black figs
4 ounces Roquefort cheese
4 ounces Dolcelatte cheese*
6 tablespoons whipping cream
1½ teaspoons mascarpone cheese**
or cream cheese

24 thin prosciutto slices
Italian parsley
Cherry tomatoes

Split each fig down center; do not cut through base. Blend next 4 ingredients until smooth. Mound 1 scant teaspoonful onto half of each fig. Press halves together to re-form fig. *(Can be prepared 1 day ahead. Cover and refrigerate.)* Roll prosciutto slices into nests. Arrange on platter. Set fig in center of each. Garnish with parsley and tomatoes and serve.

*Dolcelatte cheese is a mild Gorgonzola cheese that is available at Italian markets.

**Italian cream cheese available at Italian markets and some supermarkets.

Caviar in Potato Baskets

Assorted caviars—red, golden and black—make a pretty presentation.

Makes about 48

2 cups water
1 pound russet potatoes, peeled

2 eggs
½ red onion, finely chopped
3 tablespoons snipped fresh chives
2 tablespoons instant flour
   Salt and freshly ground pepper

Crème fraîche
Caviar (such as salmon roe, golden whitefish and black lumpfish)
Fresh parsley leaves
Chopped hard-cooked eggs
Snipped fresh chives

Preheat oven to 375°F. Oil 4 miniature nonstick muffin tins with 2-inch-wide cups. Put water in work bowl of processor. Shred potatoes in processor. Let stand in water 25 minutes.

Whisk eggs in large bowl. Add onion and 3 tablespoons chives. Drain potatoes. Press dry with towel. Add to eggs. Mix in flour. Spoon 2 tablespoons mixture into each muffin cup. Form cup by patting mixture up to rim and leaving hollow in center. Bake until potatoes are tender and edges are golden brown, about 25 minutes. Sprinkle with salt and pepper.

Place dollop of crème fraîche in each potato cup. Top with caviar. Garnish with parsley. Serve, passing eggs and snipped chives separately.

Italian Salami and Cheese Crostini

2 servings; can be doubled or tripled

6 ½-inch-thick diagonally cut French bread baguette slices
   Olive oil
1 garlic clove, flattened
   Freshly ground pepper

6 thin slices Italian dry salami
6 slices provolone cheese (smoked or regular)
   Dried oregano
6 Italian parsley leaves (optional)

Preheat broiler. Broil one side of bread slices until toasted. Brush second side of each with oil, rub lightly with garlic, then sprinkle with pepper. Broil second side until toasted. Top with salami and cheese, folding cheese under to fit. Sprinkle with oregano. Broil until cheese melts. Top with parsley.

Cheese Quesadillas with Black-Eyed-Pea Salsa

If you're short on time, use purchased corn tortillas for this delicious appetizer, snack or light main course.

4 servings

Cornmeal Tortillas
1½ cups sifted all purpose flour
½ cup white cornmeal
1 teaspoon salt
2 tablespoons solid vegetable shortening
½ cup warm water

Filling
2 ounces Monterey Jack cheese, shredded (½ cup)
2 ounces white cheddar cheese, shredded (½ cup)

2 ounces Havarti cheese, shredded (½ cup)
2 tablespoons freshly grated Parmesan cheese

1 tablespoon butter
1 tablespoon vegetable oil
4 green onions, minced
2 teaspoons minced jalapeño chilies

Sour cream
Minced fresh cilantro
Black-Eyed-Pea Salsa*

For tortillas: Combine flour, cornmeal and salt in bowl. Add shortening and cut in until mixture resembles coarse meal. Stir in water until incorporated. Gather dough into ball. Wrap in plastic. Let stand 1 hour.

For filling: Mix cheeses in bowl.

Halve dough. Cover 1 piece to prevent drying. Flatten other into disc. Cut into 4 wedges; form each into ball. Roll each out on lightly floured surface to 8-inch-diameter tortilla. Repeat with remaining dough.

Melt butter with oil on griddle or in large cast-iron skillet over medium-high heat. Set 1 or 2 tortillas on griddle. Heat lightly and turn over. Cover each with ¼ of cheese mixture, then sprinkle with green onions and jalapeños. Top each with another tortilla, pressing down. Cook until cheese melts, turning once, about 4 minutes. Repeat with remaining tortillas, filling, onions and chilies.

Cut each quesadilla into wedges. Arrange on plate. Garnish with sour cream and cilantro. Serve with salsa.

*Black-Eyed-Pea Salsa

Makes about 3 cups

1 15-ounce can black-eyed peas, drained and rinsed
1 medium red bell pepper, diced
2 tablespoons minced onion
1 tablespoon minced fresh **parsley**

1 tablespoon minced fresh cilantro
1 teaspoon minced jalapeño chili
2 tablespoons vegetable oil
2 tablespoons red wine vinegar
Salt and freshly ground pepper

Place first 6 ingredients in bowl. Mix in oil and vinegar. Season with salt and pepper. Cover and refrigerate. *(Can be prepared 1 day ahead.)*

Green Beans and Prosciutto with Herbed Mayonnaise

Use any leftover mayonnaise as a vegetable dip or a salad dressing.

4 servings

Mayonnaise
1 egg
2 tablespoons cider vinegar
2 teaspoons Dijon mustard
½ cup vegetable oil
½ cup olive oil

1½ tablespoons snipped fresh chives
Salt and freshly ground pepper

1 pound green beans, trimmed
16 paper-thin slices prosciutto

For mayonnaise: Mix egg, vinegar and mustard in processor. With machine running, gradually add both oils through feed tube in slow steady stream. Process until thickened. Mix in chives. Season with salt and generous amount of pepper. *(Can be prepared 3 days ahead. Cover and chill.)*

Blanch green beans in large pot of boiling salted water until just crisp-tender. Drain. Rinse with cold water and drain well. *(Can be prepared 1 day ahead. Cover and refrigerate.)*

Spread some mayonnaise in pool on each of 4 plates. Mound green beans in center. Drape prosciutto over beans, allowing ends of beans to show.

Shrimp with Avocado and Watercress Dip

Many supermarkets are now conveniently selling freshly shelled, deveined and cooked shrimp—the perfect "dippers" for this delicious avocado and watercress spread. For crunch, offer tortilla chips along with the shrimp.

Makes about 2¾ cups

1 bunch watercress, tough stems discarded
2 ripe avocados, halved, pitted and peeled
1 cup plain yogurt or ½ cup plain yogurt mixed with ½ cup sour cream
½ cup chopped green onions
2 tablespoons fresh lemon juice

1 tablespoon chopped drained anchovies
1 garlic clove, crushed
1 teaspoon salt

3 pounds large cooked, peeled and deveined shrimp
Tortilla chips (optional)

Blanch watercress in saucepan of boiling water 2 minutes. Drain; rinse under cold water. Wrap in double thickness of paper towels and squeeze dry. Puree watercress, avocados, yogurt, onions, lemon juice, anchovies, garlic and salt in processor. Spoon into serving bowl. Press plastic wrap onto surface and refrigerate until cold. *(Can be prepared 6 hours ahead.)*

Place bowl with dip on platter. Surround with shrimp and chips and serve.

Gravlax with Mustard-Dill Sauce

Dill-cured salmon is terrific on a buffet. Let the fish marinate three days.

20 servings

2 1- to 1½-pound center-cut salmon fillets (preferably Norwegian)
2 tablespoons coarse salt
2 tablespoons sugar
2 teaspoons coarsely ground white pepper

1 large bunch dill

Lemon slices
Fresh dill sprigs (garnish)
Mustard-Dill Sauce*
Swedish rye bread

Remove all bones from salmon using tweezers. Combine salt, sugar and pepper in small bowl. Sprinkle 1 tablespoon of mixture in glass baking dish. Spread with layer of dill. Top with 1 salmon fillet, skin side down. Spread fish with all but 1 tablespoon of salt mixture; cover with most of remaining dill. Top with second salmon fillet skin side up. Spread with remaining salt mixture, then remaining dill. Cover with plastic wrap. Top with board or tray and place 3 to 4 cans or bricks atop board as weight. Refrigerate 3 days, turning salmon and basting with brine twice a day.

Scrape all marinade and dill from salmon. Pat dry. Cut across grain into very thin diagonal slices. Arrange on platter. Garnish with lemon and dill sprigs. Serve with mustard sauce and bread.

*Mustard-Dill Sauce

Makes about 1½ cups

¼ cup Dijon mustard
2 tablespoons white wine vinegar
2 tablespoons sugar

1 teaspoon freshly ground pepper
1 cup vegetable oil
6 tablespoons minced fresh dill

Mix first 4 ingredients in medium bowl. Gradually whisk in oil. *(Can be prepared 2 days ahead. Cover and refrigerate.)* Mix in dill just before serving.

Shrimp-filled Dumplings in Basil Cream Sauce

8 servings

1 tablespoon unsalted butter
½ pound uncooked small shrimp, peeled, deveined and chopped into ¼-inch pieces
1 medium shallot, minced
2 garlic cloves, minced
3 ounces mushrooms, chopped
1 tablespoon chicken stock or canned broth
1 teaspoon white wine vinegar
½ teaspoon salt

⅓ cup ricotta cheese
⅓ cup (or more) freshly grated Parmesan cheese
2 tablespoons fresh lime juice
2 tablespoons minced fresh basil

1 12-ounce package 3¼-inch won ton wrappers
1 egg, beaten to blend (glaze)

Peanut oil (for deep frying)
Basil Cream Sauce*

Melt butter in heavy medium skillet over medium-high heat. Add shrimp, shallot and garlic and toss until shrimp begin to turn pink, about 2 minutes. Add mushrooms, stock, vinegar and salt and cook until shrimp are pink, 1 to 2 minutes. Stir in ricotta, ⅓ cup Parmesan, lime juice and basil, adding more Parmesan if liquid remains. Cool. *(Can be prepared 3 hours ahead. Cover and chill.)*

Set won ton wrapper on surface. Place 1 heaping teaspoon shrimp mixture in center. Brush edges with glaze. Bring corners and sides to center; twist top. Repeat with remaining won ton wrappers and shrimp mixture.

Heat oil in deep fryer to 375°F. Fry pockets (in batches; do not crowd) until crisp and brown, about 1 minute. Remove using slotted spoon and drain on paper towels. Divide pockets among plates. Spoon sauce around.

*Basil Cream Sauce

Makes 1⅓ cups

¼ cup (½ stick) unsalted butter
6 garlic cloves, minced
1 cup whipping cream

½ cup freshly grated Parmesan cheese (about 2 ounces)
¼ cup minced fresh basil

Melt butter in heavy medium saucepan over medium-low heat. Add garlic and stir until slightly softened, about 2 minutes. Add remaining ingredients and simmer until thickened, about 10 minutes. Serve immediately.

2 ❦ Soups and Salads

Elegant and sophisticated or down-home and hearty, make-ahead soups are perfect for easy entertaining—they can be made a day or two ahead, in most cases, or even further in advance and frozen. For a casual get-together, you might even serve a colorful buffet of soups, including both light and hearty ones, with crusty breads and breadsticks, a green salad and perhaps fruit or ice cream with buttery cookies for dessert.

Deliciously satisfying on their own, soups are also versatile—they can be partnered with a variety of different dishes to fit any occasion. Spinach Soup with Clams and "Plenty of Garlic" makes a zesty lunch or light supper accompanied with a vegetable-filled omelet. For an informal dinner party, you might serve Tomato and Cucumber Soup with Cayenne Pepper Croutons as a prelude to chicken and potatoes simply roasted with herbs, or Cream of Brie and Leek Soup with pork tenderloins or chops. For an elegant dinner, try Apple Soup with Roquefort Croutons (make it a day ahead to reduce last-minute preparation) garnished with red and green apple slices and followed with roast Cornish game hens.

Another sure winner for a first course or side dish is a fresh-tasting salad. Here you'll find some old favorites with new twists, along with some terrific surprises. For a light starter, you might try Romaine, Walnut and Radish Salad or Grapefruit, Red Onion and Avocado Salad. More hearty possibilities include Pasta Shell Salad with Walnut Pesto—add tiny shrimp, salami julienne or broccoli florets as toppings if you like—or Olive Rice Salad with bright bits of green bell pepper and red cabbage.

Salads also make fast, fabulous main courses, and the recipes here include chicken, beef, seafood and vegetarian combinations. For a truly easy entrée, try Chicken Salad with Roasted Walnuts—it takes only minutes to make with a barbecued chicken from the market or deli.

 Soups

Gazpacho with Sautéed Scallops

If you plan to serve this immediately, start with well-chilled vegetables and tomato juice. Otherwise make it at least one hour ahead and refrigerate.

2 servings; can be doubled or tripled

1 cucumber, peeled, halved lengthwise and seeded
1 green bell pepper, halved
½ small red onion, cut into 1-inch pieces
2 cups tomato juice
¼ cup olive oil
3 tablespoons red wine vinegar

⅛ teaspoon hot pepper sauce (such as Tabasco)
Salt and freshly ground pepper

1 tablespoon olive oil
¾ pound sea scallops, halved
Minced fresh cilantro

Cut half of cucumber and half of green pepper into 1-inch pieces. Place in processor with onion. Puree coarsely. Add tomato juice and process until coarse puree forms. Add ¼ cup oil, vinegar, hot pepper sauce, salt and pepper and mix to blend. Transfer to medium bowl. Cut remaining cucumber and green pepper into ⅓-inch cubes and add to soup. *(Can be prepared 1 day ahead and refrigerated.)* Divide between 2 soup bowls.

Heat 1 tablespoon oil in heavy medium skillet over high heat. Add scallops. Season with salt and pepper. Sauté until just opaque, about 2 minutes. Divide between soup bowls. Top with cilantro and serve immediately.

Chilled Avocado Lime Cream Soup

6 servings

2 tablespoons (¼ stick) butter
1 small onion, chopped
1 garlic clove, minced

4 large ripe avocados, peeled, pitted, cut into chunks
4½ cups (or more) chicken stock or canned broth

½ cup sour cream
2 tablespoons (or more) fresh lime juice
1 cup whipping cream
Salt and freshly ground white pepper
6 thin lime slices

Melt butter in heavy medium skillet over low heat. Add onion and garlic and sauté until softened, about 15 minutes. Cool onion mixture.

Transfer half of onion mixture to blender. Puree with 2 avocados, 2¼ cups stock, ¼ cup sour cream and 1 tablespoon lime juice. Transfer to bowl. Repeat with remaining onion mixture, avocados, 2¼ cups stock, sour cream and 1 tablespoon lime juice. Add to bowl. Whisk in cream. Season with salt and white pepper. Cover and refrigerate until well chilled, at least 2 and up to 8 hours. Thin soup with additional stock if desired. Adjust seasoning with additional lime juice if desired. Ladle into chilled bowls. Garnish with lime slices.

Cream of Brie and Leek Soup

Use a good-quality Brie with a creamy white rind. Start the soup several hours ahead to mellow flavors.

6 servings

½ cup (1 stick) unsalted butter
8 large leeks (white parts only), finely chopped
4 cups (or more) chicken stock or canned low-salt broth
½ cup all purpose flour

4 cups half and half
1½ pounds Brie cheese, chilled, cut into small cubes (with rind)
Salt and freshly ground pepper
2 tablespoons snipped fresh chives or minced fresh Italian parsley

Melt ¼ cup butter in heavy large deep skillet over medium heat. Add leeks and cook until translucent, stirring frequently, about 4 minutes. Add 4 cups stock and bring to boil. Reduce heat, cover and simmer until leeks are tender, about 25 minutes. Puree mixture in batches in blender.

Melt remaining ¼ cup butter in heavy large nonaluminum saucepan over medium heat. Add flour and stir 2 minutes. Blend in half and half 1 cup at a time; whisk until smooth. Add ¼ of cheese and blend until smooth and melted. Repeat with remaining cheese in batches. Strain soup through fine sieve, pressing with back of spoon. Return to saucepan. Mix in leek puree. *(Can be prepared 8 hours ahead. Cool, cover and refrigerate.)* Rewarm soup over low heat, stirring constantly. Thin with more stock if desired. Season with salt. Ladle soup into bowls. Sprinkle with pepper and chives.

Tomato and Cucumber Soup with Cayenne Pepper Croutons

6 servings

¼ cup (½ stick) unsalted butter
2 medium onions, coarsely chopped
4 small garlic cloves, minced
2¼ pounds ripe tomatoes, cored and quartered
3 large cucumbers, peeled, halved lengthwise, seeded and coarsely chopped
1 teaspoon salt
Freshly ground pepper
1½ tablespoons tomato paste

4½ cups chicken stock or canned low-salt broth
Dash of hot pepper sauce (such as Tabasco)

6 green onions (white part and all but 2 inches of green tops), cut julienne
2 tablespoons minced fresh tarragon
Cayenne Pepper Croutons*

Melt butter in heavy large saucepan over medium heat. Add onions and garlic and sauté 2 minutes. Add tomatoes and cucumbers and sauté 1 minute. Add 1 teaspoon salt; season with pepper. Add tomato paste, then mix in broth and hot pepper sauce. Bring to boil. Reduce heat and simmer until vegetables are very soft, stirring occasionally, about 30 minutes.

Puree soup in batches in blender or processor. Strain if desired. Return puree to pan. Taste and adjust seasoning. *(Can be prepared 1 day ahead. Cool, cover and refrigerate. Rewarm before serving, stirring frequently.)* Ladle soup into bowls. Garnish with green onions and tarragon. Float crouton in each bowl. Pass remaining croutons separately.

*Cayenne Pepper Croutons

Makes about 36

6 tablespoons (¾ stick) unsalted butter, room temperature
1 tablespoon minced fresh parsley
1½ teaspoons minced garlic
½ teaspoon cayenne pepper
¼ teaspoon salt

Dash of hot pepper sauce (such as Tabasco)
1 French bread baguette (about 20 inches long and 3 inches wide), cut into ¼-inch-thick rounds

Preheat oven to 300°F. Mix first 6 ingredients in small bowl. Spread mixture on both sides of bread. Arrange on baking sheet. Bake until golden brown, about 5 minutes per side.

Apple Soup with Roquefort Croutons

This hearty yet elegant soup is the perfect starter on a chilly evening. And it tastes even better when made a day ahead.

6 servings

6 tablespoons (¾ stick) unsalted butter
1¼ pounds Red Delicious apples (about 3 large), peeled, cored and sliced
1¼ pounds Granny Smith apples (about 3 large), peeled, cored and sliced
1 cup chopped onion
1 teaspoon minced garlic
5 cups chicken stock or canned broth

1½ cups whipping cream
¼ cup Calvados
Salt and freshly ground pepper

½ Red Delicious apple, cored (unpeeled)
½ Granny Smith apple, cored (unpeeled)
1 tablespoon fresh lemon juice

2 tablespoons snipped fresh chives
Roquefort Croutons*

Melt 4 tablespoons butter in heavy large saucepan or Dutch oven over medium heat. Add 1¼ pounds red apples, 1¼ pounds Granny Smith apples, onion and garlic and cook 5 minutes, stirring occasionally. Add stock and simmer until apples are very tender, about 25 minutes. Puree mixture in batches in blender or processor. Return puree to pan. Add cream and Calvados. Bring to simmer. Season with salt and pepper. *(Can be prepared 1 day ahead. Cool, cover and chill.)*

Cut each apple half into 12 thin slices. Mix with lemon juice. Melt remaining 2 tablespoons butter in heavy large skillet over medium-high heat. Add apples and sauté until golden brown, about 10 minutes.

Bring soup to simmer over medium heat. Ladle into bowls. Top each bowl with 2 red apple slices and 2 Granny Smith apple slices. Sprinkle with chives. Serve with croutons.

*Roquefort Croutons

Makes 18

4 bacon slices
18 ¼-inch-thick slices French bread baguette
4 ounces Roquefort cheese, crumbled

¼ cup (½ stick) unsalted butter, room temperature

Position rack in center of oven and preheat to 350°F. Cook bacon in heavy medium skillet until crisp. Transfer to paper towels and drain. Crumble bacon. Arrange bread slices on heavy large baking sheet. Bake until beginning to crisp, about 10 minutes. Mix cheese and butter in processor until smooth. Spread one side of each crouton with cheese mixture. *(Can be prepared 4 hours ahead. Cover croutons and store at room temperature.)*

Preheat broiler. Broil croutons 5 inches from heat source until cheese bubbles, about 2 minutes. Sprinkle with bacon. Serve warm.

Escarole and White Bean Soup

4 to 6 servings

¼ pound lean ground beef
¼ pound ground pork
1 egg, beaten to blend
2 tablespoons freshly grated Parmesan cheese
2 tablespoons seasoned dry breadcrumbs
¼ teaspoon garlic powder

8 cups chicken stock or canned broth

1 large bunch escarole, chopped
2 16-ounce cans cannellini beans,* drained
1 garlic clove, minced
½ teaspoon dried red pepper flakes
½ teaspoon dried basil, crumbled
Salt and freshly ground pepper
Additional freshly grated Parmesan cheese

Combine first 6 ingredients in medium bowl. Form into 1-inch balls. Set aside. *(Can be prepared 1 week ahead and frozen. Thaw before continuing.)*

Heat broth in large saucepan over medium heat. Stir in next 5 ingredients. Season with salt and pepper. Add meatballs and cook until firm to touch, about 30 minutes. *(Can be prepared 1 day ahead. Cover and refrigerate. Rewarm before serving.)* Ladle soup into bowls. Serve immediately, passing additional Parmesan cheese separately.

*White kidney beans available at Italian markets. If unavailable, Great Northern or navy beans can be substituted.

Chick-Pea Soup with Greens, Onions and Pasta

8 servings

14 cups water
2 cups dried chick-peas (garbanzo beans)

2 large onions, diced
1 prosciutto or ham bone or 8 ounces prosciutto or ham meat
2 whole garlic cloves

6 tablespoons olive oil

3 garlic cloves, minced
3 cups packed 1x3-inch pieces escarole or Swiss chard
3 cups chicken stock or canned broth
Salt and freshly ground pepper
½ cup pasta shells, freshly cooked
Freshly grated Parmesan cheese (preferably imported)

Combine 5 cups water and chick-peas and soak overnight.

Drain chick-peas and rinse. Place half in heavy large saucepan. Add 5 cups water, 1 onion, prosciutto bone and 2 whole garlic cloves. Bring to boil, skimming surface occasionally. Reduce heat and simmer until chick-peas are very tender, 1 hour 50 minutes.

Meanwhile, combine remaining chick-peas with 4 cups water in heavy small saucepan. Bring to boil, skimming surface. Reduce heat and simmer until tender, about 50 minutes. Drain. Return to pan. Mix in 2 tablespoons oil.

Remove bone from large pan of chick-peas. Cut off any meat and add meat to large pan of chick-peas. Puree mixture in blender until smooth. Return to pan. Heat 4 tablespoons oil in heavy large skillet over low heat. Add minced garlic and remaining onion. Cook 5 minutes, stirring occasionally. Add escarole and stir until wilted, about 5 minutes. Add to puree. Add chicken broth and chick-peas from second pan to soup. Bring to simmer, stirring frequently. Season with salt and pepper. *(Can be prepared 1 day ahead and refrigerated. Reheat before continuing, stirring frequently.)* Add pasta to soup and heat through. Ladle soup into bowls. Sprinkle with Parmesan.

Poppa's Hearty Pasta Soup with Two Beans

4 to 6 servings

2 cups small pasta (such as small shells, tubetti or small bow ties)

2 tablespoons olive oil
½ cup chopped onion
¼ cup ¼-inch red bell pepper dice
¼ cup ¼-inch green bell pepper dice
2 garlic cloves, minced
2 cups chicken stock or canned broth
1 16-ounce can whole tomatoes with liquid, pressed through food mill or sieve

1 cup frozen baby lima beans
2 tablespoons chopped parsley
Salt

1½ cups drained canned cannellini beans,* rinsed
5 ounces fresh spinach, trimmed, leaves cut into 1-inch widths

Freshly ground pepper
2 green onion tops, cut into pieces
Freshly grated Parmesan cheese

Add pasta to large pot of boiling salted water. Cook 4 minutes (pasta will be undercooked). Ladle ½ cup cooking liquid into bowl. Drain pasta; set aside.

Heat oil in heavy large saucepan over medium heat. Add onion and sauté until tender, about 5 minutes. Add bell peppers and garlic and sauté 3 minutes. Add stock, tomatoes, lima beans, 1 tablespoon chopped parsley and salt. Bring to boil over medium heat. Cover, reduce heat to low and simmer 5 minutes.

Add cannellini, pasta and reserved pasta cooking liquid to soup. Cover and simmer over low heat until pasta is tender and soup is stewlike in consistency, about 15 minutes. Fold in cut spinach. Cover, reduce heat to very low and simmer soup for 5 minutes.

Stir remaining 1 tablespoon parsley into soup. Season generously with pepper. Ladle into shallow bowls. Garnish with green onion tops and sprinkle with grated Parmesan.

*White kidney beans, available at Italian markets. If unavailable, Great Northern or navy beans can be substituted.

Spinach Soup with Clams and Plenty of Garlic

6 servings

10 garlic cloves, unpeeled
1 tablespoon plus 2 teaspoons olive oil
7 cups chicken stock or canned broth
36 tiny fresh clams, such as manila or butter clams, scrubbed

6 cups loosely packed fresh spinach leaves, cut into 1-inch-wide strips
Dash of fresh lemon juice
Salt and freshly ground pepper

Preheat oven to 400°F. Place garlic in small baking dish. Drizzle with 2 teaspoons oil. Bake until toothpick pierces garlic easily, approximately 15 minutes. Peel garlic cloves and thinly slice.

Heat remaining 1 tablespoon oil in heavy large saucepan over low heat. Add garlic and cook until golden brown, stirring frequently, about 5 minutes. Add 6 cups stock and bring to boil. Reduce heat to low, cover partially and simmer soup for 15 minutes.

Bring remaining 1 cup stock to boil in heavy medium skillet over high heat. Add clams. Cover and steam until shells open, 1½ to 3 minutes. Remove opened clams. Cook remaining clams about 5 more minutes; discard any that do not open. Divide clams among heated soup bowls using slotted spoon. Ladle clam cooking liquid into garlic stock through strainer lined with several layers of dampened cheesecloth. Add spinach. Cover tightly and cook stock over high heat until spinach wilts, about 2 minutes. Add lemon juice. Season with salt and pepper. Ladle stock over clams. Serve hot.

Mediterranean Fish and Orzo Soup

2 servings; can be doubled or tripled

¾ pound halibut, cut into 1-inch cubes
1½ tablespoons fresh lemon juice
2 teaspoons olive oil
2 tablespoons olive oil
1 large onion, halved and thinly sliced
½ 28-ounce can Italian plum tomatoes, drained
2 8-ounce bottles clam juice

¾ cup dry white wine
1 bay leaf
1 1 × 4-inch orange peel strip
⅛ teaspoon fennel seeds, crushed
⅛ teaspoon dried red pepper flakes
Salt and freshly ground pepper
½ cup orzo (rice-shaped pasta)*
1 pound clams, well scrubbed
Minced fresh parsley

Mix halibut, lemon juice and 2 teaspoons oil in small bowl. Let mixture stand while preparing soup.

Heat 2 tablespoons oil in heavy large saucepan over medium heat. Add onion and cook until translucent, stirring occasionally, about 10 minutes.

Squeeze tomatoes through fingers to break up while adding to saucepan. Add clam juice, wine, bay leaf, orange peel, fennel and pepper flakes. Simmer 10 minutes. Season with salt and pepper. Add orzo and cook 5 minutes.

Add clams to soup. Cover and cook 5 minutes. Add fish. Cover and cook until fish is opaque and clams open, about 4 minutes longer. Discard bay leaf and orange peel. Spoon soup into bowls. Garnish with parsley and serve.

*Available at Italian markets, specialty foods stores and many supermarkets.

Traditional New England Clam Chowder with Fried Leeks

Fried leeks add a new twist to this classic, served at 21 Federal in Nantucket, Massachusetts.

8 servings

5 pounds clams, scrubbed
3 cups dry white wine
4 shallots, coarsely chopped
2 bay leaves
5 cups (about) Homemade Fish Stock* or bottled clam juice

¼ pound salt pork, diced
3 tablespoons (about) unsalted butter
½ cup all purpose flour

6 leeks (white and pale green parts)
½ pound bacon slices, cut crosswise into ¼-inch-wide pieces
2 onions, finely chopped

4 celery stalks, finely chopped
Bouquet garni (4 parsley sprigs, 3 thyme sprigs, 1 bay leaf)
2 large boiling potatoes, peeled and cut into ½-inch dice
Freshly ground white pepper
Cayenne pepper

Peanut oil (for deep frying)
2 cups whipping cream
1 cup milk
8 freshly steamed clams
¼ cup minced fresh parsley
Unsalted butter

Place clams in large pot. Add wine, shallots and bay leaves and bring to boil. Reduce heat to low. Cover and steam until shells open, about 10 minutes. Discard any shells that do not open. Remove clams from shells. Finely chop clam meat in processor. Strain clam cooking liquid through sieve lined with double-thickness dampened cheesecloth. Add enough fish stock to strained clam liquid to measure 8 cups.

Blanch salt pork in pot of boiling water 4 minutes. Drain well. Pat dry on paper towels. Cook salt pork in heavy medium skillet over medium-high heat until golden brown and crisp, stirring frequently, about 10 minutes. Transfer cracklings to paper towels using slotted spoon. Add enough butter to skillet to measure 8 tablespoons fat. Add flour to skillet to make roux and stir over low heat until golden brown, about 5 minutes. Set roux aside.

Finely chop 3 leeks. Cut remaining 3 leeks julienne. Cook bacon in heavy large pot over medium heat until fat is rendered, stirring occasionally, about 10 minutes. Add chopped leeks, onions and celery and cook until vegetables soften, stirring frequently, about 4 minutes. Add clam cooking liquid and bouquet garni and bring to boil. Slowly whisk 2 cups liquid into roux. Return mixture to pot and whisk until smooth. Reduce heat and simmer chowder until liquid is reduced by ¼, about 25 minutes. Add potatoes and cook until almost tender, about 10 minutes. Stir in clams. Season with white pepper and cayenne. *(Can be prepared 1 day ahead. Refrigerate leek julienne and chowder separately. Cover cracklings and store at room temperature; rewarm in skillet before serving.)*

Heat oil in heavy deep skillet to 375°F. Add leek julienne and cook until crisp and golden brown, about 1 minute. Transfer to paper towels using slotted spoon. Bring chowder to boil. Add cream and milk and stir until heated through. Taste and adjust seasoning. Place 1 steamed clam in each bowl. Ladle chowder over. Sprinkle with cracklings and parsley. Top each with pat of butter. Sprinkle fried leeks over.

*Homemade Fish Stock

Choose bones from firm white fish, such as halibut, for making this stock. The flavor from dark-fleshed-fish bones may be too strong. The recipe doubles or triples easily.

Makes about 4 cups

3 tablespoons unsalted butter
2 celery stalks, finely chopped
1 onion, finely chopped
1 small leek, finely chopped
1 garlic clove, minced
3 pounds fish bones and/or heads from firm white fish, rinsed, cut into 4-inch pieces

Bouquet garni (5 parsley sprigs, 4 thyme sprigs, 2 bay leaves)
6 cups (about) cold water

Melt butter in heavy large pot over medium heat. Add celery, onion, leek and garlic and sauté until vegetables soften, about 8 minutes. Add fish bones. Increase heat to high and stir 2 minutes. Add bouquet garni and enough cold water to cover vegetables and bones. Bring stock to boil, skimming surface occasionally. Reduce heat and simmer until liquid is reduced to 4 cups, about 30 minutes, skimming surface occasionally. Strain through sieve. *(Can be prepared 1 day ahead, cooled, covered and refrigerated, or 1 month ahead and frozen.)*

 Side-Dish Salads

Romaine, Walnut and Radish Salad

2 servings; can be doubled or tripled

3 cups ¾-inch-wide shreds inner romaine lettuce leaves (about 1 small bunch)
4 radishes, thinly sliced
1½ teaspoons fresh lemon juice

1 teaspoon Dijon mustard
1½ tablespoons olive oil
Salt and freshly ground pepper
¼ cup chopped walnuts

Combine lettuce and radishes in large bowl. Mix lemon juice and mustard in small bowl. Gradually whisk in oil. Season with salt and pepper. Add to salad and toss to coat. Sprinkle salad with walnuts and serve.

Warm Escarole and Endive Salad

8 servings

1 bunch escarole, torn into bite-size pieces
1 bunch curly endive, torn into bite-size pieces
5 bacon slices, trimmed and cut into 1½-inch pieces
2 tablespoons olive oil
½ pound mushrooms, thinly sliced

1 red bell pepper, cut julienne
4 green onions, thinly sliced
1 teaspoon Worcestershire sauce
1 teaspoon dried thyme, crumbled
Salt and freshly ground pepper
¼ cup balsamic vinegar
1 tablespoon butter, room temperature

Place escarole and endive in large bowl. Cook bacon in heavy medium skillet over medium-high heat until crisp. Remove with slotted spoon. Drain on paper towels; add to greens. Pour off all but 2 tablespoons drippings from skillet.

Heat oil in heavy large skillet over medium heat. Add mushrooms, bell pepper and onions and stir until heated through, about 3 minutes. Stir in Worcestershire sauce and thyme. Season with salt and pepper. Add to greens. Add vinegar to skillet with reserved bacon drippings and bring to boil, scraping up any browned bits. Add butter and stir until melted. Pour over salad and toss well.

Spinach Salad with Italian Sausage

2 servings; can be doubled or tripled

4 cups packed stemmed spinach, torn into bite-size pieces (about ¾ bunch)
1 teaspoon olive oil
4 hot Italian sausages

3 green onions, sliced

3 tablespoons Sherry vinegar or red wine vinegar
1 tablespoon olive oil
1 teaspoon Dijon mustard
Salt and freshly ground pepper

Place spinach in large bowl. Heat 1 teaspoon oil in heavy large skillet over medium heat. Add sausages and cook until browned and cooked through. Transfer sausages to paper towels using slotted spoon. Drain sausages and then slice ½ inch thick.

Heat drippings in skillet over medium heat. Add green onions and stir 1 minute. Add vinegar and bring to boil, scraping up any browned bits. Mix in 1 tablespoon oil and mustard. Add sausage and toss to coat. Season with salt and pepper. Pour over spinach and toss. Adjust seasoning.

Guacamole Salad

Fried tortilla strips add texture, and beet julienne adds color to a salad inspired by this classic avocado specialty.

6 servings

Vegetable oil (for deep frying)
6 corn tortillas, cut into strips

4 large ripe avocados
½ cup diced canned green chilies
2 tablespoons minced onion
1 tablespoon fresh lemon juice
1 garlic clove, minced
1 teaspoon cracked black pepper
½ teaspoon salt

½ teaspoon ground coriander
½ teaspoon ground cumin
Hot pepper sauce (such as Tabasco)

6 red leaf lettuce leaves
1 head iceberg lettuce, shredded
2 large tomatoes, cut into wedges
1 cup beet julienne

Heat oil in heavy skillet or deep fryer to 375°F. Add tortilla strips in batches and cook until crisp, turning occasionally, about 1½ minutes. Drain on paper towels.

Peel and pit 3 avocados. Transfer flesh to bowl and mash well. Mix in next 8 ingredients. Season with hot pepper sauce to taste. Peel and pit remaining avocado. Cut flesh into cubes. Fold into mashed avocado mixture.

Line each plate with red lettuce leaf. Cover with shredded lettuce. Top with guacamole. Garnish with tomatoes and beets. Sprinkle with fried tortillas. Serve salad immediately.

Grapefruit, Red Onion and Avocado Salad

Serve this as a refreshing first course.

4 servings

1 1-pound can grapefruit sections, drained, juice reserved
2 medium avocados, peeled, pitted and chopped
¼ cup mayonnaise

2 teaspoons fresh lemon juice
 Salt and freshly ground pepper
1 small head iceberg lettuce
½ medium red onion, thinly sliced

Cut grapefruit sections into 3 pieces. Toss avocados with all but 2 tablespoons reserved juice from grapefruit. Whisk together mayonnaise, remaining 2 tablespoons grapefruit juice and lemon juice. Season with salt and pepper. Line 4 plates with lettuce. Drain avocados and toss with grapefruit. Divide grapefruit mixture among plates. Top with onion. Drizzle with dressing and serve.

Quick Mixed Cabbage and Celery Seed Slaw

A touch of fresh orange juice in the dressing adds a nice, refreshing note.

4 servings

3 tablespoons fresh orange juice
2 tablespoons white wine vinegar
2 teaspoons sugar
⅓ cup mayonnaise
⅓ cup sour cream
1 tablespoon Dijon mustard
½ teaspoon celery seeds
 Salt and freshly ground pepper
½ small head savoy cabbage (about 8 ounces), thinly sliced

½ small head red cabbage (about 8 ounces), thinly sliced
4 large green onions (white and 2 inches of pale green part), thinly sliced diagonally
4 large savoy cabbage leaves

Stir first 3 ingredients in large bowl until sugar dissolves. Mix in mayonnaise, sour cream, mustard and celery seeds. Season with salt and pepper. Mix in sliced cabbage and green onions. Cover and refrigerate at least 1 hour. *(Can be prepared 6 hours ahead.)*
 Arrange savoy cabbage leaves on plates. Fill with slaw and serve.

Grilled Corn Salad

12 servings

18 ears fresh corn in husks
1 large red bell pepper

1 bunch green onions, chopped
9 tablespoons cider vinegar

1½ tablespoons honey
¾ teaspoon ground cumin
4½ tablespoons vegetable oil
 Salt and freshly ground pepper

Prepare barbecue or smoker (low heat). Grill or smoke corn 25 minutes, turning frequently. Add bell pepper and continue grilling or smoking until corn husks are brown and bell pepper is blackened, turning frequently, about 15 more minutes. Cool corn to room temperature. Peel bell pepper; rinse if necessary. Cut bell pepper julienne or chop.
 Cut kernels from cobs. Transfer to large bowl. Mix in bell pepper and green onions. Whisk vinegar, honey and cumin in small bowl. Gradually whisk in oil. Toss with salad. Season with salt and freshly ground pepper.

White Bean, Green Bean and Red Bell Pepper Salad

Most supermarkets stock cannellini beans in the Italian section.

2 servings; can be doubled or tripled

⅓ pound green beans, trimmed and cut into 2-inch lengths
1 red bell pepper, cut into 2-inch-long strips
1 15-ounce can cannellini (white kidney) beans, kidney beans or garbanzos, drained and rinsed

2 teaspoons Dijon mustard
2 teaspoons red wine vinegar
3 tablespoons olive oil
½ teaspoon grated orange peel
½ teaspoon minced fresh tarragon (optional)
Salt and freshly ground pepper

Cook green beans in large pot of boiling salted water until crisp-tender. Drain. Refresh under cold water. Combine with red pepper and cannellini beans in medium bowl.

Blend mustard and vinegar in small bowl. Gradually whisk in oil. Mix in orange peel and tarragon. Season with salt and pepper. Mix into salad. Taste and adjust seasoning.

Olive Rice Salad

4 servings

2 cups freshly cooked rice
3 green onions, chopped
15 Kalamata olives, pitted and chopped
½ medium green bell pepper, diced
½ cup chopped red cabbage

3 tablespoons olive oil
3 tablespoons white wine vinegar
Salt and freshly ground pepper
Romaine lettuce leaves
2 medium tomatoes, quartered

Place first 5 ingredients in medium bowl. Combine oil and vinegar in jar with tight-fitting lid. Season with salt and pepper. Shake well. Pour dressing over rice and vegetables and toss. Line serving bowl with lettuce. Transfer salad to bowl. Garnish with tomatoes. Serve rice salad at room temperature.

Pasta Shell Salad with Walnut Pesto

For toppings, consider tiny shrimp, salami julienne, blanched broccoli florets and freshly grated Parmesan cheese.

16 servings

¼ cup chopped walnuts, lightly toasted
3 garlic cloves, chopped
2 cups (loosely packed) fresh basil or 2 cups spinach leaves mixed with 2 tablespoons dried basil
½ cup plus 2 tablespoons freshly grated Parmesan cheese

¾ cup olive oil
Salt

1 pound pasta shells
2 tablespoons olive oil

Grind nuts and garlic in food processor. Add basil and cheese and puree. With machine running, add ¾ cup olive oil through feed tube in thin stream. Season pesto with salt.

Cook pasta shells in large pot of rapidly boiling salted water until just tender but still firm to bite, stirring to prevent sticking. Drain. Transfer to serving bowl. Toss with 2 tablespoons olive oil. Add pesto and toss to coat.

Linguine Salad with Sesame Dressing

Condiment candidates for this salad would be sliced Chinese sausage, hot chili and/or sesame oil, green onions, toasted sesame seeds, blanched carrot matchsticks, cubed tofu, water chestnuts or peeled jicama and soy sauce.

16 servings

1½ pounds linguine

½ cup oriental sesame oil
½ cup light soy sauce
 1 tablespoon chili oil* (or to taste)
 2 teaspoons minced garlic

Salt and freshly ground pepper

 1 cup minced arugula, cilantro or watercress
 1 orange slice, twisted

Cook linguine in large pot of rapidly boiling salted water until just tender but still firm to bite, stirring to prevent sticking. Drain. Transfer to large bowl.

Combine sesame oil, soy sauce, chili oil and garlic in small bowl and whisk to blend. Season with salt and pepper. Add just enough oil mixture to linguine to coat. Cover and refrigerate linguine at least 3 and up to 8 hours.

Just before serving, add arugula to linguine and toss. Transfer to serving bowl. Top with orange slice. Pour remaining sesame dressing into small bowl and serve with pasta salad.

*Chili oil is available at oriental markets and some supermarkets.

Smoked Salmon and Pasta Salad

6 servings

½ cup dry white wine
¼ cup raspberry vinegar
¼ cup olive oil
 2 eggs
 1 tablespoon Dijon mustard
 1 shallot, minced
 1 teaspoon fresh lemon juice
Salt and freshly ground pepper

 8 ounces fusilli (corkscrew) pasta

 2 heads curly endive, torn into bite-size pieces

 1 head radicchio, torn into bite-size pieces
10 oil-packed sun-dried tomatoes, drained and coarsely chopped
10 oil-cured Italian olives,* pitted
¾ pound smoked salmon, cut julienne
 1 tablespoon snipped fresh chives

Mix first 7 ingredients in blender until smooth. Season with salt and pepper. *(Dressing can be prepared 1 day ahead. Cover and refrigerate. Bring to room temperature before continuing.)*

Cook pasta in large pot of boiling salted water until just tender but still firm to bite, stirring occasionally to prevent sticking. Drain in colander. Cool completely under running water. Drain.

Mix pasta with endive and radicchio in large bowl. Add tomatoes, olives and dressing to taste; toss well. Divide salad among serving plates. Sprinkle with smoked salmon and chives.

*Available at specialty foods stores and some supermarkets.

🍎 *Main-Dish Salads*

Southwestern Rice Salad with Cheese and Avocado

This meatless salad is a welcome addition to a warm-weather menu. Here creamy Jack cheese, avocado, crunchy jicama and rice are seasoned in the Tex-Mex style, with cumin, fresh cilantro and flecks of hot chili.

4 servings

1 jalapeño or serrano* chili
2 medium garlic cloves
6 tablespoons olive oil (preferably extra-virgin)
¼ cup fresh lemon juice
1½ teaspoons ground cumin
¾ teaspoon salt

1 medium tomato, cored, quartered and seeded
½ medium yellow bell pepper, cut into 1-inch pieces
5 green onions, trimmed, cut into 1-inch pieces

½ small jicama, peeled and cut into 1-inch pieces
½ cup loosely packed fresh cilantro leaves
2½ cups cold cooked rice (about 1 cup uncooked)

2 ripe avocados
8 ounces Monterey Jack cheese, cut into ½-inch cubes
Fresh cilantro sprigs

Insert steel knife in processor. With machine running, drop chili and garlic through feed tube and mince. Add oil, lemon juice, cumin and salt and mix 5 seconds, stopping once to scrape down sides of work bowl. Leave in work bowl.

Add tomato, bell pepper and green onions to work bowl; chop coarsely using about 10 on/off turns. Transfer tomato mixture to large bowl. Add jicama and ½ cup cilantro to work bowl and chop coarsely using on/off turns. Add jicama mixture and rice to tomato mixture and toss to combine. *(Can be prepared 1 day ahead. Cover and refrigerate.)*

Up to 2 hours before serving, peel avocados and cut into ½-inch cubes. Mix avocados and cheese into salad. Adjust seasoning. Garnish rice salad with fresh cilantro sprigs.

*A *serrano* is a very hot, small fresh green chili available at Latin American markets and some supermarkets.

Chicken Salad with Roasted Walnuts

Based on a purchased bar-becued chicken, this salad takes minutes to make. The Roasted Walnuts add a special touch; for an even easier version, just use plain walnuts.

2 servings; can be doubled or tripled

1 egg yolk
1½ tablespoons fresh lemon juice
¾ teaspoon Dijon mustard
6 tablespoons olive oil
Salt and freshly ground pepper

1 Boston lettuce head, torn into large bite-size pieces
1 1½-pound barbecued chicken, skinned, boned and shredded into bite-size pieces

3 ounces soft goat cheese, such as Montrachet or Bûcheron, crumbled
1 bunch radishes, trimmed and sliced
Roasted Walnuts*

Mix yolk, lemon juice and mustard in small bowl. Gradually whisk in oil. Season with salt and pepper.

Combine lettuce, chicken, goat cheese and radishes in large bowl. Add enough dressing to coat. Sprinkle with walnuts. Serve salad, passing any remaining dressing separately.

*Roasted Walnuts

Use these in salads or pass them with cocktails.

Makes about ¾ cup; can be doubled or tripled

¾ cup walnuts
1 teaspoon vegetable oil
2 teaspoons sugar

¼ teaspoon salt
⅛ teaspoon ground cumin
   Pinch of dried red pepper flakes

Preheat oven to 450°F. Place walnuts in small bowl. Add oil and mix to coat. Add all remaining ingredients and toss to coat. Transfer to small cake pan. Bake until brown, stirring occasionally, about 8 minutes. Serve walnuts warm or at room temperature.

Fresh Salmon Salad with Lemon Dill Dressing

Most components of this main-course salad can be prepared in advance.

4 servings

1 small cauliflower head, trimmed and cut into florets
12 ounces green beans, trimmed

¾ cup plain nonfat or lowfat yogurt
3 tablespoons fresh lemon juice
3 tablespoons olive oil
3 tablespoons chopped fresh dill or 1½ teaspoons dried dillweed
¾ teaspoon sugar
1 medium garlic clove, minced
   Salt and freshly ground pepper

¼ English hothouse cucumber (unpeeled), halved lengthwise and thinly sliced
¼ pound mushrooms, trimmed and quartered

2 green onions, trimmed and diagonally sliced ⅛ inch thick

2 ¾-pound salmon fillets (preferably center cut), about 1 inch thick

1 small head radicchio
1 small head Bibb or Boston lettuce
12 small radishes, trimmed, with small center leaves intact
2 small ripe tomatoes, cored and quartered
¼ cup dill sprigs (optional)

Place cauliflower and beans on rack set over gently simmering water in saucepan. Cover and steam until tender, about 10 minutes. Rinse under cold water. *(Can be prepared 1 day ahead. Cover and refrigerate.)*

Blend yogurt and next 5 ingredients in processor or blender. Season with salt and pepper to taste. Transfer dressing to bowl. *(Can be prepared 1 day ahead. Cover and refrigerate.)*

Combine cauliflower, beans, cucumber, mushrooms and green onions in large bowl. Toss with half of dressing. Cover; chill at least 1 hour. Refrigerate remaining dressing separately.

Place salmon on rack set over gently simmering water in saucepan. Cover and steam until just cooked through, about 10 minutes. Remove rack from over water. Cool salmon slightly. Divide salmon into 12 pieces.

Line each plate with alternating leaves of radicchio and lettuce. Cover with marinated vegetables. Top each with 3 pieces salmon. Spoon some of remaining dressing over. Garnish with radishes, tomato wedges and dill. Pass remaining dressing separately.

Beef Salad with Pepper Dressing

A nice starter or luncheon entrée. Accompany with crusty bread.

4 servings

½ cup soy sauce
6 tablespoons sugar
1 tablespoon finely grated ginger
1 tablespoon minced garlic
1 12-ounce New York (top loin) steak, 1 inch thick

8 cups bite-size pieces mixed greens (escarole, radicchio, Boston lettuce and red leaf lettuce)
¼ English hothouse cucumber, cut julienne

1⅓ cups thinly sliced red onion
¼ cup soy sauce
2 tablespoons fresh lemon juice
¾ teaspoon minced hot green chili, such as jalapeño or Thai*
2 tablespoons peanut oil
2 tablespoons olive oil

1 teaspoon sesame seeds
12 fresh cilantro sprigs

Combine first 4 ingredients in baking dish; stir to dissolve sugar. Add steak, turning to coat. Cover and refrigerate 2 hours, turning occasionally.

Prepare barbecue grill (high heat). Combine greens, cucumber and onion in large bowl. Combine ¼ cup soy sauce, lemon juice and chili in small bowl. Gradually whisk in both oils.

Grill steak until cooked to desired doneness, about 3 minutes per side for rare. Toss salad with vinaigrette. Divide salad among plates. Slice steak thinly across grain. Arrange atop salad. Sprinkle with sesame seeds. Garnish with cilantro and serve.

*Available at oriental markets.

3 ❦ *Pasta and Sandwiches*

In this chapter we present two all-time favorites—pasta and sandwiches—with all the great taste and ease of preparation that have made these dishes so popular. You'll also find some delicious new combinations of ingredients. Fettuccine with Roasted Corn and Chicken gets added flavor from broiling or roasting an ear of corn with the husk before combining it with a creamy garlic-scented sauce. Spinach, Mushroom and Goat Cheese Lasagne uses a timesaving advantage of the microwave—the noodles don't have to be precooked before the dish is assembled—and includes the traditional ricotta, mozzarella and Parmesan cheeses, along with the tangy twist of goat cheese.

Super new combinations also transform the sandwiches here into something out of the ordinary. Roasted Bell Pepper, Basil and Fontina Sandwiches are made with toasted French or Italian bread slices—serve a plate of these miniature sandwiches with soup for a warming lunch or light supper, or as elegant choices at a cocktail party. Chicken and Mustard Green Sandwiches add an irresistible new dimension to the plain old chicken sandwich—slices of juicy chicken breast and sautéed mustard greens (other greens work, too) are wedged between pieces of baguette spread with a mixture of mayonnaise and chutney. Other sandwich variations include an Italian Pizza Turnover and quick Pepperoni Pizza Bread, a rolled sandwich made with frozen bread dough.

 # Pasta

Linguine with Broccoli, Pine Nuts and Red Pepper Flakes

2 servings; can be doubled or tripled

1½ pounds broccoli, peeled and cut into florets (stems reserved for another use)

½ pound dried linguine

5 tablespoons olive oil
2 medium garlic cloves, minced
⅛ teaspoon dried red pepper flakes

2 tablespoons fresh lemon juice
⅓ cup freshly grated Parmesan cheese
Salt and freshly ground pepper
¼ cup pine nuts, toasted
Additional freshly grated Parmesan cheese

Blanch broccoli in large pot of boiling salted water until just crisp-tender, about 3 minutes. Drain and refresh under cold water. Drain well.

Cook pasta in large pot of boiling salted water until just tender but still firm to bite. Drain well.

Meanwhile, heat oil in heavy large skillet over medium-low heat. Add garlic and stir 1 minute. Add pepper flakes to skillet and stir 30 seconds. Add broccoli and stir until heated through, about 2 minutes.

Add pasta to skillet and turn to coat with oil. Add lemon juice and toss to coat. Mix in ⅓ cup Parmesan. Season generously with salt and pepper. Transfer to heated platter. Sprinkle with pine nuts. Serve, passing additional freshly grated Parmesan separately.

Fettuccine with Roasted Corn and Chicken

2 servings

1 ear corn with husk

¼ cup olive oil
8 ounces boneless chicken breast, skinned and cut into ½-inch-wide strips
1 teaspoon minced garlic
Salt and freshly ground pepper
½ cup dry white wine
1½ cups whipping cream

½ red bell pepper, diced

6 ounces fettuccine

½ cup freshly grated Parmesan cheese
¼ cup (½ stick) unsalted butter, cut into pieces, room temperature
Snipped fresh chives

Preheat broiler. Broil corn until tender, turning occasionally, about 10 minutes (husk may blacken). Husk corn. Cut off corn kernels and set aside.

Heat oil in heavy large skillet over medium heat. Add chicken and brown on all sides. Add garlic and stir 2 minutes. Season with salt and pepper. Add wine and bring to boil, scraping up any browned bits. Transfer chicken to bowl using slotted spoon. Add corn, cream and red pepper to skillet. Lower heat and simmer until reduced to thin sauce consistency, about 4 minutes.

Meanwhile, cook pasta in large pot of boiling salted water until just tender but still firm to bite, stirring occasionally. Drain.

Add chicken, pasta, half of cheese and butter to skillet and toss until heated through. Taste and adjust seasoning. Divide pasta between warm plates. Sprinkle with chives and remaining cheese. Serve immediately.

Fettuccine with Mussels and Cream

2 servings; can be doubled or tripled

2 tablespoons (¼ stick) butter
4 green onions, sliced, dark green part set aside
2 3-inch orange peel strips
⅛ teaspoon fennel seeds

2 pounds mussels, debearded
½ cup whipping cream
Salt and freshly ground pepper

½ pound fettuccine or linguine

Melt butter in heavy medium saucepan over medium heat. Add white and light green parts of green onions and cook 2 minutes. Add orange peel and fennel, then mussels. Cover and cook 5 minutes. Transfer opened mussels to bowl. Cover and continue cooking 3 minutes. Add remaining mussels to bowl, discarding any that do not open. Cover with foil to keep warm. Add cream to pan and boil until slightly thickened, adding liquid accumulated in mussel bowl, about 2 minutes. Season with salt and pepper.

Meanwhile, cook fettuccine in large pot of boiling salted water until just tender but still firm to bite. Drain well. Transfer to large bowl. Top with mussels, then sauce, discarding orange peel. Sprinkle with reserved onions.

Rigatoni with Hot Italian Sausage and Mushrooms

The sauce can be prepared two days ahead and refrigerated. Just reheat and toss with the rigatoni before serving. Offer plenty of crusty Italian bread along with the pasta.

6 servings

1 ounce (about 30 grams) dried porcini mushrooms*
1 cup hot water

1 tablespoon butter
1 large onion, finely chopped
1¼ pounds hot Italian sausages, casings removed
1 pound button mushrooms, sliced
½ teaspoon dried rosemary, crumbled
½ cup dry white wine
1 bay leaf

1 cup beef stock or canned low-salt broth

1¼ pounds rigatoni pasta

1 cup half and half
1½ cups freshly grated Parmesan cheese (about 4½ ounces)
Salt and freshly ground pepper
Chopped fresh Italian parsley
Fresh rosemary sprigs
Additional freshly grated Parmesan cheese

Rinse porcini mushrooms. Place in small bowl. Pour 1 cup hot water over and let soak until softened, about 20 minutes. Drain porcini, reserving soaking liquid. Chop porcini, discarding any hard stems. Set aside.

Melt butter in heavy large skillet over medium heat. Add onion and cook until beginning to soften, stirring occasionally, about 5 minutes. Add sausage, increase heat to high and cook just until no longer pink, breaking up with fork, about 6 minutes. Add fresh mushrooms and dried rosemary and stir until mushrooms begin to soften, about 5 minutes. Add porcini, wine and bay leaf and boil until almost all liquid evaporates, about 4 minutes. Add stock and porcini soaking liquid, discarding any sand at bottom of liquid. Simmer until sauce is syrupy, stirring occasionally, about 15 minutes. *(Sauce can be prepared 2 days ahead. Cool, then cover and refrigerate.)*

Add pasta to large pot of boiling salted water, stirring to prevent sticking. Cook until just tender but still firm to bite. Drain. Return pasta to hot pot.

Meanwhile, add half and half to sauce and boil until thickened slightly, about 2 minutes. Add sauce and 1½ cups Parmesan to pasta and stir over low heat until coated. Season with salt and pepper. Transfer to heated platter. Sprinkle with parsley. Garnish with rosemary sprigs. Serve, passing additional Parmesan separately.

*Available at specialty foods stores.

Rigatoni with Smoked Chicken and Ricotta

6 servings

1 tablespoon olive oil	1 tablespoon minced fresh oregano
1 pound rigatoni	Salt and freshly ground pepper
11 ounces smoked chicken, finely chopped	1 cup chicken stock or canned low-salt broth
4 ounces ricotta cheese	Tomato-Oregano Sauce*
¼ cup freshly grated pecorino Romano cheese (about 1 ounce)	1 large yellow bell pepper, diced
2 eggs, beaten to blend	1 large red bell pepper, diced
3 tablespoons minced fresh basil	Fresh oregano sprigs

Add oil, then pasta to large pot of boiling salted water, stirring to prevent sticking. Cook until pasta is just tender but still firm to bite, about 12 minutes. Drain. Rinse under cold water until cool. Drain well.

Mix chicken, ricotta, Romano, eggs, basil and oregano in medium bowl. Season with salt and pepper. Using narrow teaspoon, stuff each rigatoni with about 1½ teaspoons of mixture. *(Can be prepared 1 day ahead. Set rigatoni on waxed paper–lined baking sheet. Cover with plastic and refrigerate.)*

Bring stock to simmer in large shallow skillet. Carefully lower rigatoni into stock and cook until heated through, about 5 minutes. Spoon tomato sauce onto plates. Remove rigatoni from stock using slotted spoon and divide among plates. Sprinkle with bell peppers. Garnish with oregano sprigs.

*Tomato-Oregano Sauce

Makes about 5¾ cups

6 tablespoons olive oil (preferably extra-virgin)	1 cup dry red wine
¼ cup finely chopped red onion	¼ cup fresh oregano leaves
4 medium garlic cloves, minced	1 tablespoon plus 1 teaspoon tomato paste
5 pounds Italian plum tomatoes, peeled, seeded and cut into ⅛-inch dice	Salt and freshly ground pepper

Heat oil in heavy large skillet over medium-high heat. Add onion and stir 2 minutes. Add garlic and stir 30 seconds. Add tomatoes and cook 4 minutes, stirring frequently. Mix in wine, oregano and tomato paste. Reduce heat and simmer until reduced to sauce consistency, stirring frequently, about 20 minutes. Season with salt and pepper. *(Can be prepared 1 day ahead. Chill.)*

Mushroom-filled Pasta with Parmesan and Butter

6 servings

Pasta
1¼ cups (or more) all purpose flour
¼ teaspoon salt
2 large eggs
1 tablespoon milk

Filling
3 tablespoons butter
¾ pound mushrooms, finely chopped
2 ounces prosciutto, minced
2 tablespoons minced shallots
Freshly ground pepper
¼ cup whipping cream

3 tablespoons Marsala wine
Salt

2 tablespoons vegetable oil

Sauce
5 tablespoons unsalted butter
⅓ cup minced prosciutto (about 1 ounce)

3 tablespoons freshly grated Parmesan cheese
Additional freshly grated Parmesan cheese

For pasta: Mix 1¼ cups flour and salt in processor. Add eggs and milk and blend until dough begins to come together. Turn dough out onto lightly floured surface and knead until smooth and elastic, adding more flour if necessary to prevent sticking, about 3 minutes. Flatten dough and wrap in plastic. Refrigerate dough while preparing filling.

For filling: Melt butter in heavy large skillet over high heat. Add mushrooms, prosciutto, shallots and pepper. Cook until almost no liquid remains in pan, stirring frequently, about 8 minutes. Add cream and Marsala and boil until almost no liquid remains, stirring frequently, about 4 minutes. Season with salt. Cool completely.

Cut dough into 6 pieces. Flatten 1 piece of dough (keep remainder covered). Turn pasta machine to widest setting and run dough through several times until smooth and velvety, folding in thirds before each run and dusting with flour if sticky. Adjust machine to next narrower setting. Run dough through machine without folding. Repeat narrowing rollers after each run, until pasta is ⅟₁₆ inch thick, dusting with flour as necessary.

Cut dough into 2½-inch rounds using scalloped cookie cutter. Place 1 generous teaspoon filling just off center of each round. Moisten edge of side closer to filling. Fold over filling, not quite to other edge. Press edges to seal. Arrange in single layer on lightly floured, paper towel–lined baking sheets. Repeat rolling and filling, rerolling scraps and cutting out additional rounds. (*Can be prepared ahead. Cover with another towel and refrigerate 1 day, or freeze until firm and then wrap in plastic and freeze up to 1 month.*)

Add 2 tablespoons oil to large pot of boiling salted water. Add pasta and cook until just tender but still firm to bite, about 5 minutes.

Meanwhile, prepare sauce: Melt butter in heavy saucepan over medium heat. Add prosciutto and stir 1 minute.

Drain pasta; transfer to bowl. Sprinkle with 3 tablespoons cheese. Pour butter and prosciutto over. Serve, passing additional cheese separately.

Oven-baked Penne with Tomato and Eggplant

A pasta casserole.

8 servings

5 tablespoons olive oil
2 small onions, chopped
2 small celery stalks, chopped
3 pounds tomatoes, peeled, seeded and chopped
14 large fresh basil leaves, torn into strips
Salt and freshly ground pepper
Pinch of sugar (optional)

2 pounds eggplant, cut into ⅛-inch-thick rounds

Olive oil

1 pound dried penne pasta
¼ cup (½ stick) unsalted butter, sliced, room temperature
1 cup freshly grated Parmesan cheese (about 4 ounces)

¾ pound drained fresh water-packed mozzarella,* finely chopped

Heat 5 tablespoons oil in heavy large saucepan over medium-low heat. Add onions and celery and cook until vegetables soften, stirring occasionally, about 8 minutes. Add tomatoes and basil. Season with salt and pepper. Reduce heat to low and cook until almost no liquid remains in pan, stirring occasionally, about 30 minutes. Add sugar if sweeter flavor is desired. *(Can be prepared 1 day ahead; refrigerate. Bring to room temperature before continuing.)*

Sprinkle eggplant with salt and layer between paper towels on large baking sheet. Weight with another large baking sheet. Let stand 1½ hours. Pat eggplant dry with paper towels.

Heat ¼ inch olive oil in heavy large skillet over medium heat. Add eggplant in batches and cook until golden brown on both sides, about 3 minutes. Drain on paper towels.

Preheat oven to 350°F. Cook pasta in large pot of boiling salted water, stirring to prevent sticking, about 7 minutes (pasta will be undercooked and still firm). Drain well. Transfer to bowl. Add butter and half of Parmesan cheese and toss until butter melts. Season pasta with salt.

Generously butter 6-quart shallow baking dish. Spread ⅓ of tomato sauce over bottom of prepared dish. Layer with ⅓ of pasta, then ¼ of eggplant and ⅓ of mozzarella. Beginning with sauce, repeat layering twice. Cover with remaining ¼ of eggplant. Sprinkle with remaining Parmesan cheese. *(Can be prepared 8 hours ahead and refrigerated. Bring to room temperature before continuing.)* Bake until top is lightly browned, 40 minutes. Serve warm.

*Available at Italian markets, cheese shops and some specialty foods stores. Regular mozzarella can be substituted.

Spinach, Mushroom and Goat Cheese Lasagne

A big microwave advantage: The noodles don't have to be precooked before the dish is assembled.

4 servings

1 2-ounce piece Parmesan cheese (preferably imported), room temperature
8 ounces chilled part-skim mozzarella cheese
7 ounces medium mushrooms
5 ounces soft goat cheese (preferably Montrachet), crumbled

½ cup ricotta cheese
7 ounces fresh spinach, stemmed
2 cups good-quality prepared spaghetti sauce
Salt and freshly ground pepper
3 ounces broad egg noodles (not lasagne noodles)

Insert fine shredder in processor. Shred Parmesan using light pressure. Set aside. Shred mozzarella using light pressure. Set aside.

Insert thin slicer. Arrange mushrooms lengthwise in feed tube; pack tightly. Slice using light pressure. Set aside.

Insert steel knife. Blend goat cheese and ricotta until smooth, stopping once to scrape down sides of work bowl.

Combine spinach and mushrooms in 8-inch glass baking dish or shallow 6-cup rectangular baking dish. Cover with plastic; pierce once through center to allow steam to escape. Cook on High until spinach is wilted, 3 to 3½ minutes. Transfer spinach mixture to piece of waxed paper. Blot gently with paper towel to remove excess liquid.

Spread ¾ cup spaghetti sauce in bottom of same baking dish. Top with even layer of half the spinach mixture, unfolding spinach leaves as necessary. Season lightly with salt and pepper. Cover with half of noodles, arranging in single layer. Cover with half of goat cheese mixture, half of mozzarella, half of Parmesan and ¾ cup sauce. Top with remaining spinach mixture, unfolding spinach leaves. Season lightly with salt and pepper. Cover with remaining noodles, goat cheese mixture, mozzarella and Parmesan. Gently press with spatula to compress layers. Add remaining sauce.

Cover dish tightly with plastic; pierce once in center to allow steam to escape. Cook on Medium until noodles are tender, turning dish a quarter turn every 6 minutes, 20 to 27 minutes. To test for doneness, pierce noodles through plastic in several places. Let stand for 5 minutes. *(Can be prepared 1 day ahead and refrigerated. To reheat, cover and cook on High until warmed through, about 6 minutes.)* Remove plastic. Cut into squares. Transfer to plates using slotted spatula (there may be liquid in bottom of dish).

Sandwiches

Roasted Bell Pepper, Basil and Fontina Sandwiches

These miniature toasted sandwiches can be served either warm or at room temperature. Assemble them early in the day and bake just before serving.

Makes 24

¼ cup olive oil
1 garlic clove, pressed
48 ¼-inch-thick slices French or Italian bread baguettes
1 pound Fontina or provolone cheese, shredded

2 12-ounce jars roasted red peppers in oil, rinsed and drained
48 fresh basil leaves or dried basil, crumbled

Line 2 large baking sheets with foil or use nonstick baking sheets. Mix oil with garlic in bowl. Lightly brush baking sheets with some of oil mixture. Divide half of bread slices between prepared sheets. Press half of cheese over bread slices. Top with roasted peppers, trimming to fit bread if necessary. Top with remaining cheese. Cover each with 2 basil leaves or sprinkle with dried basil. Top with remaining bread. Brush bread tops with remaining oil. *(Can be prepared 8 hours ahead. Wrap tightly with plastic and refrigerate.)*

Preheat oven to 425°F. Bake sandwiches uncovered until bottoms are golden brown, about 10 minutes. Remove any melted cheese from baking sheets. Turn sandwiches over using metal spatula. Return to oven and bake until second sides are golden brown, about 5 minutes. Transfer to serving platter. Serve sandwiches hot or at room temperature.

Chicken and Mustard Green Sandwiches

If you're a fan of well-dressed sandwiches, add a little more mayonnaise and/or chutney if desired.

2 servings; can be doubled or tripled

5 tablespoons mayonnaise
¼ cup Major Grey's chutney
1 baguette, ends trimmed, halved lengthwise and crosswise
1 tablespoon butter

2 large boneless chicken breast halves, skinned
Salt and freshly ground pepper
1 bunch mustard greens or other bitter greens, stemmed

Preheat broiler. Mix mayonnaise and chutney. Spread some on cut sides of bread. Broil cut sides up until golden.

Melt butter in heavy large skillet over medium heat. Season chicken with salt and pepper. Sauté until springy to touch, about 5 minutes per side. Transfer to plate. Add greens to skillet. Season with salt and pepper. Stir until wilted, about 1½ minutes. Arrange on bottom bread pieces. Slice chicken across grain on diagonal and arrange over greens. Spread with remaining mayonnaise mixture. Top with bread and serve.

Pork Tenderloin Sandwiches with Barbecue Sauce

For a more sophisticated main course, serve the meat partnered with potatoes and vegetables. The sauce is also delicious on chicken.

8 servings

2 cups Barbecue Sauce*
1 cup creamy peanut butter
2 teaspoons minced hot chilies
Olive oil
4 whole pork tenderloins (about 1 pound each), trimmed, silver skin removed

Salt and freshly ground pepper

8 hamburger buns

Preheat oven to 375°F. Blend sauce, peanut butter and chilies in processor 1 minute, stopping to scrape down sides of bowl. Heat thin layer of oil in heavy large ovenproof skillet over medium-high heat. Pat pork dry. Season with salt and pepper. Add to skillet and sear well on all sides. Brush with some of sauce mixture. Roast in oven 25 minutes; cool slightly.

Cut pork into thin strips. Heat remaining sauce mixture in heavy medium saucepan. Toss with pork. Mound on base of 4 split buns. Cover with tops. Serve sandwiches immediately.

*Barbecue Sauce

Makes about 3 cups

2 cups catsup
¼ cup Creole or Dijon mustard
3 tablespoons light corn syrup
3 tablespoons hoisin sauce*
3 tablespoons fresh lemon juice
2 tablespoons distilled white vinegar

1 tablespoon hot pepper sauce (such as Tabasco)
1 teaspoon grated lemon peel
2 garlic cloves, minced

Mix all ingredients in bowl. Cover and refrigerate until ready to use. *(Can be prepared 3 days ahead.)*

*Available at oriental markets and oriental sections of some supermarkets.

Grilled Ham, Swiss Cheese and Sauerkraut Sandwiches

Makes 24

5 tablespoons butter, melted
Coarse-grained mustard
48 slices cocktail rye bread
½ pound Swiss cheese, shredded

1½ cups drained sauerkraut, squeezed dry
¾ pound baked ham, such as Virginia, trimmed to fit bread

Line 2 large baking sheets with foil or use nonstick baking sheets. Lightly brush each baking sheet with 1 tablespoon melted butter. Spread mustard on 1 side of each bread slice. Arrange 12 slices mustard side up on each prepared sheet. Top each with cheese, then 1 tablespoon sauerkraut. Top with ham. Cover with remaining bread slices mustard side down. Brush remaining butter over sandwiches. *(Can be prepared 6 hours ahead. Cover and refrigerate.)*

Preheat oven to 425°F. Bake sandwiches uncovered until bottoms are golden brown, about 10 minutes. Remove any melted cheese from baking sheets. Turn sandwiches over using metal spatula. Return to oven and bake until second sides are golden brown, about 5 minutes. Transfer to serving platter. Serve sandwiches warm or at room temperature.

Sandwich Crowns

12 servings

6 red bell peppers
½ cup olive oil
¼ cup balsamic vinegar*
2 small garlic cloves, minced

2 1½-pound round rye or pumpernickel loaves
Honey mustard* or Dijon mustard

12 hard salami slices
¼ pound spinach leaves, trimmed
12 provolone cheese slices
12 thin red onion rings
12 thin slices cooked turkey

Char peppers over gas flame or in broiler until blackened on all sides. Wrap in paper bag and let stand 10 minutes to steam. Peel and seed peppers. Rinse if necessary; pat dry. Cut into ¾-inch-wide strips. Combine oil, vinegar and garlic in medium bowl. Add peppers and turn to coat. Marinate at least 1 hour at room temperature. *(Can be prepared 1 day ahead. Cover tightly and refrigerate.)*

Drain peppers. Using serrated knife, cut tops off loaves and reserve. Remove insides of loaves and tops, leaving ½-inch shells. (Reserve removed bread for another use.) Spread insides of loaves and tops with thin layer of mustard. Place ½ of salami and spinach in each loaf. Add ¼ of peppers to each. Top with cheese and onion rings, then remaining peppers. Cover with turkey. Replace loaf tops. Wrap each in plastic and foil. Refrigerate overnight. Cut each into 6 wedges before serving.

*Available at specialty foods stores and also at some supermarkets.

Italian Pizza Turnover

Serve this "pizza turnover" with a salad for Sunday supper, or slice it for a delicious appetizer.

4 main-course servings

1 tablespoon olive oil
⅓ 3-pound package frozen pizza dough, thawed
8 thin slices hard salami
8 thin slices provolone cheese
8 thin slices capocollo*
1½ teaspoons Dijon mustard

¼ cup freshly grated Parmesan cheese
½ teaspoon garlic salt
½ teaspoon dried oregano, crumbled
½ teaspoon seasoned salt
¾ cup shredded mozzarella cheese

Preheat oven to 375°F. Brush 11 × 17-inch baking sheet with oil. Roll dough out on prepared sheet to edges. Arrange salami slices in lengthwise row down center of dough, leaving ½-inch space at ends. Top with provolone, then capocollo. Spread with mustard. Sprinkle with Parmesan, garlic salt, oregano and seasoned salt. Cover with mozzarella. Bring long sides of dough together atop filling and brush with water. Pinch and fold over to close. Brush short ends with water and pinch closed. Bake until golden brown, about 25 minutes. Serve warm.

*An Italian sausage available at delis and specialty foods stores.

Cabbage, Bacon and Cheese Calzone

2 servings; can be doubled or tripled

4 slices thick-cut bacon, thinly sliced
½ medium onion, thinly sliced
¼ small cabbage, thinly sliced
⅛ teaspoon dried red pepper flakes
1 tablespoon balsamic vinegar (optional)
¼ teaspoon dried thyme, crumbled
  Salt and freshly ground pepper
1½ pounds frozen bread dough, thawed

1 yolk beaten with 1 tablespoon water
6 ounces mozzarella cheese, grated
3 ounces Fontina cheese (preferably Italian), grated
2 tablespoons goat cheese (optional)

Olive oil
Dried red pepper flakes
Dried thyme, crumbled

Preheat oven to 450°F. Cook bacon in heavy large skillet over medium heat until fat begins to render, stirring frequently, about 3 minutes. Add onion, cabbage and ⅛ teaspoon red pepper flakes and cook until cabbage is tender, stirring occasionally, about 12 minutes. Add vinegar, ¼ teaspoon thyme, salt and pepper. Allow to cool.

Knead dough until smooth. Divide into 2 pieces. Roll 1 piece out on lightly floured surface to 11-inch round. Brush half of edge with yolk mixture. Spread half of mozzarella over half of dough without covering egg. Top with half of Fontina, then half of cabbage mixture, then half of goat cheese. Fold other half of dough over. Press edges together with fork to seal. Trim edges. Transfer to baking sheet. Repeat with remaining dough, cheeses and cabbage mixture.

Brush calzone with olive oil. Sprinkle with pepper and red pepper flakes. Bake until golden brown, about 13 minutes. Brush with oil again; sprinkle with thyme. Serve immediately.

4 ❦ Main Courses

The outstanding feature of the entrées here is their diversity—you'll find everything from French and Italian classics to exciting Thai and Greek specialties. But with all their variety, they have one thing in common—they're all delicious.

For a simple and sophisticated meat entrée, serve the Classic Standing Rib Roast with Claret Pan Sauce or Osso Bucco, the Italian dish of juicy veal shanks in a tomato-herb sauce. If you want poultry or fish, you might try Roast Chicken with Rosemary, Thyme and Lemon or Red Snapper with Tomato, Basil and Olive Sauce. Hearty, homey dishes for casual get-togethers and family meals include Pork Chops with Onions, Bacon and Mushrooms; Garlic Meatballs with Avgolemono Sauce, a Greek dish with a zippy lemon sauce; and Spicy Fried Chicken with the kick of cayenne pepper.

Vegetarian main courses that feature eggs, cheese and vegetables are becoming increasingly popular as alternatives to the traditional meat entrée—they're nutritious and easy to prepare, and can be served for breakfast, brunch, lunch or supper. Eggplant Sauté with Goat Cheese and Basil makes a stylish dinner served with spinach fettuccine or plump white beans—round out the meal with a cool sorbet or ice cream, brownies or fresh fruit. Italian Spicy Eggs are terrific for brunch or as a light supper with a crisp green salad.

 # Beef

Steak with Roquefort, Green Onions and Walnuts

4 servings

1½ to 2 pounds New York sirloin, rib eye, tenderloin, or top sirloin steak (¾ to 1 inch thick), trimmed
2 tablespoons (¼ stick) butter
1 tablespoon vegetable oil
   Salt and freshly ground pepper

2 tablespoons minced shallots

⅓ cup dry white wine
1 cup whipping cream
½ cup Roquefort cheese, crumbled
2 to 3 tablespoons minced green onions
3 tablespoons chopped toasted walnuts

Preheat oven to 180°F. Pat steaks dry. Melt 1 tablespoon butter with oil in heavy large skillet over medium-high heat. Add steaks (do not crowd) and cook 2 minutes, adjusting heat if necessary to prevent burning. Using tongs or spatula, turn steaks and cook about 2 more minutes for medium-rare. Transfer steaks to ovenproof platter. Season lightly with salt and pepper. Keep steaks warm in oven.

Pour off drippings from skillet. Add remaining 1 tablespoon butter and melt over low heat. Add shallots and stir 1 minute. Increase heat to high. Stir in wine and bring to boil, scraping up any browned bits. Cook until reduced to 2 tablespoons, stirring constantly, about 2 minutes. Add cream and boil until sauce thickens and lightly coats spoon, stirring constantly, about 3 minutes. Reduce heat to low. Whisk in cheese. Stir in green onions. Adjust seasoning. Transfer steaks to plates. Spoon some of sauce down center of each. Sprinkle walnuts over evenly. Serve immediately.

Steaks with Brandy, Shallot and Mustard Sauce

2 servings; can be doubled or tripled

3 tablespoons butter
1 tablespoon vegetable oil
2 1- to 1¼-inch-thick beef filet mignon steaks
   Salt and freshly ground pepper

2 large shallots, sliced

3 tablespoons brandy
1 cup beef stock or canned low-salt broth
½ teaspoon Dijon mustard
   Snipped fresh chives

Melt 1 tablespoon butter with oil in heavy large skillet over medium-high heat. Season steaks with salt and pepper. Add to skillet and cook 2 minutes per side to sear. Reduce heat to medium and cook to desired degree of doneness, about 1 minute longer per side for medium-rare. Transfer steaks to heated platter. Cover; keep warm.

Wipe out skillet. Add 1 tablespoon butter and melt over medium heat. Add shallots and sauté 1 minute. Remove from heat; cool 1 minute. Add brandy. Ignite with match. When flames subside, add stock and boil over high heat until syrupy, about 8 minutes. Whisk in mustard and remaining 1 tablespoon butter. Adjust seasoning. Spoon sauce over steaks. Garnish with snipped chives.

Classic Standing Rib Roast with Claret Pan Sauce

Simple and sophisticated. Start this about three hours before you plan to eat.

6 servings

1   6- to 8-pound standing rib roast
2   large garlic cloves, split
1   large onion, thinly sliced
     Salt and freshly ground pepper
1½   cups full-bodied dry red wine, such as Bordeaux or Cabernet Sauvignon

2   cups chicken stock or canned low-salt broth
     Fresh parsley sprigs

Preheat oven to 325°F. Trim all but ¼-inch layer of fat from meat. Place meat bone side down in shallow roasting pan slightly larger than meat. Rub garlic over meat. Leave garlic in pan. Arrange onion around meat in pan. Sprinkle meat with salt and pepper. Roast meat 20 minutes. Pour ½ cup wine over meat. Roast until thermometer inserted in center of meat registers 125°F for rare, basting frequently with pan juices, and pouring about 3 tablespoons wine over meat every 30 minutes, about 2 hours 30 minutes.

Transfer meat to heated platter, reserving drippings in pan. Tent meat with foil to keep warm. Skim fat off pan drippings. Set pan with drippings over high heat. Add stock and boil until syrupy, scraping up any browned bits and stirring frequently, about 8 minutes. Season with salt and pepper. Strain sauce. Garnish meat with parsley. Serve, passing sauce separately.

Thai Cilantro Beef and Potatoes

Although potatoes are not indigenous to Thailand, once introduced they were taken up with a passion. Called man farang, *their addition to this satisfying dish is nice for those who may not be steamed white rice fanciers.*

10 servings

½   cup coriander seeds
5   pounds beef round or chuck, trimmed, cut into ¾-inch cubes
¾   cup fish sauce (nam pla or nuoc nam)*
3½   tablespoons sugar
2   teaspoons freshly ground pepper
3   tablespoons (or more) vegetable oil

4   garlic cloves, minced
5   medium russet potatoes, peeled, cut into 1½-inch cubes
3   onions, chopped

¾   cup water

     Salt and freshly ground pepper
8   fresh cilantro sprigs, chopped

Preheat oven to 375°F. Place coriander seeds in pie pan and toast until darkened and aromatic, about 15 minutes. Cool coriander seeds slightly.

Transfer coriander seeds to mortar and crush with pestle to coarse powder. Transfer to large bowl. Add beef, fish sauce, sugar and pepper and stir to coat beef completely. Cover and marinate at room temperature 1 hour.

Add 3 tablespoons oil to wok or heavy deep skillet, tilting to coat entire surface. Add garlic and stir 15 seconds. Add potatoes and onions and cook, tossing gently, 5 minutes. Remove potato mixture using slotted spoon.

Drain beef, reserving marinade. Brown beef in wok in batches, adding more oil if necessary. Return all beef to wok. Add reserved marinade and water. Bring to boil, stirring occasionally. Reduce heat to low, cover and simmer until meat is tender, about 1½ hours, adding potato mixture for last 45 minutes of cooking.

Season beef with salt and pepper. Stir in cilantro. Transfer to heated bowl.

*Southeast Asian fish sauces, available at oriental markets and some supermarkets.

Spicy Indian Beef Stew

4 servings

2 pounds beef chuck, trimmed, cut into 2-inch squares
2½ tablespoons minced ginger

2 tablespoons coriander seeds
2 tablespoons cumin seeds
5 small dried red chilies, halved and seeded
4 green cardamom pods
4 whole cloves
1 teaspoon whole mace

½ teaspoon whole black peppercorns
20 garlic cloves, mashed
1 cup plain yogurt
Salt
¾ pound onions, cut into thin rings

Vegetable oil
1 pound onions, finely sliced lengthwise

Combine meat and ginger. Let stand 30 minutes at room temperature.

Toast coriander and cumin seeds in heavy small skillet over medium heat until lightly browned, shaking skillet frequently, 3 to 4 minutes. Transfer to spice grinder or blender. Add chilies, cardamom, cloves, mace and peppercorns and grind finely. With processor running, drop garlic cloves through feed tube and mix to paste. Add ground spice mixture to processor and blend. Scrape into bowl. Stir in yogurt. Season with salt. Mix ¼ of yogurt mixture with ¾ pound onions. Rub remaining yogurt mixture into meat.

Heat 1 inch oil in heavy 10-inch skillet over medium-high heat. Add half of remaining 1 pound onions and fry until dark brown, stirring frequently, about 10 minutes. Remove using slotted spoon and drain on paper towels. Repeat with remaining onions. Cool. Reserve oil. Crush onions coarsely.

Arrange half of meat in heavy 4-quart saucepan. Cover with half of yogurt-onion mixture. Top with half of fried onions. Repeat with remaining meat, yogurt-onion mixture and fried onions. Pour ⅓ cup reserved oil over. Cover and bring to boil. Reduce heat and simmer until meat is fork tender, about 1 hour, stirring occasionally.

Garlic Meatballs with Avgolemono Sauce

Parslied orzo and steamed broccoli make excellent accompaniments to this hearty Greek-style entrée.

8 servings

Meatballs
8 cups fresh spinach leaves (about 2 bunches)
1 teaspoon whipped butter, melted
3 slices white bread
Cold water
2½ pounds lean ground round
⅔ cup dry red wine
6 garlic cloves, pressed
1¼ teaspoons salt
1 teaspoon dried oregano, crumbled
Freshly ground pepper

Sauce
1 tablespoon potato starch or cornstarch
1½ cups chicken stock or canned broth
¼ cup strained fresh lemon juice
1 egg yolk
Salt

Lemon peel julienne
Minced fresh parsley

For meatballs: Steam spinach until just wilted. Drain well; chop. Toss spinach with butter in small bowl. Soak bread in water until softened, about 30 seconds. Squeeze out liquid. Mix bread, ground round, wine, garlic, salt and oregano in large bowl. Season with pepper. Shape mixture into sixteen 4½-inch-long, 1½-inch-wide ovals. Press finger into center of each, forming pockets. Divide spinach among pockets. Press meat up and over spinach, enclosing completely. *(Can be prepared 1 day ahead. Cover and refrigerate.)*

Bring water to boil in base of vegetable steamer. Arrange meatballs, rounded side up, on steamer rack, spacing 1 inch apart. Reduce heat to medium. Cover and cook until meat is no longer pink inside, about 15 minutes.

Meanwhile, prepare sauce: Dissolve potato starch in ¼ cup stock in heavy medium saucepan. Add remaining 1¼ cups stock and bring to boil, stirring constantly. Mix in lemon juice. Whisk yolk in medium bowl. Whisk in stock mixture. Return to saucepan and stir over low heat until thickened, about 10 minutes. Season with salt.

Arrange meatballs on heated platter. Spoon sauce over. Garnish with lemon peel and parsley and serve.

Blue Cheese Burgers

There is enough sauce for four servings, but any extra is great as a dressing for potato or other salads. Serve these burgers as is or on a bun, adding the usual lettuce, tomato and onion if you like.

2 servings; can be doubled or tripled

1 green onion, cut into 1-inch pieces (white and light green parts)
¼ cup mayonnaise
¼ cup sour cream
½ teaspoon Dijon mustard
¼ teaspoon Worcestershire sauce
¼ cup crumbled blue cheese
Salt and freshly ground pepper
⅔ to 1 pound ground beef

Chop green onion in processor. Add mayonnaise, sour cream, mustard and Worcestershire sauce and blend. Add cheese and mix well. Season with salt and pepper. *(Can be prepared 3 days ahead. Cover and refrigerate. Bring to room temperature before serving.)*

Prepare barbecue grill (medium-high heat). Form beef into two 1-inch-thick patties. Season with salt and pepper. Grill to desired doneness, about 4 minutes per side for rare. Transfer to plates. Spoon sauce over and serve.

Pop's Chili

Double this recipe and freeze half—you'll get two meals from one.

2 servings; can be doubled or tripled

1½ tablespoons vegetable oil
1 large onion, chopped
3 garlic cloves, minced
1 pound ground beef
Salt and freshly ground pepper
1 tablespoon chili powder or to taste
2 cups crushed tomatoes with added puree
1 15¼-ounce can kidney beans, drained
2 tablespoons tomato paste
1 teaspoon fresh lemon juice
Shredded cheddar cheese
Sour cream

Heat oil in heavy medium saucepan over medium-low heat. Add onion and cook 5 minutes, stirring occasionally. Add garlic and cook until onion is translucent, stirring occasionally, about 5 minutes. Add beef. Season generously with salt and pepper. Cook until beef is no longer pink, crumbling with fork. Add chili powder and stir 1 minute. Add tomatoes, beans and tomato paste. Cover and simmer 30 minutes, stirring occasionally. *(Can be prepared ahead. Cover and refrigerate 3 days or freeze up to 1 month.)*

Stir lemon juice into chili. Serve, passing cheese and sour cream.

 *Veal*

Rosemary-scented Veal with Crookneck Squash and Sun-dried Tomatoes

4 servings

⅓ cup coarsely chopped marinated sun-dried tomatoes (about 4), 3 tablespoons oil reserved
1 pound boned veal leg, cut into 2 × ½-inch slices, patted dry
2 tablespoons olive oil
½ medium red onion, coarsely chopped
1 garlic clove, minced
¼ teaspoon dried red pepper flakes
1¼ pounds crookneck squash, halved if large and thinly sliced

⅓ cup chicken stock or canned low-salt broth
3 tablespoons dry white wine
1 teaspoon instant flour
1½ teaspoons minced fresh rosemary
½ to ¾ teaspoon coarse salt
Freshly ground pepper
2 tablespoons chopped fresh parsley
2 teaspoons fresh lemon juice

Heat reserved sun-dried tomato oil in heavy large skillet or wok over medium-high heat. Add veal and stir until opaque on all sides, about 1 minute. Remove from skillet. Heat olive oil in same skillet. Add onion, garlic and pepper flakes and stir 10 seconds. Add tomatoes and squash and stir 30 seconds. Remove from skillet. Blend in stock, wine and flour and cook until reduced by half, about 1 minute. Add rosemary and cook 1 minute. Mix in salt. Season with pepper. Return veal and squash mixture to skillet. Add parsley and lemon juice and toss to heat through. Serve immediately.

Grillades and Brown Creole Sauce

Serve with the Garlic Cheese Soufflé Grits (see page 70).

8 servings

Sauce
¼ cup olive oil
¼ cup all purpose flour
1 large onion, cut into ½-inch dice
1 medium green bell pepper, cut into ½-inch dice
3 celery stalks, cut into ½-inch dice
2 large garlic cloves, minced
1 pound tomatoes, peeled, seeded and diced
6 ounces mushrooms, thinly sliced
4 cups veal stock, chicken stock or canned low-salt broth
1 cup dry red wine
2 small jalapeño chilies, seeded and minced

1 teaspoon ground cumin
1 teaspoon salt
1 teaspoon freshly ground pepper

Grillades
16 2-ounce veal loin medallions, about 1¼ inches thick
Salt
All purpose flour
Clarified butter

Garlic Cheese Soufflé Grits (see page 70)
Julienne of red, yellow and green bell peppers

For sauce: Heat oil in heavy large saucepan over medium heat until almost smoking. Mix in flour and stir until golden brown, about 1 minute. Add onion, bell pepper and celery and cook until onion is translucent, stirring occasionally, about 10 minutes. Add garlic and cook 3 minutes. Add tomatoes and cook until slightly thickened, stirring occasionally, about 10 minutes. Add mushrooms and cook until softened, stirring occasionally, about 5 minutes. Add stock, wine, chilies, cumin, salt and pepper and simmer until thick, chunky and reduced by about ⅔, stirring occasionally, 45 minutes to 1 hour. *(Can be prepared two days ahead and refrigerated. Reheat gently before serving.)*

For grillades: Pat veal dry. Season lightly with salt. Dredge in flour, shaking off excess. Heat thin layer of butter in heavy large skillet over medium-high heat. Add veal (in batches; do not crowd) and brown well on both sides. Reduce heat to medium-low and cook until veal is tender but still pink inside, about 7 minutes. Arrange veal on plates. Spoon grits on side. Top veal and grits with sauce. Garnish with bell pepper julienne and serve.

Osso Bucco

The Risotto Milanese (see page 69) is an authentic accompaniment to this dish.

12 servings

Gremolata
 2 tablespoons minced fresh parsley
 2 teaspoons grated orange peel
 2 teaspoons grated lemon peel
 2 garlic cloves, minced

Osso Bucco
 5 tablespoons butter
 5 tablespoons olive oil
 12 pieces hind veal shanks (about 1 pound each), patted dry
   All purpose flour
 1 large onion, chopped
 2 large celery stalks, chopped
 1 large carrot, chopped

 2 garlic cloves, chopped
 2 basil leaves, chopped
 2 lemon peel strips, chopped
   Salt and pepper
 ¼ cup dry white wine
 2 28-ounce cans Italian plum tomatoes, juices reserved
 2 cups (or more) beef stock or canned broth
 5 fresh parsley sprigs
 ⅓ teaspoon dried thyme, crumbled
 1 bay leaf

   Risotto Milanese (see page 69)

For gremolata: Combine all ingredients in small bowl. Cover and let stand.

For osso bucco: Position rack in lowest third of oven and preheat to 375°F. Melt butter with oil in Dutch oven over medium heat. Using kitchen twine, tie each shank in two places to keep shape. Dredge in flour, shaking off excess. Add to Dutch oven and brown well on all sides. Transfer to plate. Pour off fat from Dutch oven. Add next 6 ingredients. Season with salt and pepper and cook until vegetables soften slightly, stirring frequently, about 5 minutes. Stir in wine and cook until evaporated. Add tomatoes, beef stock, parsley, thyme and bay leaf and bring to boil. Arrange veal upright in Dutch oven; liquid should go ¾ up shanks. Cover and bake until meat is tender, basting every 20 minutes with pan juices, about 1½ hours.

Using tongs, transfer veal to platter. Discard twine; keep veal warm. Strain contents of Dutch oven into 3-quart saucepan, pressing on solids. Boil until reduced by half. Season with salt and pepper. Pour over veal. Sprinkle with gremolata. Serve with risotto.

Roasted Veal with Caramelized Apple Sauce

Tender veal is the perfect foil for the rich, Calvados-enhanced sauce. Serve with a variety of steamed vegetables and rice pilaf.

12 servings

Veal

- ½ cup olive oil
- ½ cup fresh lemon juice
- ¼ cup honey mustard
- ¼ cup dry white wine
- 1 tablespoon chopped fresh tarragon or 2 teaspoons dried, crumbled
- 1 tablespoon chopped fresh dill or 2 teaspoons dried dillweed
- 4 garlic cloves, crushed
  Freshly ground pepper
- 1 4- to 5-pound boneless veal top round or top sirloin, rolled and tied

Sauce

- 2 large tart green apples, peeled, cored and thinly sliced
- 1 tablespoon fresh lemon juice
- ¼ cup (½ stick) butter
- ¼ cup sugar
- ¼ cup Calvados or applejack
- 4½ cups veal stock, chicken stock or canned low-salt broth, boiled until reduced to 1½ cups
- 6 tablespoons (¾ stick) butter, cut into tablespoon-size pieces
  Additional Calvados
  Additional fresh lemon juice
  Salt

For veal: Combine first 8 ingredients in double plastic bag. Add veal, turning to coat. Seal; let stand 2 hours at room temperature or chill overnight.

Preheat oven to 325°F. Remove veal from marinade; reserve marinade. Set veal on rack in roasting pan and roast 1½ hours, turning and basting with marinade occasionally. *(Can be prepared 8 hours ahead and refrigerated.)*

Meanwhile, prepare sauce: Toss apples with lemon juice. Melt ¼ cup butter in heavy large skillet over medium heat. Add apples and stir to coat. Sprinkle with sugar and cook until tender and caramelized, stirring frequently, about 5 minutes. Remove from heat. Stir in Calvados. Return to heat and boil until reduced to glaze. Stir in stock and heat through. *(Can be prepared 8 hours ahead to this point. Reheat before continuing.)* Blend in 6 tablespoons butter 1 tablespoon at a time. Season to taste with additional Calvados, lemon juice and salt and pepper.

Slice veal. Arrange on plates. Spoon sauce over. Serve immediately.

 Lamb

Lamb Stroganoff with Bulgur Wheat

2 servings; can be doubled or tripled

Bulgur

- 1 tablespoon butter
- 1 cup bulgur wheat*
- 2 cups beef stock or canned broth
  Salt and freshly ground pepper

Stroganoff

- 3 to 4 shoulder blade lamb chops (cut ¾ to 1 inch thick; 1½ to 1¾ pounds)
  Salt and freshly ground pepper

- 2 tablespoons (¼ stick) butter

- 1 medium onion, chopped
- 8 ounces mushrooms, sliced
- 1½ tablespoons all purpose flour
- 1 cup beef stock or canned broth
- ¼ cup dry white wine
- 1 teaspoon minced fresh dill or ½ teaspoon dried dillweed
- ½ cup sour cream

For bulgur: Melt butter in heavy small saucepan over medium-high heat. Add bulgur and stir until golden, about 3 minutes. Add stock; season with salt and pepper. Bring to boil. Reduce heat to low, cover and simmer until liquid is absorbed, 15 minutes.

Meanwhile, prepare stroganoff: Pat chops dry. Season with salt and pepper. Melt 1 tablespoon butter in heavy large skillet over medium-high heat. Add chops and cook until firm, about 5 minutes per side. Transfer to plate.

Reduce heat to medium. Melt remaining 1 tablespoon butter in same skillet. Add onion and cook 3 minutes, stirring occasionally. Add mushrooms; season with salt and pepper. Cook until tender, stirring frequently, about 5 minutes. Add flour and stir 1 minute. Mix in stock. Boil until thickened, about 2 minutes, stirring constantly. Add wine, dill and any juices exuded by lamb. Simmer 2 minutes to blend flavors. Reduce heat to low. Mix in sour cream. Return lamb to skillet and heat through; do not boil.

Spoon bulgur onto plates. Top with lamb and sauce and serve.

*Also called cracked wheat, available at natural foods stores and supermarkets.

Lamb Chops with Mint Julep Sauce

The traditional flavors of a beloved southern drink highlight this spirited sauce. The chops can also be grilled.

4 servings

1 cup mint leaves (about 2 bunches)
½ cup sugar
¼ cup white wine vinegar
2 tablespoons bourbon

8 4-ounce lamb chops
Salt and freshly ground pepper
3 tablespoons butter
3 tablespoons vegetable oil

Finely chop mint in processor using on/off turns. Blend in sugar, vinegar and bourbon. Transfer to bowl. Cover; chill. *(Can be prepared 2 days ahead.)*

Pat lamb chops dry. Season with salt and pepper. Melt butter with oil in 2 heavy large skillets over medium-high heat. Add lamb chops and sauté to desired degree of doneness, about 4 minutes per side for medium-rare. Set 2 on each plate. Spoon sauce over.

Anglo-Indian Lamb Chop Curry with Onions and Potatoes

6 servings

6 7-ounce ¾-inch-thick lamb shoulder chops, trimmed
1½ tablespoons cider vinegar
1 tablespoon minced fresh garlic
1 tablespoon minced peeled fresh ginger
1 teaspoon salt
½ teaspoon cayenne pepper
½ cup water

¼ cup prepared chili sauce
¾ pound red potatoes, unpeeled, cut into ¼-inch-thick slices
1 medium onion, cut into ¼-inch-thick slices
1 large tomato, cut into ¼-inch-thick slices
1 tablespoon snipped fresh chives or green onion tops

Arrange lamb chops in single layer in shallow dish. Mix vinegar, garlic, ginger, salt and cayenne in small bowl. Rub spice mixture into lamb. Cover and refrigerate for at least 1 hour. *(Can be prepared 1 day ahead.)*

Transfer lamb to heavy large cast-iron skillet. Add ½ cup water and bring to boil. Reduce heat to medium and cook until lamb is tender and cooked through, turning lamb over occasionally, about 20 minutes.

Pour chili sauce around lamb. Arrange potato slices over lamb in single layer. Cover with onion and tomato slices. Cover and cook over medium heat until potatoes are tender, about 20 minutes. Divide lamb, potato, onion and tomato slices among plates. Pour sauce over. Sprinkle with chives and serve.

Leg of Lamb with Asparagus, Egg and Lemon Sauce

Serve the lamb with roasted potatoes.

8 servings

1½ pounds thin asparagus, trimmed

1 5-pound leg of lamb, trimmed
5 garlic cloves, cut into slivers
12 fresh mint leaves
Salt and freshly ground pepper

2 cups lamb or chicken stock or canned broth

¼ cup (½ stick) unsalted butter
2 medium yellow onions, diced
2 garlic cloves, minced
2 eggs
¼ cup fresh lemon juice
2 tablespoons minced fresh mint

Cook asparagus in large pot of boiling salted water until crisp-tender. Drain. Rinse with cold water and drain well. Pat dry. Cut into 2-inch pieces.

Preheat oven to 350°F. Cut slits in lamb. Roll garlic slivers in mint leaves and insert in slits. Sprinkle lamb with salt and pepper. Place on rack in roasting pan. Cook until thermometer inserted in thickest part registers 130°F for medium-rare, about 1½ hours. Transfer lamb to heated platter and keep warm.

Pour off all but 2 tablespoons fat from roasting pan. Add stock to pan and bring to boil, scraping up any browned bits. Degrease stock and set aside. Melt butter in heavy medium saucepan over medium-low heat. Add onions and cook until tender, stirring occasionally, about 8 minutes. Add minced garlic and stir 30 seconds. Add stock and boil until mixture thickens to sauce consistency, about 25 minutes. Reduce heat to low. Add asparagus to sauce and heat through. Mix eggs and lemon juice in small bowl. Slowly add to sauce, stirring constantly (do not boil or eggs will curdle). Mix in minced mint. Add salt and pepper. Serve lamb and sauce immediately.

 *Pork*

Pork Chops with Onions, Bacon and Mushrooms

6 servings

Butter
2 tablespoons (¼ stick) butter
6 ¾-inch-thick pork loin chops (5 ounces each)
Salt and freshly ground pepper
2 cups quartered mushrooms

2 medium onions, chopped

¼ pound bacon, diced
2 tablespoons all purpose flour
1½ teaspoons paprika
1 cup whipping cream
1 cup beef stock or canned broth
2 tablespoons tomato sauce
Freshly cooked rice

Preheat oven to 375°F. Butter 9 × 16-inch glass baking dish. Melt 2 tablespoons butter in heavy large skillet over high heat. Season chops with salt and pepper. Add to skillet (in batches if necessary) and sear until brown, about 2 minutes per side. Transfer to prepared baking dish. Top with mushrooms.

Add onions and bacon to same skillet and cook over medium heat until onions are translucent and bacon is crisp, stirring frequently, about 10 minutes. Mix in flour and paprika. Increase heat to medium-high. Stir in cream and broth and bring to boil, stirring constantly. Mix in tomato sauce. Season with salt and pepper. Pour sauce over mushrooms and chops. Transfer to oven and bake until chops are tender, 20 to 25 minutes. Serve with rice.

Pork Tenderloin with White Wine Sauce

2 to 4 servings

10 to 12 ounces pork tenderloin, trimmed and cut into 1-inch-thick rounds
2 teaspoons all purpose flour
Salt and pepper
¼ cup (½ stick) butter
1 large shallot, chopped

1 2½-ounce can sliced mushrooms, drained
⅛ teaspoon dried rosemary, crumbled
¼ cup dry white wine
¼ cup canned chicken broth

Pat pork dry. Place flour in plastic bag. Season with salt and pepper. Place pork in bag; close tightly and shake. Melt butter in heavy large skillet over medium heat. Add pork and shallot and cook 4 minutes. Turn pork over. Add mushrooms and rosemary and cook until mushrooms are just soft, about 1 minute. Mix in wine and broth and simmer until pork is cooked through, about 3 minutes.

Apricot- and Walnut-stuffed Pork Tenderloins

6 servings

½ cup bourbon
½ cup finely chopped dried apricots (about 3 ounces)
½ cup boiling water
6 tablespoons dried currants

¾ cup fresh white breadcrumbs
½ cup chopped walnuts (about 2 ounces)
2 tablespoons minced fresh parsley
½ teaspoon dried rosemary, crumbled
½ teaspoon salt
¼ teaspoon dried sage, crumbled
1 egg, beaten to blend

2 12- to 14-ounce pork tenderloins, trimmed of excess fat
Salt and freshly ground pepper

1 tablespoon unsalted butter
1 tablespoon vegetable oil
2 cups (about) chicken stock or canned broth

1 cup dry white wine
½ cup apricot jam, strained
1 tablespoon cornstarch dissolved in ¼ cup water

Fresh rosemary sprigs (optional)

Pour bourbon over apricots in small bowl. Let stand 20 minutes. Pour water over currants in another small bowl. Let stand 10 minutes.

Drain apricots; reserve ¼ cup soaking liquid. Drain currants. Mix apricots, currants, breadcrumbs, walnuts, parsley, dried rosemary, ½ teaspoon salt and sage in large bowl. Mix in egg.

Preheat oven to 350°F. To butterfly pork, cut each tenderloin lengthwise down center, cutting ⅔ of the way through. To flatten, cut ⅓-inch-deep slit lengthwise down centers on each half of tenderloins. Pound meat between sheets of waxed paper to thickness of ½ inch. Spread stuffing atop tenderloins. Roll up each tenderloin jelly roll fashion, starting at one long side. Tie with string to secure. Pat meat dry. Sprinkle with salt and pepper.

Melt butter with oil in heavy roasting pan over medium-high heat. Add roasts and brown on all sides, about 7 minutes. Remove roasts. Set rack in roasting pan. Arrange roasts atop rack. Mix reserved apricot soaking liquid with 1½ cups stock and pour over pork. Roast 45 minutes for medium, basting frequently with pan juices.

Transfer roasts to platter. Tent loosely with foil to keep warm. Pour pan juices into bowl. Skim off fat. Add enough stock to juices to measure 1 cup. Set roasting pan over medium-high heat. Add wine and bring to boil, scraping up any browned bits. Add pan juices. Boil until reduced by ⅓, stirring frequently, about 5 minutes. Mix in jam. Add cornstarch mixture and boil, stirring until sauce thickens and coats back of spoon, about 1 minute. Strain through sieve. Season with salt.

Remove strings from pork. Cut pork into ½-inch-thick slices. Overlap slices on plates. Pour some sauce over. Garnish with rosemary. Serve, passing remaining sauce separately.

Barbecued Spareribs with Red-Hot Sauce

The sweet-tart chili-based sauce is terrific—hot and spicy (much of its fire, though, is tamed as it cooks with the meat on the grill). Pass the remaining sauce along with the grilled ribs. Iced tea, cold beer or a chilled fruity red wine will help tame things a bit, too.

4 servings

1½ cups bottled chili sauce
⅓ cup apple jelly
2 tablespoons cider vinegar
1 tablespoon dry mustard
1 tablespoon Worcestershire sauce
1½ teaspoons hot pepper sauce (such as Tabasco)

½ teaspoon cayenne pepper

4½ to 5 pounds spareribs, preferably baby back, cut into 3-rib sections
2 teaspoons salt

Bring first 7 ingredients to boil in heavy small saucepan over medium heat, stirring occasionally. Reduce heat and simmer 1 minute. Cool completely. *(Sauce can be prepared 3 weeks ahead. Cover and refrigerate.)*

Place ribs in large pot. Add enough hot water to cover. Cover and bring to boil. Reduce heat. Add salt, cover and simmer 25 minutes. Drain well. Transfer ribs to large baking dish. Pour ¾ cup chili sauce over; turn ribs to coat. *(Can be prepared 1 day ahead. Cover and refrigerate. Bring to room temperature.)*

Prepare barbecue (high heat). Grill ribs until sauce browns slightly and ribs are heated through, brushing occasionally with additional sauce, about 5 minutes per side. Transfer to platter. Pass remaining sauce separately.

Sausage Risotto

4 servings

1 cup water
1 cup dry white wine
1 pound sweet Italian sausages

¼ cup (½ stick) butter
2 tablespoons olive oil
1 medium onion, chopped
1 medium green or red bell pepper, chopped

1 garlic clove, minced

1 cup rice
2 14½-ounce cans chicken broth
1 teaspoon fennel seeds, crushed
1 teaspoon dried sage, crumbled
Salt and freshly ground pepper
Chopped fresh parsley

Bring water and wine to boil in medium saucepan. Reduce heat. Add sausages and simmer until just cooked through but still juicy, about 12 minutes. Drain. Place sausages on plate and cut into ½-inch-thick slices; reserve sausage juices exuded on plate.

Melt butter with oil in heavy large saucepan over medium heat. Stir in onion and bell pepper. Cover and cook 6 minutes. Mix in garlic. Cover and cook until vegetables are soft, 4 minutes.

Add rice to vegetables and cook over medium heat until rice is golden, stirring occasionally, about 5 minutes. Add 1 cup broth to rice. Adjust heat so liquid barely simmers and cook until broth is absorbed, stirring occasionally. Continue adding broth 1 cup at a time, adding sausage juices, fennel and sage with last addition and cooking until rice is just tender, about 20 minutes. Stir in sausages. Season with salt and pepper. Sprinkle with parsley and serve.

 Poultry

Roast Chicken with Rosemary, Thyme and Lemon

Updating a classic, California style.

6 servings

¼ cup olive oil
1 5- to 6-pound roasting chicken, cut into 8 pieces, patted dry
1½ pounds new potatoes, unpeeled, cut into ½-inch-wide wedges
Salt and freshly ground pepper
7 tablespoons fresh lemon juice
2 tablespoons red wine vinegar

12 large thyme sprigs
10 large rosemary sprigs
2 lemons, cut into ⅛-inch-thick slices

6 lemon wedges
Fresh thyme sprigs
Fresh rosemary sprigs

Preheat oven to 400°F. Heat oil in heavy large skillet over medium-high heat. Add chicken in batches and brown on all sides, about 8 minutes. Transfer chicken to large roasting pan. Add potato wedges. Season with salt and pepper. Mix lemon juice with vinegar. Pour over chicken and potatoes. Top with 12 thyme sprigs and 10 rosemary sprigs. Layer lemon slices over. Bake until chicken and potatoes are tender, about 1 hour.

Discard lemon slices and herbs. Halve chicken breasts lengthwise. Transfer chicken and potatoes to heated platter. Garnish platter with lemon wedges, thyme and rosemary.

Country Captain Stir-fry

A variation on a southern classic, good with buttered parslied rice.

4 servings

5 tablespoons butter
4 large skinned and boned chicken breast halves, trimmed, cut into bite-size pieces and patted dry
½ large onion, thinly sliced
1 garlic clove, minced
1½ teaspoons curry powder
¾ teaspoon coarse salt
¾ teaspoon fresh thyme leaves or ⅛ teaspoon dried, crumbled
⅛ teaspoon cayenne pepper
⅛ teaspoon sugar

6 ounces green bell pepper, thinly sliced
6 ounces red bell pepper, thinly sliced
1 pound tomatoes, peeled, seeded and cut into 1-inch strips
½ cup chicken stock or canned broth
⅓ cup raisins
3 tablespoons toasted slivered almonds
2 tablespoons chopped fresh parsley

Melt 3 tablespoons butter in heavy large skillet or wok over medium-high heat. Add chicken and sauté until just opaque, about 2 minutes. Remove from skillet. Melt remaining butter in same skillet. Add onion and garlic and stir 10 seconds.

Blend in curry, salt, thyme, cayenne and sugar. Add bell peppers and cook 30 seconds. Add tomatoes, stock and raisins, bring to boil and cook until reduced by half. Return chicken and any exuded juices to skillet and heat through. Stir in almonds and parsley and serve.

Thai Chicken with Fresh Basil

The particular variety of basil used for this dish in Thailand is called holy basil, or bai gaprow. *It is very difficult to find here, but any member of the basil family works just fine. Fresh mint can also be used. A delicious introduction to Thai cooking.*

4 servings

3 tablespoons vegetable oil
2 tablespoons coarsely chopped garlic
¾ cup lightly packed thinly sliced fresh basil leaves
2 serrano chilies, stemmed, seeded and cut lengthwise into thin strips
1 pound boned chicken breast, skinned and cut crosswise into 1¼ × 1-inch strips

3 tablespoons fish sauce (nam pla or nuoc nam)*
2 tablespoons water
2 teaspoons sugar
Thai Steamed Rice**

Heat oil in wok or heavy large skillet over high heat until piece of garlic added sizzles immediately. Add garlic and stir until golden brown, about 10 seconds. Add ½ cup basil leaves and chilies and stir-fry just until basil wilts, about 1 minute. Add chicken and stir-fry until springy to touch, about 3 minutes. Add fish sauce, water and sugar and stir-fry until sauce bubbles and thickens slightly, about 2 minutes. Add remaining ¼ cup basil and stir-fry just until wilted, about 5 seconds. Transfer to shallow dish. Serve immediately with steamed rice.

*Southeast Asian fish sauces, available at oriental markets and some supermarkets.

**Thai Steamed Rice

If the bag of jasmine rice says "New Crop," reduce the water in this recipe to 2½ cups.

4 servings

2 cups jasmine rice or other long-grain rice

3 cups cold water

Rinse and drain rice 3 times. Place in heavy 3-quart saucepan. Add water. Bring to boil over high heat. Reduce heat to low and stir vigorously with bamboo rice paddle or wooden spoon, scraping bottom of pot. Cover and cook 20 minutes without lifting lid. Remove from heat and let stand covered 10 minutes. Fluff gently with fork or rice paddle and serve.

Chicken Sauté with Artichokes and Pancetta

Orzo tossed with butter and grated Parmesan cheese is a fitting accompaniment to this Italian-flavored dish.

4 servings

3 tablespoons olive oil
1¼ pounds skinned and boned chicken breasts, trimmed, cut into 1-inch squares and patted dry
½ medium onion, chopped
2 ounces pancetta,* chopped
1 garlic clove, minced
Pinch of dried red pepper flakes
1 6-ounce jar marinated quartered artichoke hearts, drained, halved and patted dry

⅓ cup chicken stock or canned broth
⅓ cup Niçoise olives, pitted and quartered
3 tablespoons dry white wine
1 teaspoon minced fresh rosemary
1 teaspoon minced fresh thyme
1 cup frozen tiny peas
2 tablespoons chopped fresh basil
Freshly ground pepper

Heat 1½ tablespoons oil in heavy large skillet or wok over medium heat. Add chicken and cook until almost opaque on all sides, tossing frequently, about 2½ minutes; do not cook through. Remove from skillet. Heat remaining oil in same skillet over high heat. Add onion, pancetta, garlic and pepper flakes and stir 1½ minutes. Add artichokes, stock, olives, wine, rosemary and thyme and cook 1 minute. Return chicken with any exuded juices to skillet and stir 30 seconds. Add peas and cook 30 seconds. Remove from heat. Stir in basil. Season with pepper.

*Pancetta, unsmoked bacon cured in salt, is available at Italian markets.

Prosciutto-wrapped Chicken with Three Cheeses

Serve this rich main course on a bed of spinach.

4 servings

1 egg, beaten to blend
1 tablespoon water
1 cup all purpose flour
⅛ teaspoon freshly ground pepper
8 medium boneless chicken breast halves, skinned
¼ cup (½ stick) butter

4 thin slices Gruyère cheese
4 thin slices mozzarella cheese
⅓ cup chicken stock or canned broth

4 thin slices prosciutto
4 thin slices Fontina cheese

Preheat oven to 350°F. Combine egg and water in small bowl. Combine flour and pepper in another bowl. Pat chicken dry. Dip into egg mixture. Dredge in seasoned flour. Melt butter in heavy large ovenproof skillet over medium-high heat. Add chicken (in batches if necessary) and brown well, 4 minutes per side. Transfer to plate.

Top 4 chicken breasts with 1 slice Gruyère and 1 slice mozzarella. Top with remaining chicken. Return to skillet. Pour in broth. Transfer to oven, cover and bake chicken until opaque, about 10 minutes.

Preheat broiler. Wrap prosciutto around chicken. Top with Fontina cheese. Broil until cheese melts, about 3 minutes.

Smoked Chicken with Goat Cheese and Herbs

6 servings

2 garlic cloves (unpeeled)
Olive oil

½ cup goat cheese, such as Montrachet, room temperature
½ cup minced fresh parsley
2 tablespoons (¼ stick) unsalted butter, room temperature
1 shallot, minced
1½ teaspoons minced fresh rosemary
1½ teaspoons minced fresh thyme
1¼ teaspoons herbes de Provence*
Salt and freshly ground pepper

1 5½- to 6-pound chicken, excess fat trimmed

2 rosemary sprigs
2 thyme sprigs
1 garlic clove, peeled
1 tablespoon olive oil (preferably extra-virgin)

4 cups hickory chips, soaked in water to cover 1 hour and drained

1 cup chicken stock or low-salt canned broth

Kale leaves (optional)

Preheat oven to 350°F. Rub unpeeled garlic with olive oil. Place on sheet of foil and roast 20 minutes. Maintain oven temperature at 350°F.

Peel roasted garlic and mash in small bowl. Mix in goat cheese, parsley, butter, shallot, ½ teaspoon rosemary, ½ teaspoon thyme and ¼ teaspoon herbes de Provence. Season with salt and freshly ground pepper.

Line shallow roasting pan with foil. Pat chicken dry. Season cavity with salt and pepper. Loosen skin over breast meat and top of legs by sliding hand between skin and meat. Spread goat cheese mixture under skin over breast meat and top of legs. Place any remaining mixture in cavity. Add rosemary and thyme sprigs to cavity. Rub garlic clove over skin of chicken; add garlic to cavity. Truss to hold shape. Sprinkle chicken with salt and pepper. Rub with remaining 1 teaspoon rosemary, 1 teaspoon thyme and 1 teaspoon herbes de Provence. Place in prepared pan. Sprinkle with extra-virgin olive oil. Roast 1 hour.

Meanwhile, prepare barbecue grill (high heat). Add hickory chips to fire; cover until smoky, about 5 minutes.

Place chicken on grill rack, reserving pan juices. Cover and smoke until chicken juices run clear when thigh is pierced, about 15 minutes.

Meanwhile, degrease pan juices. Combine with stock in small saucepan. Boil until reduced to ⅔ cup.

Line platter with kale. Transfer chicken to prepared platter. Serve, passing pan juices separately.

*A dried herb mix available at specialty foods stores and some supermarkets. Basil and/or marjoram can be substituted.

Paella

If clams are unavailable, mussels can be substituted in this classic from Spain. Complete the meal with a salad, bread, cheese, and sorbet and fruit for dessert.

6 servings

¼ cup olive oil
1 3-pound chicken, cut into 8 pieces, trimmed of excess fat
Salt and freshly ground pepper
8 ounces uncooked medium shrimp, peeled and deveined, tails left intact

1⅔ cups chopped onions
1 red bell pepper, diced
1 green bell pepper, diced
¾ cup diced smoked ham (about 3½ ounces)
4 medium garlic cloves, minced
2 bay leaves
½ teaspoon saffron threads, crushed
Generous pinch of dried thyme, crumbled

1½ cups drained canned Italian plum tomatoes
1 cup (or more) water
12 small clams, scrubbed or mussels, scrubbed and debearded
1½ cups Arborio* or other short-grain rice
1½ cups chicken stock or canned broth
½ cup peas (about 8 ounces unshelled)
12 pimiento-stuffed green Spanish olives, sliced
Fresh thyme sprigs (optional)
Fresh lemon wedges (optional)

Heat ¼ cup oil in 14- to 15-inch paella pan or heavy deep 12-inch skillet over medium-high heat. Add chicken. Season with salt and pepper. Cook until golden brown on all sides, turning occasionally, about 10 minutes. Transfer chicken to plate. Add shrimp to pan and sauté until shrimp begin to turn pink, about 1 minute. Transfer shrimp to plate with chicken.

Add onions and peppers to paella pan. Cook over medium heat until slightly softened, stirring frequently, about 10 minutes. Add ham, garlic, bay leaves, saffron and thyme. Season with salt and pepper. Stir 1 minute. Add tomatoes and bring to boil, breaking up tomatoes with fork. Set aside.

Bring 1 cup water to boil in heavy medium saucepan over high heat. Add clams. Cover tightly and steam until shells open, 2 to 5 minutes. Remove opened clams. Cook remaining clams about 5 more minutes; discard any that do not open. Transfer clams to another plate. Tent with foil to keep warm. Strain clam cooking liquid into measuring cup through strainer lined with several layers dampened cheesecloth. Add water to measure 1½ cups.

Add rice to tomato mixture in paella pan and stir over medium heat until rice is translucent, about 5 minutes. Add stock and clam cooking liquid. Increase heat and bring to boil. Cook 5 minutes, stirring frequently. Tuck chicken and shrimp into rice mixture. Sprinkle peas over. Reduce heat and simmer paella 15 minutes, shaking pan occasionally to prevent sticking. Arrange clams around edge of pan. Cook until almost all liquid is absorbed and rice is tender, about 5 minutes. Remove pan from heat. Cover tightly with foil and let stand 5 minutes. Adjust seasoning. Sprinkle with olives. Garnish with thyme if desired. Serve, passing lemon wedges if desired.

*Italian short-grain rice, available at Italian markets and specialty foods stores.

Acadian Pepper Chicken

4 servings

½ cup (1 stick) butter
2 tablespoons freshly ground pepper
2 tablespoons fresh lemon juice
1 tablespoon paprika
1 tablespoon dried basil, crumbled
1 tablespoon dried oregano, crumbled
3 garlic cloves, minced

2 bay leaves, crumbled
2 teaspoons dried rosemary, crumbled
1 teaspoon cayenne pepper
1 teaspoon freshly grated nutmeg
½ teaspoon salt
1 3-pound chicken, cut into 8 pieces

Freshly cooked rice

Melt butter in heavy large skillet over medium-low heat. Add next 11 ingredients and cook until spices are aromatic, stirring occasionally, about 5 minutes. Remove from heat and let cool. Add chicken, turning to coat thoroughly. Cover and refrigerate 2 to 4 hours.

Cover chicken and cook over medium-low heat until juices run clear when thigh is pierced with sharp knife, turning occasionally, about 25 minutes. Serve immediately with rice.

Spicy Fried Chicken

12 servings

8 cups all purpose flour
2 tablespoons paprika
2 tablespoons cayenne pepper
2 tablespoons salt
4 teaspoons dried thyme, crumbled
4 cups milk

4 eggs
4 frying chickens, cut into serving pieces, patted dry

Vegetable oil (for deep frying)

Mix first five ingredients in large bowl. Whisk milk and eggs in another large bowl. Dredge chicken in flour mixture, shaking off excess. Dip in milk mixture, allowing excess to drip into bowl. Dredge in flour mixture.

Heat 2 inches of oil in heavy large skillet to 360°F. Fry chicken in batches (do not crowd) until cooked through and coating is golden brown, about 20 minutes for white meat and 25 minutes for dark. Remove using tongs. Drain chicken on paper towels. Serve hot or at room temperature.

Chicken and Chorizo Stew

6 servings

1½ cups lightly salted water
1 cup long-grain rice

3 teaspoons dried oregano
8 whole black peppercorns
4 garlic cloves, minced
2 teaspoons olive oil
1 teaspoon white wine vinegar
1 teaspoon salt
3½ pounds chicken pieces

4 tablespoons (about) olive oil
1 pound Spanish chorizo or sweet Italian sausage, casings removed

1 pound eggplant (unpeeled), cut into 1-inch cubes
3 green bell peppers, coarsely chopped
2 large onions, coarsely chopped
6 large tomatoes, peeled, seeded and chopped or 5½ cups chopped drained canned plum tomatoes
2 cups chicken stock or canned broth
½ teaspoon ground saffron

Bring salted water to boil in heavy medium saucepan over medium heat. Add rice, cover and cook 12 minutes. (Rice will not be tender; water will not be absorbed.) Set aside.

Combine oregano, peppercorns, garlic, 2 teaspoons oil, vinegar and salt in mortar and crush with pestle until well mixed. Rub chicken pieces with half of oregano mixture; set remainder aside. Let stand 15 minutes.

Meanwhile, heat 2 tablespoons oil in heavy large skillet over medium-high heat. Add chorizo and cook until no longer pink, crumbling with fork, 10 to 15 minutes. Remove from skillet.

Add 1 tablespoon oil to same skillet if necessary and heat over medium-high heat. Add chicken pieces and brown on all sides, about 10 minutes. Remove chicken pieces from skillet.

Add 1 tablespoon oil to same skillet if necessary and heat over medium heat. Add eggplant, bell peppers, onions and remaining oregano mixture and sauté until tender, about 10 minutes.

Preheat oven to 400°F. Oil large ovenproof casserole dish. Spread rice with liquid in prepared dish. Place chicken and sausage atop rice. Top with eggplant mixture. Sprinkle with chopped tomatoes. Heat stock in small saucepan over medium heat until bubbles form around edge. Add saffron and stir to dissolve. Pour stock over tomatoes. Cover casserole tightly. Bake 40 minutes. Uncover and bake 5 more minutes. Serve immediately.

Tortillas with Chicken, Chilies and Cheese

8 servings

Sauce
- 4 cups (or more) water
- 2 6-ounce cans tomato sauce
- 2 4-ounce cans whole green chilies, drained and diced
- 1 green bell pepper, diced
- 1 small onion, diced
- 5 to 7 jalapeño chilies, seeded and sliced
- 1½ teaspoons salt

- 3 cups chicken stock or canned broth

- 2 large whole chicken breasts, split

- 8 10-inch flour tortillas
  Vegetable oil
- 1 cup shredded Monterey Jack cheese (about 4 ounces)
- 1 cup shredded cheddar cheese (about 4 ounces)

- ½ head iceberg lettuce, chopped
  Sour cream
  Guacamole
  Sliced green onions

Combine 2 cups water, tomato sauce, canned chilies, bell pepper, onion, sliced jalapeños and salt in heavy large skillet. Bring sauce to boil. Reduce heat and simmer 3 hours, stirring occasionally and adding water as necessary to maintain original level. Continue simmering without adding water until sauce is reduced by three-quarters, about 40 minutes. *(Can be prepared 1 day ahead. Cool, cover and refrigerate.)*

Meanwhile, bring broth to boil in heavy large saucepan. Reduce heat to low and add chicken. Simmer until just springy to touch, about 12 minutes. Remove chicken from broth and cool. (Reserve broth for another use.) Skin, bone and shred chicken.

Brush both sides of 1 tortilla lightly with oil. Arrange ¼ cup chicken, 2 tablespoons of each cheese and 2 tablespoons sauce down center. Fold one side over center and then roll up. Repeat with remaining tortillas, chicken, cheese and 14 tablespoons sauce (you will have sauce left over).

Bring water to boil in base of steamer. Place flautas seam side down on steamer rack. Cover and cook until cheese is melted, about 5 minutes. Arrange lettuce on large platter. Top with flautas. Drizzle remaining sauce down center. Top with sour cream, guacamole and green onions.

Cornish Game Hens with Figs and Thyme

6 servings

- 1 quart water
- ¾ pound dried figs (preferably Black Mission)

- ½ cup (about) olive oil
- 6 1½-pound Cornish game hens, halved
  Salt and freshly ground pepper
- 1½ cups chopped carrots (about 2 large)
- 1½ cups chopped onions (about 2 small)
- 2 cups dry red wine

- 6 cups chicken stock or canned low-salt broth
- 8 fresh thyme sprigs
- 6 garlic cloves, crushed
- 4 bay leaves, halved

- 2 tablespoons cornstarch dissolved in 2 tablespoons water
- ¼ cup (½ stick) chilled unsalted butter, cut into pieces
  Additional fresh thyme sprigs
  Braised Endive (see page 65)

Bring 1 quart water to boil in heavy large saucepan. Add figs. Reduce heat and simmer until soft but not mushy, 15 to 30 minutes depending upon moistness of figs. Drain figs.

Preheat oven to 400°F. Heat ¼ cup oil in heavy large skillet over medium-high heat. Add hens in batches and brown on all sides, adding more oil as necessary. Drain on paper towels. Season hens with salt and pepper. Pour all but 2 tablespoons oil from skillet. Add carrots and onions. Reduce heat to medium and sauté 5 minutes. Add wine and bring to simmer, scraping up any browned bits. Arrange hens breast side up in 2 heavy large roasting pans. Divide vegetable-wine mixture between pans. Add 3 cups stock, 4 thyme sprigs, 3 garlic cloves and 2 bay leaves to each pan. Bake hens 30 minutes, basting frequently with juices. Add figs and bake until hens are tender, 10 minutes more.

Transfer hens and figs to large platter. Tent with foil to keep warm. Strain pan juices into heavy medium saucepan, reserving vegetables. Degrease juices, then boil until reduced to 1½ cups, about 20 minutes. Reduce heat to medium-low. Whisk in cornstarch mixture and stir until thickened. Whisk in butter. Stir 2 tablespoons reserved vegetables into sauce if desired. Spoon sauce over hens. Garnish with thyme sprigs and serve with endive.

Roast Turkey with Herbs and Aromatic Vegetables

The stuffing—a fragrant mixture of herbs and vegetables—scents the bird while it roasts but is not meant to be eaten.

8 servings

1½ bunches fresh thyme, coarsely chopped (about 1 cup)
1½ bunches fresh sage, coarsely chopped (about 1¼ cups)
1½ bunches fresh basil, coarsely chopped (about 1¼ cups)
1½ bunches fresh oregano, coarsely chopped (about 1 cup)
 2 tablespoons (¼ stick) unsalted butter, room temperature
 2 tablespoons coarsely ground pepper
 2 tablespoons coarse salt
1½ tablespoons dried thyme, crumbled
1½ tablespoons rubbed or ground sage
1½ tablespoons dried oregano, crumbled
1½ tablespoons dried basil, crumbled

1 12- to 14-pound turkey (neck and giblets reserved for Corn Bread Dressing with Giblets and Mushrooms, see following recipe), rinsed and patted dry
2 small onions, cut into ¼-inch-thick slices
2 carrots, cut into ¼-inch-thick rounds
2 celery stalks, cut into ¼-inch pieces
2 leeks, cut into ¼-inch-thick rounds
1 whole garlic head, halved crosswise

Olive oil
Herb Butter (see page 76)

Fresh herbs

Preheat oven to 450°F. Mix first 11 ingredients in medium bowl. Rub mixture into turkey cavity. Pack onions, carrots, celery, leeks and garlic into cavity. Truss turkey with string.

Rub turkey skin with oil. Place turkey on rack set in heavy large roasting pan. Roast 30 minutes. Reduce oven temperature to 325°F. Brush turkey with some of Herb Butter. Roast 30 minutes. Brush with Herb Butter. Roast turkey until thermometer inserted in thickest part of thigh registers 170°F, basting occasionally with accumulated pan juices, about 2¼ hours.

Transfer turkey to platter. Degrease pan juices. Let turkey stand 20 minutes. Garnish with fresh herbs. Serve turkey with pan juices.

Corn Bread Dressing with Giblets and Mushrooms

Plenty for a special Thanksgiving dinner, but supplement by passing a basket of dinner rolls if your tradition dictates.

8 servings

Corn Bread
  3 tablespoons solid vegetable shortening or bacon drippings
  1 cup unbleached all purpose flour
  1 tablespoon baking powder
  2 teaspoons sugar
  1 teaspoon salt
  2 cups yellow cornmeal
  2 cups milk
  2 eggs, beaten to blend

Dressing
  4 cups (about) chicken stock or canned broth
    Neck and giblets (reserved from turkey)

  1 bouquet garni made with 3 thyme sprigs, 2 bay leaves and 5 whole black peppercorns

  2 ounces dried mushrooms, such as shiitake or porcini*

  ¾ cup (1½ sticks) unsalted butter
  4 shallots, finely chopped
  2 large garlic cloves, finely chopped
  ¼ pound button mushrooms, sliced
  2 tablespoons chopped fresh parsley
  1 tablespoon fresh thyme leaves or 1 teaspoon dried, crumbled
  ¼ teaspoon rubbed or ground sage

  Salt and freshly ground pepper

For corn bread: Preheat oven to 425°F. Place shortening in heavy 10-inch-diameter ovenproof skillet with 3-inch-high sides (preferably cast iron). Place in oven to heat skillet and melt shortening while preparing batter. Sift flour, baking powder, sugar and salt into large bowl. Mix in cornmeal, then milk and eggs. Remove skillet from oven. Cool slightly. Brush shortening up sides of skillet, then pour shortening into batter; mix well. Pour batter into skillet. Bake until golden brown and tester inserted in center comes out clean, about 25 minutes. Invert corn bread onto rack and cool. Reduce oven temperature to 300°F.

Cut corn bread into ¾-inch cubes. Place on baking sheet. Bake until edges form crust, stirring occasionally, about 35 minutes. Cool completely. *(Can be prepared 2 days ahead. Place in plastic bag and let stand at room temperature.)*

For dressing: Bring 2 cups stock, turkey neck, heart and gizzard and bouquet garni to simmer in heavy small saucepan. Cover and simmer until giblets are very tender, about 1½ hours. Add liver and simmer until no longer pink, approximately 15 minutes.

Strain giblet broth into measuring cup; reserve neck and giblets. Add enough additional stock to measure 2 cups liquid if necessary. Return giblet broth to saucepan and bring to simmer. Remove from heat. Add dried mushrooms. Let stand 20 minutes to soften. Strain giblet broth, reserving mushrooms and broth. Cut off tough mushroom stems. Squeeze mushrooms dry and slice. Remove meat from turkey neck. Finely chop meat and giblets.

Butter 9 × 11 × 2-inch baking dish. Melt ¾ cup butter in heavy large skillet over medium-high heat. Add shallots and garlic and cook until softened, stirring occasionally, about 6 minutes. Add button mushrooms and soaked dried mushrooms and sauté 3 minutes. Add parsley, thyme and sage.

Coarsely crumble corn bread into large bowl. Add mushroom-and-herb mixture and giblet mixture. Moisten with reserved giblet broth and enough additional stock just to hold crumbs together. Season with salt and pepper. Spoon dressing into prepared dish. *(Can be prepared 1 day ahead. Cover and refrigerate. Bring dressing to room temperature before baking.)*

Preheat oven to 350°F. Bake dressing until golden brown, 30 minutes.

*Available at specialty foods stores and some supermarkets.

❦ Fish and Shellfish

Salt-baked Fish with Garlic Oil

Baking in salt produces a very moist yet not salty result; the garlic oil makes this simple offering something special.

6 servings

¾ cup olive oil (preferably extra-virgin)

3 large garlic cloves, minced

2 2- to 2¼-pound bass or snappers, scaled and cleaned, heads and tails left intact, room temperature

Freshly ground pepper

1 lemon, cut into ¼-inch-thick rounds

12 cups (about) coarse salt

1 cup water

Heat ½ cup oil in heavy small skillet over medium-low heat. Add garlic and cook until softened, stirring occasionally, about 5 minutes; do not brown. Transfer oil and garlic to bowl. Cool. Mix in remaining ¼ cup oil.

Preheat oven to 450°F. Sprinkle fish inside and out with pepper. Place lemon rounds inside fish. Fill large roasting pan ⅓ full with coarse salt. Arrange fish atop salt, cutting off tails if necessary to fit in pan. Cover fish with salt. Sprinkle ½ cup water over salt atop each fish. Gently pack moist salt around fish. Bake fish for 30 minutes.

Break salt crust using heavy mallet or cleaver. Pry salt free with sharp knife if necessary. Transfer fish to work surface, brushing off salt with pastry brush. Cut top fillet off each fish. Remove skin. Arrange skinned side up on heated platter. Debone and skin remaining fillets. Arrange on serving platter. Serve, passing garlic oil separately.

Monkfish in Red Bell Pepper Sauce

6 servings

4 large red bell peppers

10 tablespoons (1¼ sticks) unsalted butter, room temperature

2 small onions, coarsely chopped

2 plum tomatoes, chopped
   Salt and freshly ground pepper

½ cup fish stock or bottled clam juice

2 monkfish fillets (about 1½ pounds each), dark meat and any bones removed

2 tablespoons (¼ stick) unsalted butter, melted

¼ cup whipping cream

1 tablespoon (or more) fresh lemon juice

2 large bunches arugula, stemmed (about 4 ounces) or 1 large bunch spinach

Lemon wedges

Char peppers over gas flame or in broiler until blackened on all sides. Wrap in paper bag and let stand 10 minutes to steam. Peel and seed. Rinse if necessary. Coarsely chop peppers.

Melt 4 tablespoons butter in heavy large skillet over medium-low heat. Add onions and cook until softened, stirring occasionally, about 7 minutes. Add peppers, tomatoes, salt and pepper and cook until vegetables are very soft, stirring

*Traditional New England Clam Chowder
with Fried Leeks*

Brian Le

Clockwise from top left: Minted Chick-Pea Dip; Spicy Cheddar Cheese Spread; Roasted Bell Pepper, Basil and Fontina Sandwiches; Grilled Ham, Swiss Cheese and Sauerkraut Sandwiches; Marinated Cauliflower with Orange and Thyme; Country-style Pâté (recipe not included); Cornichons and Pickled Onions (recipes not included); Goat Cheese Marinated in Rosemary and Lemon; Shrimp with Avocado and Watercress Dip; Tamari Mixed Nuts

*Monkfish in Red Bell Pepper
Sauce; Mushroom-filled Pasta
with Parmesan and Butter; Peaches
Baked with Amaretti, Almonds
and Chocolate; Green Beans with
Parsley and Mint*

E.K. Waller

Fresh Salmon Salad
with Lemon Dill Dressing

Clockwise from top right:
Blackberry Corn Muffin Cake;
Blueberry-Carrot Picnic Cake;
Strawberry Rhubarb Crumble;
Blueberry-Lime Shortcake

*Grand Marnier Cheesecake with
Strawberries and Candied Orange Peel*

Aaron Rezny

frequently, about 20 minutes. Add stock and simmer 5 minutes, stirring occasionally. Puree mixture in processor. Strain into heavy small saucepan. *(Can be prepared 1 day ahead. Cool. Cover and refrigerate.)*

Preheat oven to 375°F. Fold narrow tail under so fillet is of even thickness. Tie fillet at 1-inch intervals to hold shape. Repeat with remaining fillet. Brush fillets with melted butter. Roast on rack in baking pan until just springy to touch, about 25 minutes.

Meanwhile, rewarm puree over medium heat. Add cream and bring to simmer. Gradually whisk in 4 tablespoons butter. Add lemon juice to taste. Remove from heat. Melt remaining 2 tablespoons butter in heavy medium skillet over medium heat. Add arugula and stir until wilted, about 1 minute. Divide among serving plates.

Cut string off fillets. Cut fillets into 1-inch-thick slices. Arrange atop arugula. Pour some of sauce over. Garnish with lemon wedges. Serve, passing remaining sauce separately.

Grilled Swordfish and Japanese Eggplant with Sesame Sauce

4 servings

2 6-ounce long thin Japanese eggplants, halved crosswise
Olive oil
½ cup chicken stock or canned broth
2½ tablespoons soy sauce
1 tablespoon oriental sesame oil
1½ teaspoons rice vinegar

8 4-ounce ¾-inch-thick swordfish pieces
Salt and freshly ground white pepper
Sesame Sauce*
Toasted Sesame Seeds**
Minced fresh parsley

Prepare barbecue (high heat) or heat cast iron skillet until hot. Using fork, score eggplant lengthwise. Using knife, cut across eggplant at ⅓-inch intervals to fan; do not cut through base. Rub with olive oil. Grill or cook in skillet 5 minutes per side; eggplant should be firm. Blend next 4 ingredients in bowl. Add eggplant. Cover and refrigerate at least 6 hours. *(Eggplant can be prepared 1 day ahead.)*

Prepare barbecue (high heat) or heat cast iron skillet until hot. Rub fish with olive oil. Season with salt and pepper. Grill or cook in skillet 3 minutes per side (turn on grill to form crosshatch markings). Fan eggplant half at top of each plate. Overlap two swordfish pieces in center of plate. Ladle 3 tablespoons sauce over. Sprinkle with 1 tablespoon sesame seeds. Top with minced fresh parsley.

*Sesame Sauce

Makes ¾ cup

1 tablespoon oriental sesame oil
5 tablespoons thinly sliced shallots
3 tablespoons sliced peeled fresh ginger
4 teaspoons sliced garlic
1 cup plus 1½ teaspoons rice vinegar
1 cup dry white wine

½ bay leaf
1¼ cups chicken stock or canned broth
¾ cup veal stock, chicken stock or canned low-salt broth
1 tablespoon tahini (sesame seed paste)
1 tablespoon soy sauce

Heat oil in heavy medium skillet over medium-high heat. Add shallots, ginger and garlic and stir 1 minute. Add 1 cup vinegar, wine and bay leaf and boil until reduced to glaze, about 25 minutes. Add stocks, tahini and soy sauce and boil until reduced to ¾ cup, about 20 minutes. Strain through fine sieve into heavy small saucepan. Stir in remaining 1½ teaspoons vinegar. Keep Sesame Sauce warm in water bath.

**Toasted Sesame Seeds

Makes ¼ cup

¼ cup sesame seeds   2 teaspoons chopped fresh parsley

Preheat oven to 400°F. Spread seeds on baking sheet. Bake until toasted, about 8 minutes, tossing every 2 minutes. Stir in parsley. Transfer to bowl.

Red Snapper with Tomato, Basil and Olive Sauce

Come barbecue weather, the sauce will be good with grilled swordfish steaks.

2 servings; can be doubled or tripled

2 red snapper fillets or any firm white fish, such as sea bass or halibut
Olive oil
Fresh lemon juice
Freshly ground pepper

Sauce
12 ounces plum tomatoes, peeled, seeded and chopped
4 Mediterranean olives, such as Kalamata or Niçoise, pitted and slivered

1 small shallot, minced
3 tablespoons minced fresh basil or 3 tablespoons minced fresh parsley mixed with ½ teaspoon dried basil, crumbled
3 tablespoons olive oil
1 tablespoon balsamic or red wine vinegar
Salt and freshly ground pepper

Preheat broiler. Rub fish with olive oil and lemon juice. Season with pepper. Let stand while preparing sauce.
    For sauce: Combine all ingredients in small bowl and mix well.
    Sprinkle fish with salt. Broil flat side down until just opaque, about 9 minutes per inch of thickness. Transfer fish to plates. Spoon sauce over.

Trout with Pecan Butter and Bacon

8 servings

1 cup all purpose flour
Salt and freshly ground pepper
8 whole rainbow trout with heads, cleaned (about 8 ounces each)
12 tablespoons (1½ sticks) butter

¾ cup chopped pecans
⅓ cup fresh lemon juice
3 tablespoons minced fresh parsley
6 slices cooked bacon, crumbled
Lemon wedges

Preheat oven to lowest setting. Season flour with salt and pepper. Dredge each trout in flour, shaking off excess. Melt 3 tablespoons butter in heavy large skillet over medium-high heat. Add 4 trout and cook about 9 minutes per inch of thickness, turning once. Transfer to platter. Keep warm in oven. Repeat with 3 more tablespoons butter and remaining trout.
    Wipe skillet clean. Melt remaining 6 tablespoons butter in same skillet over high heat. Add pecans and cook until heated through, about 3 minutes. Add lemon juice and parsley. Season with salt and pepper. Pour over fish. Sprinkle with bacon and garnish with lemon wedges. Serve immediately.

Mediterranean Mussels and Shrimp

A small salad and warm French bread for sopping up the broth is all that's needed to complete a nice light lunch or supper.

2 servings

1 tablespoon unsalted butter
2½ tablespoons finely chopped onion
1 garlic clove, minced
½ cup dry white wine
½ cup water
¼ teaspoon fennel seeds
¼ teaspoon salt

⅛ teaspoon freshly ground pepper
½ pound large mussels, scrubbed and debearded
½ pound uncooked unshelled large shrimp
2 tablespoons minced fresh parsley

Melt butter in heavy large shallow skillet over medium heat. Stir in onion and garlic. Cover and cook 1 minute. Mix in wine, water, fennel, salt and pepper and bring to boil. Reduce heat to medium-high. Add mussels, cover and steam 5 minutes. Remove opened mussels. Add shrimp and cook until remaining mussels open and shrimp are just opaque, about 4 minutes. Discard any mussels that do not open. Return opened mussels to skillet. Toss with 1 tablespoon parsley. Divide shellfish among heated bowls. Spoon broth over. Sprinkle with remaining 1 tablespoon parsley and serve.

Scallops with Walnuts and Shallots

The scallops take a quick ten minutes. Basil Rice (see page 68) and some simple baked squash would be appropriate side dishes.

4 servings

5 tablespoons butter
1 cup sliced shallots (about 8 large)
  Freshly ground pepper
⅓ cup dry white wine
1⅔ pounds bay scallops
  Salt

1 cup walnut pieces, toasted (about 3½ ounces)
¼ cup chopped fresh Italian parsley

Basil Rice (see page 68)

Melt butter in heavy large skillet over medium-high heat. Add shallots and pepper and sauté until golden brown, about 4 minutes. Add wine and boil until syrupy. Add scallops. Season with salt. Stir until just opaque, about 3 minutes. Mix in walnuts and parsley.

Mound Basil Rice over half of 4 shallow soup bowls. Spoon scallop mixture onto other half and serve.

Sauté of Scallops with Ginger and Zucchini

Don't forget to serve some crisp and crusty French bread alongside.

2 to 4 servings

1 tablespoon unsalted butter
2 medium zucchini, cut into ½-inch dice
2 medium shallots, chopped
1 garlic clove, minced
1 teaspoon minced fresh peeled ginger
  Pinch of cayenne pepper
¼ cup whipping cream
3 tablespoons dry white wine

1½ pounds bay scallops or sea scallops, quartered
½ cup 2 × ¼-inch red bell pepper strips
2 teaspoons instant flour
1½ tablespoons chopped fresh parsley
1½ teaspoons fresh lemon juice
1 teaspoon chopped lemon peel
¾ teaspoon coarse salt
  Freshly ground pepper

Melt butter in heavy large skillet or wok over high heat. Add zucchini, shallots, garlic, ginger and cayenne and stir 30 seconds. Add cream and wine and cook until thickened, about 2 minutes. Add scallops and bell pepper and cook 1 minute, shaking pan occasionally. Stir in flour and cook 1 minute. Add parsley, juice, peel, salt and pepper. Serve immediately.

Garlic Shrimp

Soak the wooden skewers in water before using them; that way they won't burn on the barbecue.

12 servings

¾ cup (1½ sticks) butter
10 large garlic cloves, minced
2 tablespoons fresh lemon juice
1 teaspoon cayenne pepper

36 uncooked large shrimp, peeled and deveined, tails left intact
Fresh rosemary sprigs

Prepare barbecue (high heat) or preheat broiler. Melt butter in heavy small saucepan over low heat. Add next 3 ingredients and simmer 1 minute. Thread shrimp on wooden skewers. Brush with seasoned butter. Grill shrimp until pink, about 3 minutes. Turn and grill until opaque, about 1 minute, basting with butter. Line platter with rosemary. Top with shrimp. Serve immediately.

Eggs, Cheese and Vegetables

Italian Spicy Eggs

Try these for brunch or as a light supper. You can make a double (or triple) recipe of the sauce and freeze the remainder to enjoy later.

2 servings

3 tablespoons olive oil
½ small onion, minced
2½ pounds tomatoes, peeled, seeded and chopped
2 tablespoons torn fresh basil leaves
2 tablespoons minced fresh parsley
Salt and freshly ground pepper

4 large eggs

4 ⅓-inch-thick slices Italian bread
Olive oil

6 tablespoons freshly grated Parmesan cheese (about 1 ounce)

Heat 3 tablespoons oil in heavy 10-inch skillet over medium heat. Add onion and cook until softened, stirring occasionally, about 6 minutes. Add tomatoes and bring to simmer. Mix in basil, parsley, salt and pepper. Increase heat to high and cook until almost no liquid remains in pan, stirring frequently, about 15 minutes. *(Can be prepared 1 day ahead. Cover and refrigerate. Rewarm before continuing.)*

Press back of large spoon into tomato mixture in 4 places, spacing evenly apart and forming wells. Carefully break 1 egg into each well. Season eggs with salt and freshly ground pepper. Cover and cook over low heat until eggs are soft-poached, about 6 minutes.

Meanwhile, preheat broiler. Brush both sides of bread with oil. Place on baking sheet. Broil bread until golden brown on both sides.

Sprinkle cheese over eggs. Divide toast between shallow bowls. Gently spoon eggs and sauce over toast.

Smoked Salmon with Soft Scrambled Eggs and Caviar

4 servings

8 ounces smoked salmon, sliced paper thin, room temperature

4 tablespoons (½ stick) unsalted butter
8 eggs, beaten to blend
4 tablespoons whipping cream
Salt and freshly ground pepper

Snipped fresh chives
Sour cream
2 ounces sevruga, salmon or golden whitefish caviar
Warm toasted brioche

Preheat oven to 200°F. Arrange salmon slices in single layer on 4 ovenproof plates. Set aside.

Melt 1 tablespoon butter in heavy large nonaluminum skillet over low heat. Add eggs and 2 tablespoons cream to skillet. Whisk until eggs thicken, about 5 minutes. Add remaining 2 tablespoons cream and 3 tablespoons butter and whisk until thick and creamy, about 2 more minutes. Season with salt and freshly ground pepper.

Warm salmon in oven until just heated through. Spoon eggs atop salmon. Sprinkle with chives. Place 2 dollops of sour cream on each side of eggs. Top sour cream with caviar. Serve, passing brioche separately.

Omelet Duke of Alba Style

A savory version of a classic Spanish tapa. Serve the omelet warm or at room temperature, and pass some crusty bread alongside. A platter of fresh fruit will round the meal out nicely.

6 to 8 servings

1 large red bell pepper
1 large green bell pepper
Olive oil

3 tablespoons olive oil
1½ cups coarsely chopped onions
½ pound boiling potatoes, peeled, quartered lengthwise and thinly sliced crosswise
Salt and freshly ground pepper

2 garlic cloves, thinly sliced
1 cup well-drained canned Italian plum tomatoes
2 tablespoons minced fresh parsley

8 eggs, beaten to blend

12 pimiento-stuffed green Spanish olives, sliced

Brush peppers lightly with oil. Char peppers over gas flame or in broiler until blackened on all sides. Place in paper bag and let stand 10 minutes to steam. Peel and seed. Rinse if necessary; pat dry. Cut into ¾-inch dice.

Heat 3 tablespoons oil in heavy 10-inch skillet (preferably nonstick) over medium heat. Add onions and sauté until softened, about 7 minutes. Add peppers and potatoes. Season with salt and pepper. Cook until potatoes soften slightly, stirring occasionally, about 7 minutes. Add garlic and stir 2 minutes. Add tomatoes and cook until potatoes are tender and liquid has reduced slightly, breaking up tomatoes with fork, 15 minutes. Add parsley.

Season eggs with salt and pepper. Pour mixture over vegetables, separating vegetables with spoon so egg covers bottom of skillet. Reduce heat to low and cook until bottom and sides of eggs are set but center is still loose, shaking skillet occasionally to prevent sticking, about 15 minutes.

Preheat broiler. Place skillet in broiler 6 inches from heat source and cook until omelet is set and top is light golden, about 2 minutes; do not overcook. Cool omelet slightly. Run knife around edge of pan to loosen. Invert omelet onto platter. Serve warm or at room temperature, cutting into wedges and arranging olives around edges.

Eggs Baked with Shiitake Mushrooms, Leeks and Prosciutto

These creamy eggs have a rich flavor and soufflélike texture. A good part of the recipe can be completed the day before.

12 servings

8 tablespoons (1 stick) unsalted butter
5 cups leek julienne (white and 1 inch of pale green parts) (about 5 medium)
½ pound fresh shiitake mushrooms* or button mushrooms, stemmed and cut into ¼-inch-wide strips
½ pound paper-thin slices prosciutto, cut into ¼-inch-wide strips

5 cups whipping cream
12 large eggs
1 teaspoon freshly grated nutmeg
1 teaspoon salt
Freshly ground pepper
2½ cups freshly grated Gruyère cheese (about 8 ounces)
Minced fresh parsley

Using 1 tablespoon butter for each, butter two 3-quart shallow baking dishes. Melt remaining 6 tablespoons butter in heavy large skillet over medium heat. Add leeks and sauté until softened, about 8 minutes. Add mushrooms and sauté 5 minutes. Add prosciutto and sauté 2 minutes. Spread half of mixture over bottom of each dish. *(Can be prepared 1 day ahead. Cover and refrigerate.)*

Preheat oven to 375°F. Whisk cream, eggs, nutmeg, salt and pepper in large bowl. Stir in 2 cups cheese. Pour over vegetable mixture in baking dishes. Stir to mix vegetables with cream. Sprinkle remaining cheese over. Bake until knife inserted in centers comes out clean and tops are golden brown, about 30 minutes. Cool 10 minutes. Sprinkle with parsley and serve.

*Two ounces dried shiitake mushrooms can be substituted. Cover with hot water and let stand 30 minutes to soften. Drain.

Eggplant Sauté with Goat Cheese and Basil

Serve hot from the stove or room temperature atop buttered spinach fettuccine.

4 servings

¼ cup plus 1 tablespoon olive oil
¼ pound carrots, peeled and cut into 3 × ⅛-inch strips
½ pound eggplant, cut into 3 × ¼-inch strips
2 tablespoons water
1 teaspoon coarse salt
½ small red onion, coarsely chopped
2 garlic cloves, minced
¼ teaspoon dried red pepper flakes

1 pound Italian plum tomatoes, peeled, seeded and quartered
2 tablespoons dry white or red wine
1 tablespoon balsamic vinegar
½ cup chopped fresh basil leaves
3 tablespoons pine nuts, toasted
Freshly ground pepper
4 ounces goat cheese (preferably imported), crumbled

Heat ¼ cup oil in heavy large skillet or wok over high heat. Add carrots and stir 45 seconds. Add eggplant and stir 2 minutes. Add water and stir 1 minute. Transfer to bowl. Toss with ½ teaspoon salt. Heat remaining oil in same skillet over high heat. Add onion, garlic and pepper flakes and stir 10 seconds. Add tomatoes and cook 10 seconds. Add remaining salt and wine and cook until sauce thickens, about 1½ minutes. Remove from heat. Stir in carrot-eggplant mixture, vinegar, basil and pine nuts. Season with pepper. Spoon onto plates immediately, or let stand 10 minutes. Crumble goat cheese over each serving.

5 ❦ Side Dishes and Condiments

Side dishes provide that indefinable "something" that completes a terrific meal. The vegetables, rice and grains, breads and condiments in this chapter will round out any meal and provide that little something extra that lifts it out of the ordinary.

The exciting vegetable side dishes range from the traditional, such as Stuffed Acorn Squash, a perfect go-with for a holiday ham or pork chops, to the more exotic, such as refreshing Green Beans with Parsley and Mint. Rice and grains provide nice textural contrast as well as great flavor—depending on your entrée, you might want to serve a zesty accompaniment like Spiced Rice with Green Peppers and Cashews or creamy, satisfying Risotto Milanese, made with Italian short-grain rice.

Homemade breads enhance any meal—breakfast, brunch, lunch, dinner, afternoon tea—and with the variety here, you'll be inspired to whip up a basket of fresh-baked rolls, biscuits or breads to include in your next menu. Well-flavored yeast breads include Rosemary Rolls, little dinner rolls enhanced with sautéed garlic, Black Olive Focaccia, a large flat loaf filled with chopped olives, and Almond Butter Crown, the perfect sweet touch for breakfast or late-afternoon tea. There are also some easy quick breads, such as Buttermilk Cheddar Biscuits and Provolone, Sun-dried Tomato and Basil Bread.

To complete the chapter, we offer a veritable relish tray full of zippy condiments. Some, such as a simple Herb Butter or Garlic-Cayenne Butter, would be delightful served in crocks with crusty bread. Other imaginative combinations, including sweet and crunchy Three-Onion Relish, fragrant with orange and Italian herbs, would add spark to entrées such as hamburgers or grilled fish.

 Vegetables

Green Beans with Parsley and Mint

Mint and lemon add a refreshing note to this colorful side dish.

6 servings

1½ pounds green beans, trimmed
¼ cup olive oil (preferably extra-virgin)
 3 tablespoons minced fresh mint
 3 tablespoons minced fresh parsley
   Salt and freshly ground pepper

2 tablespoons fresh lemon juice
4 teaspoons grated or shredded lemon peel

Cook beans in large saucepan of boiling salted water until just tender, about 5 minutes. Drain. Refresh in bowl of ice water. Drain well. Transfer beans to large bowl. Mix in oil, mint, parsley, salt and pepper. *(Can be prepared 1 hour ahead. Cover and let stand at room temperature.)* Just before serving, mix in lemon juice and grated lemon peel. Serve at room temperature.

Broccoli with Anchovies

Leftovers are terrific tossed with pasta.

10 servings

4 large broccoli heads

1 cup olive oil (preferably extra-virgin)
8 garlic cloves, minced

16 anchovy fillets, rinsed and minced
½ to ¾ teaspoon dried red pepper flakes
   Salt

Cut off broccoli florets leaving 1-inch-long stems. Peel stalks; cut into 1-inch-long pieces. Cook florets and stalks in large pot of boiling salted water until just tender, about 3 minutes. Drain. Refresh in bowl of cold water. Drain well; pat dry. Set aside.

Heat oil in heavy very large deep skillet over low heat. Add garlic and cook until golden brown, stirring occasionally, about 3 minutes. Add anchovies and ½ teaspoon pepper flakes and mash with spoon. Add broccoli and toss until heated through. Season with salt. Taste, adding remaining ¼ teaspoon pepper flakes if desired. Transfer to large bowl. Serve broccoli warm or at room temperature.

Collard and Mustard Greens with Bacon

8 servings

4 ounces slab bacon, cut into ¼-inch pieces
1 small onion, minced
2 large bunches collard greens, stemmed
1 bunch mustard greens, stemmed

½ cup chicken stock or canned broth
   Salt and freshly ground pepper
   Hot pepper sauce (such as Tabasco), optional

Cook bacon in heavy large skillet over medium heat until fat is rendered. Reduce heat to low. Add onion and cook until softened, stirring occasionally, about 10 minutes. Add all greens and stock. Cover and cook until greens are just tender, stirring occasionally, about 25 minutes. Season with salt and pepper. *(Can be prepared 4½ hours ahead. Let stand at room temperature. Rewarm before continuing.)* Sprinkle greens with hot pepper sauce if desired.

Deviled White Beans with Tomatoes

Offer the beans as an accompaniment to grilled sausages or chicken.

4 to 6 servings

¼ cup olive oil
1 small onion, chopped
4 small garlic cloves, minced
½ teaspoon (or more) dried red pepper flakes
1 pound Swiss chard, stemmed and coarsely chopped
1 4-ounce piece prosciutto, cut into ¼-inch dice

2 cups canned cannellini beans,* rinsed and drained
4 small tomatoes, peeled, cored and quartered
¼ cup minced fresh parsley
   Salt and freshly ground pepper

Heat oil in heavy large skillet over medium heat. Add onion and garlic and cook until onion is translucent, stirring occasionally, about 10 minutes. Add ½ teaspoon pepper flakes and stir 1 minute. Add chard and prosciutto and stir until chard wilts, about 2 minutes. Add beans, tomatoes and parsley. Season with salt and pepper. Cover and cook 5 minutes. Uncover and cook 5 minutes to blend flavors, stirring occasionally. Taste, adding more pepper flakes for spicier flavor. *(Can be prepared 1 day ahead. Cool, cover and refrigerate. Rewarm over low heat, stirring occasionally.)* Serve hot.

*White kidney beans available at Italian markets. If unavailable, Great Northern or navy beans can be substituted.

Braised Endive

6 servings

4½ tablespoons unsalted butter
6 large Belgian endive, each cut lengthwise into quarters
1 cup chicken stock or canned low-salt broth

1½ tablespoons fresh lemon juice
   Salt and freshly ground pepper

Melt butter in heavy large skillet over medium heat. Add endive and cook 3 minutes, turning endive occasionally. Add stock and simmer until almost all liquid evaporates, about 8 minutes. Mix in lemon juice. Season with salt and pepper. *(Can be prepared 4 hours ahead. Cool, cover and refrigerate. Rewarm over low heat before serving.)*

Potato Cheese Pie

6 servings

3 pounds baking potatoes, peeled and cut into 1-inch chunks
2 garlic cloves

6 tablespoons (¾ stick) butter, cut into pieces
½ cup freshly grated Parmesan cheese
⅓ cup half and half
2 eggs, beaten to blend
Salt and freshly ground pepper
Cayenne pepper

½ cup minced green onions
1 cup grated sharp cheddar cheese
3 tablespoons freshly grated Parmesan cheese
2 tablespoons dry breadcrumbs
2 tablespoons (¼ stick) butter, cut into pieces

Preheat oven to 350°F. Butter 10-inch glass pie plate. Combine potatoes and garlic in large pot. Cover with cold water and bring to boil. Continue boiling until potatoes are tender, about 10 minutes. Drain, then return potatoes and garlic to pot. Shake over medium heat until potatoes are dry, 2 minutes.

Mash potatoes with garlic and 6 tablespoons butter. Add ½ cup Parmesan, half and half and eggs and mash until fluffy. Season with salt, pepper and cayenne. Stir in green onions. Spoon half of potato mixture into prepared pie plate, spreading evenly. Cover with cheddar cheese, pressing lightly with back of spoon. Top with remaining potato mixture, spreading evenly. Sprinkle with 3 tablespoons Parmesan and breadcrumbs. Dot with 2 tablespoons butter. Bake until golden brown and crusty, about 45 minutes.

Mushroom and Bacon Baked Tomatoes

6 to 8 servings

5 bacon slices, diced
3 tablespoons butter
½ pound mushrooms, sliced
2 large onions, sliced
1 garlic clove, minced
1 tablespoon all purpose flour
Salt and freshly ground pepper

10 medium tomatoes, cut into ½-inch-thick slices
½ cup grated Parmesan cheese
3 tablespoons dry breadcrumbs

Preheat oven to 350°F. Grease 9-inch square baking dish. Cook bacon in heavy medium skillet over medium-high heat until crisp, about 7 minutes. Transfer bacon to paper towels, using slotted spoon. Add 2 tablespoons butter to bacon drippings and melt. Add mushrooms, onions and garlic and cook until onions are soft, stirring occasionally, about 8 minutes. Mix in bacon and flour. Season with salt and pepper.

Place half of tomato slices in prepared baking dish. Spoon half of mushroom mixture over tomatoes. Sprinkle with ¼ cup Parmesan. Repeat with remaining tomato slices, mushroom mixture and Parmesan. Sprinkle with breadcrumbs. Dot with remaining 1 tablespoon butter. Bake until breadcrumbs brown, about 25 minutes. Serve hot.

Grilled Zucchini

*2 servings; can be doubled
or tripled*

3 tablespoons olive oil
2 garlic cloves, minced
2 teaspoons soy sauce
Freshly ground pepper

2 zucchini, trimmed and cut
lengthwise into ½-inch-thick
strips
Salt

Combine first 4 ingredients in glass baking dish. Add zucchini and turn to coat. Let stand until ready to cook.

Prepare barbecue grill (medium-high heat). Cook zucchini until browned and tender, about 4 minutes per side. Season with salt and pepper. Transfer zucchini to plates and serve.

Fall Vegetable Puree

*A delicious alternative to
the usual Thanksgiving
mashed potatoes.*

8 servings

1½ pounds turnips, peeled and cut
into 1-inch pieces
1½ pounds rutabagas, peeled and cut
into 1-inch pieces
1½ pounds carrots, peeled and cut
into 1-inch-long pieces

6 garlic cloves

½ cup (1 stick) unsalted butter, cut
into pieces
Salt and freshly ground pepper

Cook turnips, rutabagas, carrots and garlic in large pot of boiling salted water until all vegetables are tender, about 20 minutes. Drain well. Puree vegetables in batches in processor, stopping occasionally to scrape down sides of bowl. Transfer to heavy saucepan.

Add butter to puree. Stir over medium heat until excess liquid evaporates and mixture thickens, about 15 minutes. Season with salt and pepper. *(Can be prepared 1 day ahead. Cool, cover and refrigerate. Rewarm over medium heat, stirring frequently.)* Spoon puree into bowl and serve.

Stuffed Acorn Squash

2 servings

1 acorn squash, halved crosswise
and seeded
1 tablespoon butter, melted
Salt and freshly ground pepper

1 large carrot, peeled and chopped

1 zucchini, chopped
1 crookneck squash, chopped
2 tablespoons (¼ stick) butter,
melted
¼ teaspoon freshly grated nutmeg

Preheat oven to 375°F. Place acorn squash cut side up on baking sheet. Drizzle 1 tablespoon butter over. Season with salt and freshly ground pepper. Turn squash over. Bake until tender, about 40 minutes.

Meanwhile, cook carrot, zucchini and crookneck squash in medium saucepan of boiling water until soft, about 10 minutes. Drain. Transfer to blender or food processor. Add 2 tablespoons melted butter and nutmeg. Puree. *(Can be prepared 1 day ahead. Cover squash and filling separately and refrigerate. Rewarm filling in saucepan and squash in oven.)*

Divide filling between squash halves. Serve immediately.

Vegetable "Stew" Provençal

This boldly colored and flavored assortment of vegetables is delicious either hot or cold. Try splashing on some balsamic or red wine vinegar just before serving.

4 to 6 servings

2 tablespoons olive oil
1 garlic clove, minced
1 tablespoon tomato paste
2 small zucchini, trimmed and cut into ½-inch cubes
½ pound eggplant, cut into ½-inch cubes
½ pound ripe tomatoes, cored and cut into ½-inch cubes
1 medium red bell pepper, cut into ½-inch cubes
1 small red onion, cut into ½-inch cubes

¼ pound mushrooms, cut into ½-inch cubes
Salt and freshly ground pepper
¼ cup chopped fresh parsley (preferably Italian)
¼ cup chopped fresh basil or 2 teaspoons dried, crumbled
1 teaspoon minced fresh thyme or ¼ teaspoon dried, crumbled
½ teaspoon minced fresh rosemary or pinch of dried, crumbled

Heat olive oil in heavy large skillet over low heat. Add garlic and sauté 1 minute. Stir in tomato paste. Add zucchini, eggplant, tomatoes, bell pepper, onion and mushrooms. Cover and cook until vegetables are tender but not mushy, about 15 minutes. Season with salt and generous amount of pepper. Combine parsley, basil, thyme and rosemary. Stir into vegetables. Adjust seasoning. Serve vegetables warm or cold.

❦ *Rice and Grains*

Basil Rice

Makes about 3½ cups

3 cups water
½ teaspoon salt
1½ cups rice

¾ cup sliced fresh basil or Italian parsley

Bring water to boil in heavy medium saucepan. Add salt. Stir in rice. Cover, reduce heat to low and cook until water is absorbed, about 20 minutes. Turn off heat and let stand 5 minutes. Mix in basil with fork. Serve immediately.

Spiced Rice with Green Peppers and Cashews

A delicious side dish or vegetarian entrée.

2 to 4 servings

¼ cup vegetable oil
1 teaspoon mustard seeds
1 teaspoon minced fresh ginger
¾ cup chopped green bell pepper
1½ cups cooked basmati rice
½ teaspoon turmeric

½ teaspoon Indian chili powder*
Salt
1 8-ounce container plain yogurt, beaten
¼ cup raw cashews
2 tablespoons minced cilantro

Heat oil in heavy large skillet over medium-high heat. Add mustard seeds and cover. When seeds stop popping, stir in ginger. Add bell pepper and stir 2 minutes. Reduce heat to medium. Add rice, turmeric and chili powder. Season with salt. Cover and cook until heated through, about 5 minutes. Fold in yogurt, cashews and cilantro.

*Available at Indian markets. If unavailable, substitute cayenne pepper.

Risotto Milanese

12 servings

1 cup (2 sticks) butter
2 small onions, chopped
4 ounces beef marrow, diced
　Freshly ground pepper
1 cup dry white wine
4 cups Arborio rice*
　Salt
10 cups (about) beef stock or canned low-salt broth

1 teaspoon saffron threads, crushed and dissolved in ¼ cup warm water
2½ cups freshly grated Parmesan cheese (about 8 ounces)
　Italian parsley

Melt 5 tablespoons butter in heavy large pot over medium-low heat. Add onions and marrow and cook until onions are translucent, stirring occasionally, about 10 minutes. Season with pepper. Add wine and boil until evaporated. Add rice and stir to coat all grains completely. Season with salt. Stir in 6 cups broth and saffron and bring to boil. Reduce heat and simmer until all liquid is absorbed, stirring frequently. Continue adding enough of remaining broth 1 cup at a time until rice is just tender but still firm to bite, stirring frequently; risotto should be creamy but not mushy. Remove from heat. Stir in remaining butter and ¼ cup Parmesan cheese. Let stand 1 minute. Transfer to platter. Garnish with parsley. Serve immediately, passing remaining cheese separately.

*Italian short-grain rice. Available at Italian markets and specialty foods stores.

Corn and Barley Casserole

Prepare this creamy side dish one day ahead, then bake just before serving.

6 servings

6 ears corn, husked
1 cup barley

2 red bell peppers

1 pound sliced bacon
1 jalapeño chili, seeded and minced

1 teaspoon ground cumin
3 cups whipping cream
½ teaspoon salt
　Freshly ground pepper

Cook corn in a large pot of boiling salted water until just tender, about 5 minutes. Remove corn. Add barley to water and cook 30 minutes, skimming surface occasionally. Drain. Rinse under cold water and drain well. Transfer to large bowl. Cut kernels off corn cobs. Add to barley.

Char bell peppers over gas flame or in broiler until blackened on all sides. Wrap in paper bag and let stand 10 minutes to steam. Peel and seed. Rinse if necessary; pat dry. Chop 1 pepper; add to barley mixture. Thinly slice second pepper and set aside for garnish.

Cook bacon in heavy large skillet over medium heat until crisp. Drain on paper towels. Break into small pieces. Add half of bacon to barley mixture. Mix in half of jalapeño and ½ teaspoon cumin. Combine cream, ½ teaspoon salt, pepper and remaining bacon, jalapeño and ½ teaspoon cumin in heavy small saucepan. Boil until reduced by half, about 15 minutes. Blend into barley mixture. Adjust seasoning. Transfer mixture to 10-cup casserole. Cover with foil. *(Can be prepared 1 day ahead. Refrigerate barley and sliced pepper separately. Bring to room temperature before continuing.)*

Preheat oven to 350°F. Bake casserole until heated through, about 25 minutes. Garnish with bell pepper slices.

Garlic Cheese Soufflé Grits

8 servings

2 tablespoons (¼ stick) butter
2 teaspoons minced garlic
5 cups water
¾ teaspoon salt
½ teaspoon freshly ground white pepper
¼ teaspoon dry mustard
¼ teaspoon ground turmeric

1 cup regular grits

4 eggs, separated, room temperature
6 ounces sharp cheddar cheese, grated (about 1½ cups)
Dash of hot pepper sauce (such as Tabasco)

¼ teaspoon cream of tartar

Melt butter in heavy medium saucepan over medium heat. Add garlic and stir until golden brown. Add water and salt and bring to boil. Stir in pepper, mustard and turmeric.

Gradually stir in grits and return to boil. Reduce heat to medium-low and cook 15 minutes, stirring frequently. Transfer 2 cups cooked grits to large bowl. (Reserve any remainder for another use.) Stir in yolks. Blend in cheese and hot pepper sauce. *(Can be prepared several hours ahead. Reheat before continuing.)*

Preheat oven to 400°F. Butter and flour one 4-cup or four 6-ounce soufflé dishes. Using electric mixer, beat whites and cream of tartar until stiff but not dry. Gently fold ¼ of whites into grits. Fold grits into remaining whites. Divide mixture among prepared dishes. Bake until puffed and browned, about 20 minutes. Serve immediately.

 *Breads*

Homemade Melba Toast

Makes 30

1 loaf thinly sliced white bread
¾ cup (1½ sticks) salted butter

6 garlic cloves, crushed

Preheat oven to 300°F. Using serrated knife, trim crusts off each slice of bread; cut bread in half. Melt butter in heavy small saucepan over low heat. Add garlic and simmer 5 minutes. Brush both sides of bread with garlic butter. Arrange bread on baking sheets. Bake until lightly browned, turning once, about 25 minutes. Cool. Store in airtight container. *(Can be prepared 2 days ahead.)*

Buttermilk-Sesame Crackers

Toasting the sesame seeds heightens their flavor.

Makes about 7 dozen

1⅔ cups unbleached all purpose flour
½ cup sesame seeds
⅓ cup cornstarch
¾ teaspoon salt
¾ teaspoon baking powder
¼ teaspoon baking soda

½ cup (1 stick) chilled unsalted butter, cut into pieces
⅓ cup (or more) buttermilk
1½ teaspoons snipped fresh chives
1½ teaspoons minced fresh parsley

Mix first 6 ingredients in processor. Cut in butter using on/off turns until mixture resembles coarse meal. Combine ⅓ cup buttermilk, chives and parsley in bowl. Gradually add buttermilk mixture to processor and blend until soft, slightly crumbly dough forms, adding more buttermilk 1 teaspoon at a time if necessary to bind dough. Divide dough in half. Gather into balls; flatten into discs. Wrap in plastic and refrigerate at least 20 minutes. *(Can be prepared 1 day ahead and refrigerated.)*

Preheat oven to 375°F. Roll 1 dough piece out on lightly floured surface to thickness of ⅛ inch. Cut out rounds using 2-inch plain or scalloped cookie cutter. Pierce rounds with fork. Transfer to heavy large baking sheet, spacing ½ inch apart. Repeat with second dough piece. Bake crackers until light golden brown, about 12 minutes. Transfer to rack and cool completely. (Crackers will crisp as they cool.) *(Can be prepared 1 week ahead. Store airtight.)*

Herb and Buttermilk Breadsticks

These are chewy and breadlike. If you prefer a crisp texture, bake the breadsticks for an additional 20 minutes in a 200°F oven.

Makes 24

1 envelope dry yeast
⅓ cup warm water (105°F to 115°F)
1 tablespoon honey
1 cup buttermilk
3 tablespoons vegetable oil
1 teaspoon salt
1 teaspoon minced fresh parsley or ½ teaspoon dried, crumbled
1 teaspoon minced fresh oregano or ½ teaspoon dried, crumbled

1 teaspoon minced fresh basil or ½ teaspoon dried, crumbled
3¼ cups (about) unbleached all purpose flour
⅓ cup plus 1 teaspoon olive oil
½ cup cornmeal
6 medium garlic cloves, pressed
Coarse salt

Sprinkle yeast over water and honey in medium bowl; stir to dissolve. Let stand 5 minutes. Mix in buttermilk, vegetable oil, salt, parsley, oregano, basil and enough flour ½ cup at a time to form soft dough. Turn dough out onto lightly floured surface and knead until smooth and elastic, about 5 minutes. Lightly grease large bowl with 1 teaspoon olive oil. Add dough, turning to coat entire surface. Cover bowl and refrigerate until doubled in volume, about 2 hours.

Preheat oven to 400°F. Line 3 large baking sheets with parchment. Sprinkle evenly with cornmeal. Punch dough down. Knead on lightly floured surface until smooth. Divide dough into 24 pieces. Roll each piece between palms and work surface to 10-inch-long rope. Transfer ropes to prepared sheets, spacing 1½ inches apart. Mix remaining ⅓ cup oil and garlic in bowl. Brush over breadsticks. Sprinkle lightly with coarse salt. Bake until breadsticks are deep golden brown, 15 to 20 minutes. Cool slightly on wire rack. Serve breadsticks warm or at room temperature.

Croutons with Orange Rouille

A variation on a traditional southern French accompaniment to fish soups. It is also delicious spooned over freshly cooked vegetables or as a dip for crudités.

2 servings; to double or triple, use more bread

1 7-ounce jar roasted red peppers, drained and rinsed
1 garlic clove, minced
¾ teaspoon grated orange peel
½ teaspoon salt
⅛ teaspoon cayenne pepper

⅛ teaspoon fennel seeds, crushed
1 egg yolk
½ cup olive oil

4 ½-inch-thick slices Italian or French bread

Finely chop roasted peppers with next 5 ingredients in processor. Add yolk and puree until smooth. With machine running, gradually add oil through feed tube. *(Can be prepared 1 week ahead. Cover and refrigerate.)*

Preheat broiler. Broil bread until brown on both sides. Spread one side generously with rouille. Broil to heat through, about 30 seconds.

Buttermilk Cheddar Biscuits

Makes about 18

2 cups unbleached all purpose flour
1½ cups shredded medium or sharp cheddar cheese (about 6 ounces)
2 teaspoons baking powder
½ teaspoon baking soda
7 tablespoons chilled unsalted butter, cut into pieces

⅔ to ¾ cup buttermilk
½ teaspoon sugar
½ teaspoon salt
1 egg yolk

Preheat oven to 425°F. Lightly grease heavy large baking sheet. Mix flour, ½ cup cheese, baking powder and soda in medium bowl. Cut in butter until mixture resembles grainy meal. Mix ⅔ cup buttermilk with sugar and salt in small bowl; stir to dissolve. Whisk in yolk. Add to flour mixture and stir until dough gathers into ball, adding more buttermilk 1 teaspoon at a time if necessary to bind dough.

Knead dough on lightly floured surface until just smooth, about 30 seconds. Flatten dough with hands to thickness of ½ inch. Cut out rounds using 2-inch biscuit or cookie cutter. (Do not twist cutter while cutting through dough or biscuits will rise unevenly.) Transfer rounds to prepared sheet. Reduce oven temperature to 400°F. Bake 10 minutes. Sprinkle biscuits with remaining 1 cup cheese. Bake until cheese melts and biscuits are golden brown, about 20 minutes. Cool on rack. Serve warm.

Rosemary Rolls

Sautéed garlic and rosemary enhance these little dinner rolls. Inspired by those from the Emilia-Romagna region of Italy.

Makes about 16

1 ounce fresh yeast cake or 1 envelope dry yeast
1 cup water, lukewarm (95°F) for fresh yeast, warm (105°F to 115°F) for dry yeast
6 tablespoons olive oil
3 tablespoons minced fresh rosemary or 1 tablespoon dried, crumbled

1 garlic clove, minced
3½ cups (or more) unbleached all purpose flour, sifted
2 teaspoons salt
3 tablespoons (about) coarse salt
2 tablespoons (¼ stick) unsalted butter, melted

Dissolve yeast in water in small bowl. Let stand 10 minutes. Heat oil in heavy small skillet over low heat. Add rosemary and garlic and stir 2 minutes. Remove from heat and cool slightly.

Mound 3½ cups flour on work surface or in bowl; make well in center. Add dissolved yeast, rosemary mixture and 2 teaspoons salt to well. Mix ingredients in well, then incorporate flour. Knead dough on lightly floured surface until smooth and elastic, adding more flour if necessary, about 10 minutes.

Form dough into ball. Place on floured surface. Dust with flour. Cut cross in center of dough. Cover with towel and let dough rise until doubled in volume, about 1½ hours.

Flour baking sheets. Punch dough down. Knead on lightly floured surface until smooth. Roll out to ¼-inch-thick square. Cut into 2-inch-wide strips. Roll each up jelly roll fashion, starting at 1 short end. Arrange seam side down on prepared sheets. Cut 3 score lines in top of each with small sharp knife. Sprinkle with coarse salt. Cover with towel and let rise until almost doubled in volume, about 50 minutes.

Preheat oven to 450°F. Bake rolls until golden brown, about 20 minutes. Brush with melted butter. Cool on rack. Serve warm or at room temperature.

Provolone, Sun-dried Tomato and Basil Bread

A quick batter bread.

Makes 3 loaves

2¼ cups unbleached all purpose flour
2 teaspoons baking powder
1 teaspoon salt
1 teaspoon freshly ground pepper
½ teaspoon baking soda
1 cup grated provolone cheese (about 4 ounces)
⅓ cup drained oil-packed sun-dried tomatoes (oil reserved), chopped

¼ cup chopped fresh parsley
1¼ teaspoons dried basil, crumbled
2 eggs
3 tablespoons vegetable oil
1 teaspoon sugar
1¼ cups buttermilk

Preheat oven to 350°F. Grease three 5½ × 3⅛ × 2¼-inch loaf pans. Combine first 5 ingredients in large bowl. Using fork, mix in provolone, tomatoes, parsley and basil. In another bowl, whisk eggs, vegetable oil, sugar and 2 tablespoons oil reserved from tomatoes. Mix in buttermilk. Add to dry ingredients and stir until just combined. Divide among prepared pans.

Bake breads until tester inserted in center comes out clean, about 50 minutes. Cool in pans on rack 5 minutes. Invert onto rack and cool completely. *(Can be prepared 3 days ahead. Wrap in foil and refrigerate.)* Serve bread at room temperature, thinly sliced.

Sourdough Skillet Breads

These breads occasionally expand into balloon shapes during cooking, but don't worry if they don't—they will be delicious anyway.

Makes 16

1 cup chilled plain whole milk yogurt
1½ cups boiling water
1 tablespoon golden brown sugar
2 teaspoons dry yeast
½ cup Sourdough Starter*

2½ cups unbleached all purpose flour
2 tablespoons plus 1 teaspoon olive oil
1 tablespoon salt
5 cups (about) whole wheat flour

Place yogurt in large bowl. Gradually stir in water. Cool to 105°F to 115°F. Add sugar and yeast; stir to dissolve. Mix in starter, then all purpose flour. Stir until thick batter begins to form, about 3 minutes. Mix in 2 tablespoons oil and salt. Mix in enough whole wheat flour 1 cup at a time to form stiff dough. (Dough can also be mixed in heavy-duty mixer.) Turn dough out onto lightly floured surface and knead until smooth and elastic, adding more whole wheat flour if necessary to prevent sticking, about 12 minutes.

Grease large bowl. Add dough, turning to coat entire surface. Cover bowl tightly with plastic wrap. Let dough stand at least 24 hours and up to 36 hours at room temperature.

Punch dough down (dough will be spongy). Divide into 16 pieces. Using lightly floured hands, flatten 1 piece on floured surface into 4-inch round (dough will be sticky). Roll out on lightly floured surface into 1/8-inch-thick round, adding more flour if necessary to prevent sticking (keep remaining dough covered).

Using paper towel, rub remaining 1 teaspoon oil onto heavy griddle or large skillet. Heat over medium-high heat. Invert round into skillet, top side down, using lightly floured tart pan bottom as aid. Cook 30 seconds. Turn and cook until bottom begins to brown (dough will puff up), about 2 minutes. Turn bread over and cook until first side begins to bubble and brown, pressing gently with clean towel, about 1 minute. Transfer to rack. Repeat flattening, rolling and cooking with remaining dough pieces, rubbing skillet occasionally with oiled paper towel and rolling one round while another cooks. *(Can be prepared 1 day ahead. Cool completely. Stack breads in 2 batches and wrap in paper bag or foil. Rewarm wrapped breads in 300°F oven until heated through, about 10 minutes.)* Serve skillet breads warm.

*Sourdough Starter

Makes about 3 cups

2 cups unbleached all purpose flour	1/8 teaspoon dry yeast
2 cups warm water (105°F to 115°F)	

Mix all ingredients in large bowl. Stir until elastic batter forms, about 7 minutes. Transfer to large glass or ceramic container with lid. Let stand at room temperature until sour aroma develops, 3 to 5 days, stirring once a day.

To maintain starter: Replenish starter every time you use it with equal parts of warm water and flour. For example, if you remove 3/4 cup starter, then add 3/4 cup lukewarm water and 3/4 cup unbleached all purpose flour. If you don't bake often, discard 1/2 of starter and replenish it with warm water and all purpose flour every 2 months.

Black Olive Focaccia

Filled with chopped olives, this large flat loaf is great with an antipasto platter, salad or pasta.

1 large loaf

1 ounce fresh yeast cake or 1 envelope dry yeast
1 cup water, lukewarm (95°F) for fresh yeast, warm (105°F to 115°F) for dry yeast

3 cups (or more) unbleached all purpose flour
1 cup oil-cured black olives (about 8 ounces), pitted and chopped

1/4 cup olive oil
1 teaspoon salt

Olive oil
6 tablespoons olivada*

Coarse salt

Dissolve yeast in water in small bowl. Let yeast stand 10 minutes.

Mound 3 cups flour on work surface or in large bowl; make well in center. Add dissolved yeast, chopped olives, ¼ cup oil and 1 teaspoon salt to well. Mix ingredients in well, then incorporate flour. Knead dough on lightly floured surface until smooth and elastic, adding more flour if sticky, 10 minutes.

Dust dough with flour and place in large bowl. Cover with kitchen towel. Let dough rise in warm draft-free area until doubled, about 1½ hours.

Grease large baking sheet with olive oil. Punch dough down. Knead on lightly floured surface until smooth, about 2 minutes. Cut dough in half. Roll 1 piece out on lightly floured surface to 11 × 7-inch rectangle. Transfer to prepared sheet. Spread with olivada, leaving 1-inch border. Roll remaining dough piece out to 11 × 7-inch rectangle. Place atop first piece. Press edges with fork to seal. Let dough rise in warm draft-free area 30 minutes.

Preheat oven to 400°F. Brush dough with olive oil. Sprinkle with coarse salt. Bake until loaf sounds hollow when tapped on bottom, about 40 minutes. Transfer to rack and cool. Serve warm or at room temperature.

*An olive paste available at Italian markets and specialty foods stores. If unavailable, puree pitted oil-cured olives.

Almond Butter Crown

An almond-filled treat perfect for breakfast or late-afternoon tea.

Makes 1 large loaf

Dough
- 3 cups all purpose flour
- 1¼ cups (2½ sticks) chilled unsalted butter, cut into pieces

- 2 envelopes dry yeast
- ¼ cup sugar
- ¼ cup warm water (105°F to 115°F)
- ½ cup evaporated milk, room temperature
- 2 large eggs, room temperature
  Seeds from 6 cardamom pods, crushed

- 1 teaspoon salt

Filling
- ½ cup (1 stick) unsalted butter, room temperature
- ½ cup sugar
- ½ cup almond paste
- 1 teaspoon almond extract

- ¼ cup sliced almonds

  Powdered sugar

For dough: Place flour in processor. Add butter and cut in using on/off turns until butter is size of kidney beans. Transfer to large bowl. Cover and refrigerate while dissolving yeast.

Sprinkle yeast and pinch of sugar over warm water in medium bowl; stir to dissolve. Let stand until foamy, about 5 minutes. Mix in milk, eggs, cardamom, salt and remaining sugar. Pour over flour-butter mixture and stir just until flour is moistened. Cover and chill at least 5 hours. *(Can be prepared 1 day ahead.)*

Punch dough down. Dust hands with flour. Pat dough out on lightly floured surface to 20-inch square. Fold dough over into 3 equal sections as for business letter. Press edges lightly with rolling pin to seal. Turn dough so one short side faces you. Roll dough out into 6½ × 30-inch rectangle. Starting at one short side, fold dough over into thirds, forming 6½ × 10-inch rectangle. Wrap dough in plastic. Refrigerate while preparing filling.

For filling: Using electric mixer, cream butter with sugar, almond paste and almond extract.

Butter 12-cup bundt pan. Sprinkle bottom with sliced almonds. Unwrap dough. Roll dough out on lightly floured work surface into 9 × 24-inch rectangle. Spread filling over. Starting at one long side, roll dough up jelly roll style. Cut dough crosswise into eight slices. Arrange dough slices cut side down in bottom of prepared pan, spacing evenly apart. Let rise in warm draft-free area until almost doubled in volume, about 1½ hours.

Preheat oven to 375°F. Bake loaf until top is dark golden brown, about 45 minutes. Turn bread out onto rack. *(Can be prepared ahead. Cool completely. Wrap tightly. Store 1 day at room temperature or freeze up to 1 month. Rewarm before continuing.)* Sift powdered sugar over. Serve warm.

 Condiments

Herb Butter

Makes about 1¼ cups

1 cup (2 sticks) unsalted butter, room temperature
2 tablespoons minced fresh parsley
1 tablespoon minced fresh sage or 1 teaspoon rubbed or ground sage
1 tablespoon fresh lemon juice
2 teaspoons minced fresh thyme or ½ teaspoon dried, crumbled

2 teaspoons minced fresh basil
½ teaspoon minced fresh oregano or pinch of dried, crumbled
1 small garlic clove, finely chopped Salt and freshly ground pepper

Beat all ingredients in medium bowl to blend. *(Can be prepared 4 days ahead. Cover and refrigerate. Bring to room temperature before using.)*

Garlic-Cayenne Butter

Spread this spicy butter on crusty French bread.

Makes ½ cup

½ cup (1 stick) unsalted butter, room temperature
2 tablespoons minced fresh parsley

1 teaspoon cayenne pepper
1 garlic clove

Puree all ingredients in processor until smooth. Transfer to bowl. *(Can be prepared 1 day ahead. Cover and refrigerate. Bring flavored butter to room temperature before using.)*

Three-Onion Relish

A sweet and crunchy mixture, fragrant with orange and Italian herbs. It adds a real spark to the familiar hamburger and is equally good on grilled fish, especially trout or snapper. Another favorite use: as a topping for an Italian sausage sandwich.

Makes about 1 cup

½ cup ⅛-inch dice red onion
½ cup ⅛-inch dice sweet yellow onion (such as Maui, Vidalia or Spanish)
¼ cup minced green onions
2 tablespoons minced fresh Italian parsley
2 tablespoons olive oil (preferably extra-virgin)
1 tablespoon fresh lemon juice
1 tablespoon fresh orange juice

1 tablespoon chopped orange pulp
1 teaspoon chopped fresh oregano leaves or ¼ teaspoon dried, crumbled
1 teaspoon fresh thyme leaves or ¼ teaspoon dried, crumbled
1 teaspoon finely shredded orange peel
½ teaspoon salt
⅛ teaspoon freshly ground pepper

Mix all ingredients in large bowl. *(Can be prepared 4 hours ahead; chill.)* Serve cold or at room temperature.

Cranberry-Pecan Conserve

Makes about 3 cups

1½ cups sugar
½ cup fresh orange juice
¼ cup water
1 tablespoon grated orange peel
½ teaspoon grated peeled fresh ginger

4 cups cranberries
½ cup chopped toasted pecans (about 2 ounces)

Bring first 5 ingredients to simmer in heavy large saucepan over medium heat, stirring until sugar dissolves. Add cranberries and cook until berries pop, stirring occasionally, about 5 minutes. Stir in pecans. Pour into bowl. Cool, cover and refrigerate until well chilled. *(Can be prepared 4 days ahead.)*

Bread and Butter Pickles

Makes about 8 cups

2½ pounds pickling cucumbers, rinsed and cut into ⅛-inch-thick rounds
4 small onions, halved and sliced paper-thin
¼ cup coarse salt
10 ice cubes

2½ cups sugar
2½ cups cider vinegar
1 tablespoon yellow mustard seeds
1½ teaspoons celery seeds
1 teaspoon ground turmeric
2 whole cloves

Mix first 4 ingredients in large bowl. Cover with plastic wrap and weight with heavy object. Refrigerate 4 hours.

Drain cucumbers; pat dry. Transfer to large nonaluminum pot. Add remaining ingredients. Bring just to boil, stirring occasionally. Spoon some of pickles into clean hot jar to within ½ inch from top.* Ladle cooking liquid over to within ½ inch from top. Place lid on jar; seal tightly. Repeat with remaining pickles and cooking liquid. Arrange jars in large pot. Cover with boiling water by at least 1 inch. Cover pot and boil 5 minutes.

Remove jars from water bath. Cool to room temperature. Press center of each lid. If lid stays down, jar is sealed. Store in cool dry place up to 6 months. Refrigerate pickles after opening. (If lid pops up, pickles can be stored in refrigerator for up to 1 week.)

*Freshly made pickles that have not been processed in water bath will keep up to 1 week in refrigerator.

Sweet Onion Marmalade

Southerners classically serve a relish tray as part of their Thanksgiving feast. Pass this marmalade along with cranberry conserve and pickles for a new version of that tradition.

Makes about 2 cups

¼ cup olive oil
2 pounds onions, halved lengthwise and cut into ½-inch-wide wedges
2 tablespoons sugar
1 teaspoon (or more) freshly ground white pepper
1 teaspoon (or more) freshly ground black pepper

⅛ teaspoon ground allspice
⅛ teaspoon ground cloves
¼ cup balsamic vinegar or red wine vinegar
¼ cup chicken stock or canned broth
Salt

Heat oil in heavy large skillet over medium heat. Add onions and cook until softened, stirring frequently, about 15 minutes. Add sugar, 1 teaspoon white pepper, 1 teaspoon black pepper, allspice and cloves and cook 10 minutes, stirring frequently. Add vinegar and cook 5 minutes, stirring occasionally. Add stock; reduce heat to low. Cover and cook 35 minutes, stirring occasionally. Season with salt. Taste, adding more pepper if desired. *(Can be prepared 4 days ahead; refrigerate. Bring to room temperature before serving.)*

6 ❧ Desserts

The desserts in this chapter are a sampler of irresistible treats. The best desserts of 1988 include an abundance of old-fashioned favorites such as Deep-Dish Cranberry Apple Raisin Pie, Strawberry Rhubarb Crumble and Black Bottom Devil's Food Cake. But that doesn't mean there are no surprises—delicious new twists include Pumpkin Caramel Custards with Rum-flavored Cream, Banana and Toblerone Sundae (a luscious version of a banana split) and Blueberry-Lime Shortcakes, a refreshing take on a summer tradition.

Along with the down-home, you'll find plenty of sophisticated show-stoppers, from Pecan Lace Baskets with Peach and White Chocolate Mousse to Grand Marnier Cheesecake with Strawberries and Candied Orange Peel. There's even a fabulous version of the old holiday stand-by—White Chocolate Fruitcake includes white chocolate both in the cake and drizzled on top.

Cookies and candies finish off the chapter with a sweet flourish—here, too, you'll find an assortment of homey treats like Lemon Cooler Cookies, Peanut Butter Chocolate Chip Cookies with Glazed Peanuts and Buttery Hazelnut Toffee. Elegant possibilities include delicate Brown Sugar Almond Crisp cookies, Coffee Spice Caramels and Ginger-Orange Macadamia Bark.

🍎 *Fruit Desserts*

Glazed Strawberries

Enjoy these on their own, or use as a garnish for a fancy dessert. You will need to work quickly, as the glaze thickens and hardens as it cools.

Makes 32

32 6- to 8-inch wooden skewers	2 cups sugar
32 large strawberries	1 cup water

Insert skewer halfway into each strawberry through stem. Place on baking sheet.

Oil another large baking sheet. Cook sugar and water in heavy medium saucepan over low heat, stirring occasionally until sugar dissolves. Increase heat and boil without stirring until syrup registers 280°F (soft-crack stage) on candy thermometer, brushing down any sugar crystals on sides of pan with wet pastry brush. Remove from heat. Immediately dip 1 berry into syrup. Tap skewer on sides of pan, allowing excess glaze to drip back into pan. Place on oiled sheet. Repeat with remaining berries and glaze, working quickly. *(Can be prepared 1 hour ahead. Let stand in cool dry place; do not refrigerate.)*

Melon Sauce with Cantaloupe Wedges and Raspberries

8 servings

6 tablespoons sugar	½ cup whipping cream, whipped
4 large egg yolks	2 1-pound cantaloupes, seeded and
1 cup milk, scalded	cut into wedges
1 teaspoon vanilla extract	Fresh raspberries or sliced
1 tablespoon melon liqueur, dark rum or Grand Marnier	strawberries

Combine sugar and yolks in heavy medium saucepan and mix well. Whisk in warm milk. Stir custard over medium-low heat until mixture thickens and leaves path on spoon when finger is drawn across, about 3 minutes; do not boil. Strain into bowl. Stir in vanilla. Press piece of plastic wrap onto surface of custard. Refrigerate until chilled, at least 1 and up to 8 hours.

Stir melon liqueur into custard. Fold in whipped cream. Arrange cantaloupe wedges on plates. Top with sauce. Sprinkle with berries.

Plums with Cream and Brandy Sauce

Try this sauce over any seasonal fruit. Serve with cookies for crunch.

2 servings; can be doubled or tripled

3 plums, pitted and sliced	½ cup chilled whipping cream
3 tablespoons slivovitz or other brandy	1 egg yolk
3 tablespoons sugar	¾ teaspoon vanilla extract
¼ teaspoon grated lemon peel	

Combine first 4 ingredients in medium bowl. Stir to blend. Let stand at least 30 minutes (or up to 2 hours), stirring occasionally. Drain plums, reserving liquid.

Using electric mixer, beat cream until peaks form. Mix in yolk and vanilla. Beat in plum liquid and continue beating until sauce mounds in spoon. *(Can be prepared 1 hour ahead. Cover and refrigerate plums and sauce separately. Gently mix sauce before using.)*

Divide most of plums between 2 large stemmed glasses. Spoon sauce over. Top with remaining plums.

Honeyed Fig, Pear and Kumquat Compote

A wine syrup fragrant with star anise and cinnamon imparts an exotic flavor to the fruit. The compote is equally delicious for breakfast or served over vanilla ice cream.

6 servings

Figs and Pears
1 8-ounce package dried Calimyrna figs
2½ cups water

2 cups dry white wine
3 tablespoons honey
3 whole star anise
1 3¼-inch piece cinnamon stick

3 Bosc pears (ripe but firm), quartered, cored and peeled

Kumquats
¾ pound kumquats, stem ends removed, halved lengthwise and seeded
¼ cup water
¼ cup dry white wine
¼ cup honey
1 whole star anise
¼ teaspoon cinnamon

Vanilla ice cream (optional)

For figs and pears: Combine figs and water in small bowl. Cover and let soak overnight at room temperature.

Bring figs, soaking liquid, wine, honey, star anise and cinnamon to boil in heavy large saucepan. Reduce heat, cover and simmer until knife pierces figs easily, about 45 minutes.

Transfer figs to large bowl using slotted spoon. Reduce heat, add pears to liquid and simmer until knife pierces pears easily, about 12 minutes.

Meanwhile, cool figs slightly. Cut off stems; halve figs lengthwise. Return to bowl. Add pears to figs using slotted spoon. Boil poaching liquid until reduced to ⅔ cup, about 15 minutes. Pour over figs and pears.

For kumquats: Bring kumquats, water, wine, honey, star anise and cinnamon to boil in heavy medium saucepan. Boil over medium-high heat until liquid is reduced to 2 tablespoons, stirring frequently, about 12 minutes. Add kumquats with their poaching liquid to figs and pears. Cover and refrigerate until well chilled. *(Compote can be prepared 4 days ahead.)*

Remove star anise and cinnamon stick. Spoon compote into bowls. Serve with vanilla ice cream if desired.

Southern Comfort Peach and Blueberry Compote

Lush, ripe peaches and blueberries in a laid-back "sippin' whisky" and blossom honey syrup.

4 servings

¼ cup Southern Comfort or other whiskey
3 tablespoons orange blossom or other fragrant honey
3 tablespoons fresh lemon juice
1 tablespoon chopped fresh mint leaves

3 large peaches
1 cup fresh blueberries

4 fresh mint sprigs

Cook first 4 ingredients in heavy small saucepan over low heat, stirring until honey dissolves. Cool completely. *(Syrup can be prepared 1 day ahead. Cover and refrigerate.)*

Blanch peaches in large pot of boiling water 30 seconds. Drain; rinse under cold water. Slip off skins. Thinly slice peaches. Transfer peaches to large bowl. Gently mix in blueberries and syrup. Refrigerate until well chilled. *(Can be prepared 4 hours ahead.)*

Spoon compote into serving bowls. Garnish with mint sprigs and serve.

Fall Apple Bake

Apples baked under a crisp pecan topping.

12 servings

8 medium-size tart apples, peeled, cored and sliced
1 cup firmly packed golden brown sugar
2 tablespoons all purpose flour
½ teaspoon cinnamon

2 tablespoons fresh orange juice
1 tablespoon fresh lemon juice

1 tablespoon grated orange peel
¾ cup all purpose flour
¼ teaspoon salt
6 tablespoons (¾ stick) chilled unsalted butter
½ cup chopped pecans
Whipped cream

Preheat oven to 375°F. Butter 2½-quart soufflé dish or deep casserole. Mix apples, ½ cup sugar, 2 tablespoons flour and cinnamon in large bowl. Transfer to prepared pan.

Combine orange juice, lemon juice and orange peel and pour over. Mix ¾ cup flour, salt and remaining ½ cup sugar in medium bowl. Add butter and cut in until mixture resembles coarse meal. Add pecans. Spread over apples. Bake until apples are just tender and top is brown, about 50 minutes. Serve warm, topped with whipped cream.

Peaches Baked with Amaretti, Almonds and Chocolate

A simple, delicious way to cook peaches.

6 servings

6 medium peaches, halved, pitted and cut into eighths
¼ cup maraschino liqueur or Grand Marnier

½ cup crushed amaretti* cookies or almond macaroons
½ cup finely chopped toasted almonds (about 2 ounces)

1 tablespoon unsweetened cocoa powder
¼ cup (½ stick) chilled unsalted butter, diced
Sweetened whipped cream or vanilla ice cream (optional)

Arrange peaches in 8 × 11-inch oval baking dish. Pour liqueur over; toss gently. Let stand 30 minutes.

Preheat oven to 375°F. Combine cookies, almonds and cocoa in small bowl. Add butter and rub with fingertips until mixture resembles coarse meal. Sprinkle over peaches. Bake until peaches are tender and topping browns, about 20 minutes. Cool slightly. Serve warm or at room temperature with whipped cream or vanilla ice cream if desired.

*Italian macaroons available at Italian markets and some supermarkets.

Strawberry Rhubarb Crumble

A classic pairing of red summer fruits, baked under a buttery crunch of brown sugar, almonds and oats. Serve it slightly warm, drizzled with cream.

8 servings

Topping
  1 cup unbleached all purpose flour
  ¾ cup firmly packed golden brown sugar
  ½ cup whole unblanched almonds (about 3 ounces)
  ½ cup rolled oats
  1 teaspoon ground allspice
  ¾ cup (1½ sticks) chilled unsalted butter, cut into pieces

Filling
  3 pints strawberries, stemmed and halved

  6 cups ½-inch chunks fresh rhubarb (about 1¾ pounds)
  1½ cups sugar
  ¾ cup unbleached all purpose flour
  1 tablespoon vanilla extract
  2 teaspoons ground allspice

  Whipping cream

For topping: Place ingredients in order listed in processor. Blend until crumbly, about 45 seconds. *(Can be prepared 1 day ahead. Cover and refrigerate.)*

For filling: Mix first 6 ingredients in large bowl. Cover and let stand 30 minutes, stirring occasionally.

Position rack in center of oven and preheat to 375°F. Spoon filling into 9 × 14 × 2-inch baking dish. Sprinkle with topping. Bake until top browns and filling bubbles, about 40 minutes.

Cool slightly. Spoon into dishes. Serve, passing cream separately.

❦ *Mousses, Puddings and Soufflés*

Warm Indian Pudding with Gingered Pears

This old-fashioned treat will "weep," but if you serve it with heavy cream, no one will be able to tell. Start the pears one day ahead.

8 servings

Gingered Pears
  8 small firm pears (preferably Bosc), peeled, cored and cut into thick chunks
  ⅔ cup sugar
  2 tablespoons grated lemon peel
  4 tablespoons fresh lemon juice
  1 tablespoon finely chopped crystallized ginger

  ½ cup water

Pudding
  4 cups milk
  ⅔ cup plus 2 tablespoons yellow cornmeal
  ⅔ cup molasses
  3 tablespoons butter
  2 eggs, beaten to blend
  1½ teaspoons ground allspice
  ¾ teaspoon salt

  Whipping cream

For pears: Combine pears, sugar, peel, 2 tablespoons juice and ginger in large nonaluminum bowl. Let stand overnight at room temperature.

Drain pears, reserving juices. Transfer juices to heavy medium saucepan. Simmer until large bubbles form on surface. Add pears and simmer 5 minutes. Add remaining 2 tablespoons lemon juice and simmer until mixture is thick and slightly caramelized, stirring frequently to prevent sticking, about 20 minutes. Remove from heat. Stir in water. *(Can be prepared 2 days ahead. Cool completely, cover and refrigerate. Reheat gently before serving.)*

For pudding: Preheat oven to 300°F. Butter 1½-quart shallow baking dish. Bring milk just to boil in heavy medium saucepan over medium heat. Whisk in cornmeal and stir until simmering, about 4 minutes. Remove from heat. Whisk in next 5 ingredients. Turn batter into prepared dish. Bake 45 minutes; pudding will not be firm and will weep. Cool 20 minutes.

To serve: Rewarm pears over medium heat. Spoon warm pudding into bowls. Top with pears. Drizzle with cream.

Souffléed Rice Pudding

A surprisingly light and delicate dessert, based on a recipe from restaurant Cabo Mayor in Madrid.

6 to 8 servings

5 cups milk
⅔ cup plus 2 tablespoons sugar
2 teaspoons lemon peel julienne
½ cinnamon stick

½ cup short-grain rice

1 tablespoon plus ½ teaspoon unflavored gelatin

5 large egg whites, room temperature
¼ teaspoon cream of tartar

Macerated Strawberries*
Fresh mint sprigs

Bring 4 cups of milk, ⅔ cup sugar, lemon and cinnamon to boil in heavy medium saucepan, stirring until sugar dissolves. Remove pan from heat. Cover and let mixture steep 30 minutes.

Discard cinnamon stick. Return mixture to boil. Mix in rice. Reduce heat to low. Cover and simmer until mixture is thick and pasty, stirring frequently during last 30 minutes, about 1½ hours. Cool completely.

Lightly oil 10- to 12-cup ring mold. Sprinkle gelatin over remaining 1 cup milk in heavy small saucepan. Let stand 5 minutes to soften. Stir over low heat until gelatin dissolves.

Puree rice mixture in blender or processor until almost smooth. Transfer to large bowl. Stir in gelatin mixture. Beat egg whites with cream of tartar in medium bowl until soft peaks form. Gradually beat in remaining 2 tablespoons sugar and beat until almost stiff but not dry. Fold ¼ of whites into rice mixture to lighten. Gently fold in remaining whites. Spoon mixture into prepared mold. Refrigerate overnight.

Run small knife around sides of mold. Dip mold into hot water 3 seconds. Unmold onto platter. Spoon strawberries around pudding. Garnish with mint sprigs and serve.

*Macerated Strawberries

Makes about 3 cups

4 cups hulled strawberries, halved if large
2 tablespoons (or more) sugar, preferably superfine

1 teaspoon (or more) fresh lemon juice

Mash 1¼ cups berries with 2 tablespoons sugar in large bowl using potato masher or spoon. Let stand 1 hour. Add remaining strawberries and 1 teaspoon lemon juice. Cover and refrigerate until well chilled. *(Can be prepared 6 hours ahead.)* Taste, adding more sugar or lemon juice if desired.

Pumpkin Caramel Custards with Rum-flavored Cream

In this rendition of a classic dessert, pumpkin custard is poured inside caramel-lined soufflé dishes. When baked, the coating melts into a syrupy sauce. Prepare these at least four hours ahead.

6 servings

⅔ cup sugar
¼ cup water

1¾ cups whipping cream
1¼ cups canned solid pack pumpkin
½ teaspoon cinnamon
⅛ teaspoon ground cloves
    Generous pinch of freshly grated nutmeg

4 large egg yolks
2 large eggs
1½ cups sugar

1 cup chilled whipping cream
1½ tablespoons powdered sugar
1½ tablespoons dark rum
    Cinnamon

Preheat oven to 350°F. Cook ⅔ cup sugar and water in heavy small saucepan over low heat, swirling pan occasionally, until sugar dissolves. Increase heat and boil without stirring until syrup turns deep caramel color. Pour syrup into bottom of six 1-cup soufflé dishes. Set aside at room temperature.

Stir 1¾ cups cream, pumpkin, ½ teaspoon cinnamon, cloves and nutmeg in heavy medium saucepan over medium heat until lukewarm. Using electric mixer, beat yolks and eggs in large bowl to blend. Gradually beat in 1½ cups sugar. Add pumpkin mixture; beat until just blended. Pour into soufflé dishes.

Place soufflé dishes into large deep baking pan. Add enough hot water to baking pan to come halfway up sides of dishes. Bake until knife inserted into centers comes out clean, about 1 hour. Transfer custards to rack and cool 1 hour. Invert custards onto plates. Cover loosely and refrigerate at least 4 hours. *(Can be prepared 1 day ahead.)*

Whip 1 cup cream to soft peaks. Gradually add powdered sugar and rum and beat until stiff. Spoon cream over sides of custards. Sprinkle cream with cinnamon and serve.

Pecan Lace Baskets with Peach and White Chocolate Mousse

8 servings

Mousse
1 envelope unflavored gelatin
6 tablespoons sweet white wine, such as Sauternes or late harvest Riesling
10 ounces white chocolate, coarsely chopped
¾ cup peach puree (from about 1 peeled 8-ounce peach)
2 tablespoons powdered sugar
4 egg yolks

2 cups chilled whipping cream

Peach Sauce
1½ pounds peaches
½ cup sweet white wine, such as Sauternes or late harvest Riesling

2 tablespoons sugar

Baskets
1 cup pecans (3½ ounces)
½ cup blanched almonds (3 ounces)
½ cup (1 stick) unsalted butter, melted
½ cup sugar
1 tablespoon light corn syrup
2 tablespoons milk
3 tablespoons bread flour

    Sliced fresh peaches
    Sliced fresh strawberries
    Fresh mint sprigs

For mousse: Sprinkle gelatin over wine in small bowl. Set bowl into pan of simmering water and stir gelatin until dissolved. Melt chocolate in large double boiler over gently simmering water; stir until smooth. Whisk in dissolved gelatin, peach puree, powdered sugar and egg yolks. Cool.

Beat cream until soft peaks form. Fold into peach mixture. Pour into bowl. Cover and refrigerate until set, at least 4 hours. *(Can be prepared 1 day ahead.)*

For sauce: Drop peaches into boiling water. Drain, refresh and peel. Cut into slices. Transfer to processor. Add wine and sugar and puree. Cover and refrigerate until well chilled. *(Can be prepared 1 day ahead.)*

For baskets: Chop pecans and almonds in processor using on/off turns until size of Grape-Nuts. Pour butter into bowl. Stir in sugar and corn syrup. Mix in nuts and milk. Fold in flour. Chill batter until set, at least 4 hours.

Preheat oven to 375°F. Grease baking sheet. Using ¼-cup ice cream scoop, set 2 scoops batter on prepared sheet. Top with waxed paper. Using hand, flatten each into 4-inch circle; remove paper. Bake until caramel colored, about 12 minutes. Let cookies stand until just cool enough to handle. Working quickly, cut 1 line from edge to center of each. Using spatula as aid, immediately lift cookies and press into flat-bottomed custard cups to form basket. Cool. Remove from cups. Repeat with remaining batter.

To assemble: Set 1 basket on each plate. Using two spoons, form mousse into ovals. Place in baskets. Surround with sauce and peach slices. Garnish with strawberries and mint.

Salzburg Soufflé with Strawberry Kirsch Sauce

A quick, lemony version of the airy Austrian dessert Salzburger *Nockerln.*

4 servings

Sauce
- 1 pint strawberries, hulled
- 3 tablespoons sugar
- 1 tablespoon kirsch
- ¼ teaspoon vanilla extract

Soufflé
- 3 large eggs, separated, room temperature
- ⅛ teaspoon cream of tartar
- ¼ cup sugar
- 1½ tablespoons all purpose flour
- 1 teaspoon grated lemon peel
- 1 teaspoon vanilla extract

Powdered sugar

For sauce: Puree half of berries with sugar, kirsch and vanilla in processor. Pour into medium bowl. Slice remaining berries and mix into puree. Cover and let stand 25 minutes at room temperature. *(Can be prepared 6 hours ahead. Refrigerate. Bring sauce to room temperature before serving.)*

For soufflé: Position rack in lowest third of oven and preheat to 350°F. Butter 10-inch glass pie dish. Using electric mixer, beat whites and cream of tartar until soft peaks form. Gradually beat in ¼ cup sugar and continue beating until stiff but not dry. Beat yolks in another bowl until pale yellow and slowly dissolving ribbon forms when beaters are lifted. Blend in flour, lemon peel and vanilla. Fold in 1 heaping spoonful whites to lighten mixture. Carefully fold in remaining whites.

Spoon soufflé in 4 heaping mounds in prepared dish. Bake until top is golden brown, about 14 minutes. Sift powdered sugar over soufflé. Spoon sauce onto plates. Gently separate soufflé into 4 mounds. Place 1 atop sauce on each plate. Serve immediately.

🍎 *Frozen Desserts*

Banana and Toblerone Sundae

The flavors of a banana split in a delicious sundae. Rather than make the ice cream, you could buy some honey-vanilla and stir in toasted almonds.

6 servings

Honey-Almond Ice Cream
- 4 cups half and half
- 6 egg yolks
- ¾ cup honey

- 1 cup unblanched whole almonds, toasted and coarsely chopped (about 6 ounces)

Toblerone Sauce
- 6 3.5-ounce Toblerone milk chocolate bars, chopped
- 1 cup whipping cream

- 6 large bananas, sliced
  Whipped cream
  Toasted chopped almonds

For ice cream: Scald half and half in heavy medium saucepan. Whisk yolks in medium bowl. Gradually whisk in half and half. Return to saucepan and stir over medium-low heat until mixture thickens and leaves path on back of spoon when finger is drawn across, about 6 minutes; do not boil. Strain into medium bowl. Mix in honey. Whisk 1 minute to cool. Refrigerate custard until well chilled (or chill over ice water, whisking occasionally).

Transfer custard to ice cream maker and process according to manufacturer's instructions, adding almonds when ice cream is almost set. Freeze in covered container several hours. *(Can be prepared 4 days ahead.)*

For sauce: Cook chocolate with 1 cup cream in heavy medium saucepan over low heat, stirring until smooth.

Scoop ice cream into sundae dishes. Top with bananas. Spoon warm sauce over. Top with whipped cream. Sprinkle almonds over and serve.

Raspberry and Vanilla Sundae

A sophisticated ending to any dinner party. Don't forget that vanilla beans can be rinsed and reused. If using Tahitian vanilla beans, which are intensely flavored, use half the amount called for.

6 servings

Vanilla Bean–Cognac Ice Cream
- 4 cups half and half
- 2 6-inch vanilla beans, split lengthwise

- 6 egg yolks
- 1 cup sugar
- 3 tablespoons Cognac or brandy (optional)

Raspberry-Zinfandel Sauce
- 3 cups red Zinfandel wine

- 1½ cups frozen unsweetened raspberries
- 1 cup sugar
- 1 6-inch and 1 3-inch piece vanilla bean, split lengthwise

- 3 cups fresh raspberries
  Toasted sliced almonds
  Fresh mint sprigs

For ice cream: Place half and half in heavy medium saucepan. Scrape in seeds from vanilla beans; add pods. Scald half and half. Remove from heat and let steep 15 minutes.

Whisk yolks and sugar to blend in medium bowl. Reheat half and half. Gradually whisk 2 cups into yolks. Return to saucepan. Stir over medium-low heat until mixture thickens and leaves path on back of spoon when finger is drawn across, about 7 minutes; do not boil. Strain into medium bowl. Whisk 1 minute to cool. Stir in Cognac. Refrigerate custard until well chilled (or chill over bowl of ice water, whisking occasionally).

Transfer custard to ice cream maker and process according to manufacturer's instructions. Freeze in covered container several hours. *(Ice cream can be prepared 4 days ahead.)*

For sauce: Bring Zinfandel, frozen berries, sugar and vanilla beans to boil in heavy medium saucepan, stirring until sugar dissolves. Reduce heat and simmer 5 minutes. Increase heat and boil until reduced to 1½ cups, stirring occasionally, about 10 minutes. Strain into bowl, pressing on berries to extract as much pulp as possible. Cool to room temperature. *(Can be prepared 3 days ahead. Cover and refrigerate. Bring to room temperature before using.)*

Scoop ice cream into sundae dishes. Spoon sauce over. Top with fresh raspberries. Sprinkle with almonds. Garnish with mint sprigs and serve.

Frozen Double Chocolate Mousse

10 servings

Crust
- ⅔ **cup chocolate wafer cookie crumbs**
- ⅓ **cup graham cracker crumbs**
- ¼ **cup (½ stick) unsalted butter, melted**

Dark Chocolate Mousse
- 4 **ounces semisweet chocolate, finely chopped**
- 2 **ounces unsweetened chocolate, finely chopped**
- 6 **egg yolks**

- ¾ **cup sugar**
- ½ **cup Frangelico liqueur**
- 1¼ **cups chilled whipping cream**

White Chocolate Mousse
- ¾ **cup whipping cream**
- 10 **ounces white chocolate, chopped**

- 3 **tablespoons Frangelico liqueur**
- 1⅓ **cups chilled whipping cream**

- 2 **ounces semisweet chocolate, coarsely chopped**
- 1 **tablespoon unsalted butter**

For crust: Preheat oven to 350°F. Mix all crumbs in bottom of 9½-inch springform pan. Pour butter over. Mix with fork until well blended. Press mixture firmly onto bottom of pan. Bake 8 minutes. Cool crust on rack.

For dark chocolate mousse: Stir both chocolates in double boiler over barely simmering water until smooth and melted. Cool to lukewarm. Using electric mixer, beat yolks to blend in large bowl. Gradually add sugar and beat until pale yellow and slowly dissolving ribbon forms when beaters are lifted. Blend in Frangelico, then melted chocolate. Whip cream in another bowl until soft peaks form. Fold ⅓ of cream into chocolate mixture. Gently fold in remaining cream. Pour mixture into crust; smooth top. Freeze until set, about 30 minutes.

For white chocolate mousse: Bring ¾ cup cream to boil in heavy small saucepan. Reduce heat and simmer 2 minutes. Finely chop white chocolate in processor. Pour hot cream through feed tube and blend until mixture is smooth, about 1 minute. Transfer to medium bowl. Cool completely.

Stir Frangelico into white chocolate mixture. Using electric mixer, whip 1⅓ cups cream in medium bowl until peaks form. Fold ⅓ of cream into white chocolate mixture. Gently fold in remaining cream. Pour over dark chocolate mousse; smooth top. Freeze until top of mousse sets.

Spicy Fried Chicken; Grilled Corn Salad; Garlic Shrimp; Homemade Melba Toast; Sliced Tomatoes

Lynn St. John

Rigatoni with Smoked Chicken and Ricotta

Kathryn Kleinman

Apple Soup with Roquefort Croutons; Cornish Game Hens with Figs and Thyme; Braised Endive; Mixed Green Salad; Pumpkin Caramel Custards with Rum-flavored Cream

Jerry Friedman

Roast Turkey with Herbs and Aromatic
Vegetables; Fall Vegetable Puree; Corn
Bread Dressing with Giblets and Mush-
rooms; Collard and Mustard Greens
with Bacon; Bread and Butter Pickles;
Cranberry-Pecan Conserve; Sweet
Onion Marmalade

Alan Krosnick

Black Bottom Devil's Food Cake;
Hazelnut Pastry Crescents with
Chocolate and Apricot Filling;
Herb and Buttermilk Breadsticks;
Buttermilk-Sesame Crackers;
Buttermilk Cheddar Biscuits

Raspberry and Vanilla Sundae

Brian Leatart

Buttery Hazelnut Toffee and Ginger-Orange Macadamia Bark in box; Raspberry Creams; Double-Decker Mint Patties in silver cups; Peanut Butter Dreams; Rocky Road Fudge

Cover mousse and freeze at least 24 hours. Run knife around edge of pan to loosen. Release pan sides from mousse. Smooth sides of mousse with icing spatula. Return to freezer.

Stir 2 ounces semisweet chocolate and butter in heavy small saucepan over low heat until melted and smooth. Cool to lukewarm. Spoon into parchment cone or pastry bag fitted with small plain tip. Pipe chocolate in decorative pattern around edge of mousse. Freeze until chocolate sets, about 10 minutes. *(Can be prepared 2 days ahead. Cover with plastic wrap.)* Cut into wedges to serve.

Ice Cream Cheesecake with Cognac Cherries

Cream cheese adds its subtle tang and richness to the ice cream filling. Use a premium ice cream for best results. You can purchase a sponge cake or make one from your favorite recipe.

10 servings

Cheesecake
1 30-ounce jar pitted sour cherries in light syrup,* drained, juices reserved
½ cup Cognac

1 9-inch round sponge cake or 1 pound cake
1 8-ounce package cream cheese, room temperature
¼ to ⅓ cup canned sweetened condensed milk

2 teaspoons vanilla extract
1 quart vanilla ice cream, slightly softened

Sauce
⅓ cup sugar
1 tablespoon cornstarch dissolved in 2 tablespoons water
1 teaspoon unsalted butter

Sweetened whipped cream

For cheesecake: Combine cherries with Cognac in medium bowl. Let stand 1 hour at room temperature.

Drain cherries, reserving Cognac. Mix Cognac with reserved cherry juices and 10 cherries in bowl; chill.

Line bottom of 9-inch springform pan with parchment. Cut sponge cake horizontally into ¾-inch-thick round; reserve trimmings for another use. Place cake layer in bottom of pan. (If using pound cake, cut into ¾-inch-thick slices. Trim and fit cake pieces tightly in bottom of pan.) Using electric mixer, beat cream cheese in large bowl until smooth. Blend in ¼ cup condensed milk and vanilla. Cut ice cream into chunks; blend into cream cheese until just combined; do not let melt. Taste, blending in remaining milk if sweeter flavor is desired.

Pour half of ice cream mixture over cake in pan; smooth top. Arrange drained cherries over, allowing some to touch sides of pan. Gently pour remaining filling over. Cover with plastic wrap and freeze overnight. *(Can be prepared 2 days ahead.)*

For sauce: Strain cherry-Cognac juices into small saucepan; pat cherries dry. Add sugar to juices and bring to boil. Add cornstarch mixture and stir until mixture boils and thickens, about 2 minutes. Cool slightly (sauce will be thin). *(Can be prepared 2 days ahead. Cover and refrigerate sauce and cherries separately. Rewarm sauce over low heat, stirring constantly.)* Stir in butter.

Run sharp wet knife around sides of cheesecake. Release pan sides. Transfer cheesecake cake side down to platter. Spoon whipped cream into pastry bag fitted with star tip. Pipe 10 rosettes around top edge of cheesecake. Top each with cherry. Serve immediately, ladling warm sauce around each slice.

*Available at Middle Eastern markets and some specialty foods stores.

Frozen Lemon Soufflé with Berry Sauce

A creamy soufflé with an intense lemon flavor.

8 servings

1½ cups sugar
1 cup plus 1 tablespoon fresh lemon juice
1 cup (2 sticks) unsalted butter, cut into pieces
14 large egg yolks
2 tablespoons grated lemon peel

3 large egg whites, room temperature

2 cups chilled whipping cream

1 tablespoon sugar
1 teaspoon vanilla extract
   Candied Lemon Peel*
   Berry Sauce**

Fold 24-inch-long sheet of foil lengthwise in thirds. Brush one side with oil. Wrap foil, oiled side in, around top of 1½-quart soufflé dish, extending 4 inches above rim. Tie with string to secure. Bring first 5 ingredients to boil in heavy large nonaluminum saucepan over medium heat, whisking constantly. Boil just until very thick, about 5 seconds (do not overcook or mixture will curdle). Pour lemon mixture into large bowl. Set bowl over larger bowl filled with ice and water. Cool completely, stirring frequently.

Using electric mixer beat whites in medium bowl to soft peaks. Fold into lemon mixture. Whip 1½ cups cream to soft peaks. Fold into lemon mixture. Pour into prepared dish. Freeze overnight. *(Can be prepared 2 days ahead.)*

Remove foil collar from soufflé. Return soufflé to freezer. Using electric mixer, whip remaining ½ cup cream with 1 tablespoon sugar and vanilla in bowl to medium-stiff peaks. Spoon into pastry bag fitted with medium star tip. Pipe 8 rosettes of cream around outer edge of soufflé. Sprinkle candied peel over each rosette. Serve soufflé, passing sauce separately.

*Candied Lemon Peel

Candied peel adds a festive touch to most any dessert. Try it over mousses, cakes and ice cream.

Makes about ¼ cup

2 large lemons

½ cup sugar
½ cup water

Remove lemon peel in large strips using vegetable peeler. Cut strips into julienne. Blanch peel in medium saucepan of boiling water 1 minute. Drain. Repeat blanching once.

Cook ¼ cup sugar and ½ cup water in heavy small saucepan over low heat, stirring until sugar dissolves. Increase heat and bring to boil. Add peel. Reduce heat and simmer 15 minutes. Drain peel. Toss peel in remaining ¼ cup sugar to coat. Separate peel strands on plate. Let stand 30 minutes at room temperature to dry. *(Can be prepared 1 week ahead. Store at room temperature in airtight container between layers of waxed paper.)*

**Berry Sauce

Delicious over ice cream.

Makes about 1⅓ cups

1 10-ounce package frozen raspberries or strawberries in syrup, thawed

¼ cup crème de cassis

Puree berries in processor. Strain through sieve into bowl. Mix in cassis. Cover and refrigerate until well chilled. *(Can be prepared 1 day ahead.)*

🍒 *Pies, Tarts and Pastries*

Deep-Dish Cranberry Apple Raisin Pie

8 servings

Crust
1¼ cups unbleached all purpose flour
¼ teaspoon salt
¼ cup chilled solid vegetable shortening, cut into pieces
3 tablespoons chilled unsalted butter, cut into pieces
¼ cup (about) ice water

Filling
2½ pounds tart green apples such as Granny Smith, cored, peeled and very thinly sliced
⅓ cup unbleached all purpose flour
1½ cups cranberries
1 cup sugar
⅓ cup finely shredded orange peel
1 cup golden raisins
½ cup fresh orange juice

1 egg, beaten to blend
1 tablespoon sugar
Orange sherbet swirled with vanilla ice cream

For crust: Combine flour and salt in processor. Add shortening and butter and cut in until mixture resembles coarse meal. Mix in enough water 1 tablespoon at a time to form soft, crumbly dough. Turn dough out onto lightly floured surface. Gather into ball; flatten into disc. Wrap in plastic and refrigerate at least 45 minutes. *(Can be prepared up to 1 day ahead.)*

For filling: Mix apples and flour in large bowl. Finely chop cranberries, 1 cup sugar and orange peel in processor. Add to apples. Mix in raisins and orange juice. Cover and let stand 30 minutes at room temperature.

Position rack in center of oven and preheat to 400°F. Spoon filling into 10-cup soufflé dish or casserole. Roll dough out on heavily floured surface to 11-inch round. Brush outer edges of dish with water. Place dough atop dish. Trim to ½-inch overhang. Crimp edges, pressing to dish sides. Pierce dough with knife in several places. Bake 15 minutes. Reduce oven temperature to 375°F. Brush top of dough with egg; sprinkle with 1 tablespoon sugar. Bake until top is deep golden brown, about 45 minutes. Cool 30 minutes on rack. Serve pie warm with orange sherbet.

Lime and Toffee Tart

A buttery cookie-crust base is filled with a luscious lime curd and sprinkled with a toffee topping.

8 servings

Crust
¾ cup (1½ sticks) unsalted butter, room temperature
¼ cup plus 2 tablespoons sugar
1 small egg, room temperature
¼ teaspoon vanilla extract
Pinch of salt
1¾ cups plus 2 tablespoons all purpose flour

Filling
1¼ cups sugar
1 cup (2 sticks) unsalted butter, cut into pieces, room temperature
1 cup fresh lime juice
11 large egg yolks
1 tablespoon plus 1½ teaspoons grated lime peel

Toffee Sprinkles*

For crust: Using electric mixer cream butter with sugar in medium bowl until light, stopping occasionally to scrape down sides of bowl. Beat in egg, vanilla and salt. Add flour and stir until dough comes together. Roll dough out between sheets of waxed paper to thickness of ¼ inch. Peel off top sheet of paper. Invert dough onto 11-inch-diameter tart pan with removable bottom. Peel off top sheet of paper. Press dough into pan; trim edges. Refrigerate 1 hour.

Preheat oven to 350°F. Bake crust until golden brown, piercing with fork if dough puffs, about 25 minutes. Cool on rack.

For filling: Bring first 5 ingredients to boil in heavy large nonaluminum saucepan over medium heat, whisking constantly. Boil just until thickened, about 5 seconds (do not overcook or mixture will curdle). Pour into prepared crust. Refrigerate until set, about 4 hours. *(Can be prepared 1 day ahead.)*

Remove tart from pan. Transfer to platter. Sprinkle toffee over and serve.

*Toffee Sprinkles

This rich toffee is also great over ice cream.

Makes about 1 cup

1 cup sugar
1 cup water
2 tablespoons whipping cream

3 tablespoons unsalted butter, cut into pieces

Lightly oil large baking sheet. Cook sugar and water in heavy medium saucepan over low heat, stirring occasionally until sugar dissolves. Increase heat and boil without stirring until sugar turns caramel color, about 8 minutes. Remove from heat. Stir in cream, then butter (mixture will bubble vigorously). Stir until butter melts. Pour onto prepared sheet. Freeze toffee until firm, about 20 minutes. Break toffee into 2-inch pieces. Coarsely chop toffee in processor using on/off turns. *(Can be prepared 1 day ahead. Store in airtight jar in freezer.)*

Pineapple-Strawberry Pizza

A fresh, creative take on everyone's favorite "pie." Any combination of seasonal fruit can be used to top this butter crust. Galette is the French term for this type of free-form tart.

8 to 10 servings

Galette Dough
1⅓ cups all purpose flour
1½ tablespoons sugar
2 teaspoons grated lemon peel
¼ teaspoon salt
10 tablespoons (1¼ sticks) chilled unsalted butter, cut into pieces
3 tablespoons (about) water

1 egg yolk beaten with 2 tablespoons whipping cream (glaze)

½ medium pineapple, peeled
1 tablespoon sugar
1 pint strawberries, stemmed and halved

Glaze
¼ cup strained apricot preserves
3 tablespoons Grand Marnier

Whipped cream

For dough: Combine first 4 ingredients in bowl of electric mixer fitted with paddle or in processor. Blend in butter until mixture resembles coarse meal. Mix in enough water to bind dough. Gather dough into ball; flatten to disc. Wrap and refrigerate 30 minutes.

Roll dough out on lightly floured surface to 12-inch-diameter round. Brush off any excess flour. Transfer dough to baking sheet or pizza pan. Brush surface with egg glaze. Fold edge in to form rim. Brush with egg glaze. Pierce all over with fork. Freeze 30 minutes.

Preheat oven to 375°F. Core pineapple, discarding core, and cut crosswise into ⅛-inch-thick slices, reserving any juices for glaze. Overlap pineapple slices in circular pattern atop pastry. Sprinkle with 1 tablespoon sugar. Bake until crust is golden brown, about 35 minutes. Transfer to rack. Arrange strawberries decoratively over pineapple.

For glaze: Boil preserves, Grand Marnier and reserved pineapple juice in heavy small saucepan until reduced to glaze, about 5 minutes.

Brush glaze over fruit and edge of crust. *(Can be prepared 6 hours ahead.)* Serve at room temperature, passing whipped cream separately.

Pumpkin Pie with Ginger Whipped Cream

Makes 2 pies

Filling
- 2 1-pound cans solid pack pumpkin
- 2 cups firmly packed golden brown sugar
- 4 large eggs
- ¼ cup (½ stick) butter, melted
- 2 tablespoons all purpose flour
- 2 teaspoons ground ginger
- 2 teaspoons cinnamon
- 1 teaspoon freshly grated nutmeg
- 1 teaspoon salt
- 1 teaspoon freshly ground pepper
- 3 cups half and half

Crust
- 2½ cups unbleached all purpose flour
- 3 tablespoons sugar
- ½ teaspoon salt
- ½ cup chilled solid vegetable shortening
- 5 tablespoons chilled unsalted butter, cut into ½-inch pieces
- 6 tablespoons (about) ice water

Ginger Whipped Cream*
Chopped crystallized ginger

For filling: Mix all ingredients except half and half in large bowl until well blended. Mix in half and half. *(Can be prepared 2 days ahead. Cover and chill. Bring to room temperature before using.)*

For crust: Combine first 3 ingredients in large bowl. Add shortening and butter and cut in until mixture resembles coarse meal. Mix in enough water to form soft dough. Gather dough into ball; divide in half. Flatten each half into disc. Wrap in waxed paper and refrigerate until well chilled, at least 1 hour. *(Can be prepared 1 day ahead.)*

Roll 1 dough piece out between sheets of waxed paper to ⅛- to ¼-inch-thick round. Transfer to 9-inch pie pan, using paper as aid; discard paper. Double edges over and crimp, forming ½-inch-high edges. Repeat rolling and crimping with second dough piece, forming second pie crust. Pierce crusts with fork. Freeze 20 minutes.

Position rack in center of oven and preheat to 400°F. Line each crust with foil and fill with dried beans or pie weights. Bake 10 minutes. Remove foil and beans. Bake until crusts are light brown, about 10 minutes. Reduce oven temperature to 375°F.

Divide filling between crusts. Bake until centers no longer move when pan is shaken, about 70 minutes. Cool completely on rack. Cut pies into wedges. Top each with dollop of Ginger Whipped Cream. Sprinkle chopped ginger over.

*Ginger Whipped Cream

Makes about 3 cups

1½ cups chilled whipping cream
¼ cup sour cream
3 tablespoons sugar

3 tablespoons dark rum
¾ teaspoon vanilla extract
¼ cup minced crystallized ginger

Whip cream with sour cream and sugar until peaks form. Beat in rum and vanilla. Fold in ginger. *(Can be prepared 8 hours ahead; refrigerate.)*

Brownie Walnut Pie

Offer this dense, moist chocolate pie with scoops of coffee ice cream.

8 servings

Pie Crust Dough*

Filling
¾ cup (1½ sticks) unsalted butter, cut into pieces
3 ounces unsweetened chocolate, chopped
1½ teaspoons instant coffee granules
1½ cups firmly packed golden brown sugar

3 large eggs, room temperature
1 cup unbleached all purpose flour
1 teaspoon salt
½ teaspoon cinnamon
1 cup chopped walnuts (about 3½ ounces)

Coffee ice cream

Position rack in center of oven. Place heavy large baking sheet on rack and preheat to 400°F. Roll dough out on lightly floured surface to ⅛-inch-thick round. Transfer dough to 9-inch pie pan. Crimp edges, trimming excess dough. Pierce bottom with fork. Line crust with parchment or foil. Fill with dried beans or pie weights. Place on baking sheet in oven and bake 10 minutes. Remove paper and weights. Reduce oven temperature to 350°F. Bake on sheet until crust is pale golden brown, about 10 minutes more. Transfer crust to wire rack and cool while preparing filling. Leave baking sheet in oven and maintain oven temperature.

For filling: Melt butter and chocolate with coffee in top of double boiler over simmering water, stirring until smooth. Cool to room temperature.

Using electric mixer, beat sugar and eggs in large bowl until thick and glossy. Stir in chocolate mixture. Combine flour, salt and cinnamon. Add to chocolate mixture with walnuts and stir until just combined.

Pour filling into prepared crust. Place on baking sheet in oven and bake until top forms crust and filling rises around edges but still moves in center when pan is shaken, about 30 minutes. Transfer to rack and cool at least 4 hours. *(Can be prepared 1 day ahead. Cover and let stand at room temperature.)* Serve with coffee ice cream.

*Pie Crust Dough

Makes one 9- or 10-inch pie crust

1½ cups unbleached all purpose flour
1½ tablespoons sugar
⅛ teaspoon (generous) salt
½ cup chilled solid vegetable shortening, cut into pieces

¼ cup (½ stick) chilled unsalted butter, cut into pieces
4 tablespoons (about) ice water

Mix flour, sugar and salt in medium bowl. Add shortening and butter and cut in until mixture resembles coarse meal. Mix in enough water 1 tablespoon at a time to bind dough. Gather dough into ball; flatten into disc. Wrap in plastic. Chill at least 30 minutes. *(Can be prepared 1 day ahead.)*

Cherry Vareniki

These terrific dessert dumplings are the ultimate for pasta lovers: They're like spiced cherry-filled ravioli.

Makes 36

⅓ cup sour cream
1 egg
1 egg yolk
1 teaspoon salt
1½ cups all purpose flour

1 16-ounce can tart red pitted cherries in syrup

14 tablespoons plus 1½ teaspoons sugar

3 tablespoons cornstarch
⅛ teaspoon cinnamon
2 pinches of ground cloves
1 egg white, beaten to blend
1 12-ounce jar sour cherry preserves

6 tablespoons (¾ stick) butter, melted
1 pint sour cream, stirred

Blend ⅓ cup sour cream, egg, yolk and salt in processor 2 seconds. Add flour and mix until dough forms ball, 20 to 30 seconds, stopping once to scrape down sides of bowl. Gather dough. Wrap in plastic; flatten into disc. Refrigerate 2 hours or up to 1 day.

Set cherries in colander over bowl and let drain; do not discard syrup.

Cut dough into 8 pieces. Roll 1 piece out (keep remainder covered to prevent drying) in pasta machine or by hand to thickness of generous ¹⁄₁₆ inch. Cut out scant 3-inch rounds. Gather scraps; reroll and cut out additional rounds. Repeat rolling and cutting with remaining dough, forming 36 rounds.

Line baking sheet with several layers of paper towel. Using fork, blend 8 tablespoons sugar, cornstarch, cinnamon and cloves in medium bowl. Brush 1 dough round lightly with egg white. Place ¼ teaspoon preserves in center of dough. Roll two cherries in sugar mixture, covering completely. Set cherries atop preserves. Fold 1 side of dough over filling. Press edges to seal, leaving ¼- to ½-inch air space around filling. Place vareniki on prepared sheet. Repeat with remaining dough, preserves, cherries and sugar mixture. *(Can be prepared 3 hours ahead. Cover vareniki with plastic and let stand at room temperature.)*

Pour reserved cherry syrup into heavy small saucepan. Stir in 1½ teaspoons sugar and boil until reduced to ⅓ cup. Let stand at room temperature.

Bring two large pots of salted water to boil. Add 18 vareniki to each and cook until tender but still firm to bite, stirring occasionally to prevent sticking, 10 to 12 minutes. Drain well.

To serve, place 6 vareniki in each of 6 shallow soup bowls. Spoon 1 tablespoon melted butter over each serving. Sprinkle each with 1 tablespoon of remaining sugar. Top with dollop of sour cream. Drizzle with 1 tablespoon cherry syrup. Serve immediately.

Rum Raisin Calas

An old-time New Orleans street vendor snack with a new twist.

Makes 16

1 cup raisins
1 cup dark rum

½ cup all purpose flour
3 tablespoons sugar
2 teaspoons baking powder
½ teaspoon cinnamon
¼ teaspoon salt

⅛ teaspoon freshly grated nutmeg
2 eggs, room temperature
½ teaspoon vanilla extract
2 cups cooked long-grain rice (⅔ cup uncooked)

Peanut oil (for deep frying)
Powdered sugar

Bring raisins and rum to simmer in heavy small saucepan. Remove from heat. Cover and let stand until plump, about 30 minutes; drain raisins.

Mix flour, sugar, baking powder, cinnamon, salt and nutmeg in large bowl, then sift. Beat eggs and vanilla to blend in large bowl. Mix in raisins and cooked rice. Stir in dry ingredients.

Preheat oven to 200°F. Line baking sheet with paper towels. Heat oil in deep fryer or heavy large saucepan to 350°F. Drop batter by 2 tablespoonfuls into oil (in batches; do not crowd) and fry until golden brown, 7 to 9 minutes. Remove using slotted spoon and keep warm in oven on prepared baking sheet while frying remaining calas. Dust with powdered sugar.

Cinnamon Apple Ring Fritters

Serve with vanilla ice cream if you like.

2 servings; can be doubled or tripled

⅓ cup half and half
1 egg
1 tablespoon applejack or Calvados (optional)
1 tablespoon sugar
½ teaspoon vanilla extract
½ cup all purpose flour
½ teaspoon baking powder

⅛ teaspoon salt
2 tablespoons sugar
¼ teaspoon cinnamon

Vegetable oil for frying
2 Golden Delicious apples, cored and cut into ¼-inch-thick rounds

Mix first 5 ingredients in processor to blend. Add flour, baking powder and salt. Mix until just smooth using on/off turns. Transfer to bowl. Let stand at room temperature at least 30 minutes. *(Can be prepared 2 hours ahead.)*

Mix 2 tablespoons sugar and cinnamon in small bowl. Set aside.

Heat ½ inch oil in heavy large skillet to 350°F. Sprinkle apples with cinnamon sugar. Dip in batter and add to pan in batches (do not crowd). Fry until golden brown, about 1 minute per side. Drain on paper towels. Sprinkle with more cinnamon sugar and serve.

Hazelnut Pastry Crescents with Chocolate and Apricot Filling

Delicious to enjoy with coffee or tea.

Makes 48

Pastry
3 cups (or more) unbleached all purpose flour
1 envelope fast-rising dry yeast
1 teaspoon baking soda
1 cup (2 sticks) chilled unsalted butter, cut into pieces
1 cup buttermilk
3 egg yolks
2 tablespoons sugar
¼ teaspoon salt

Filling
1½ cups apricot preserves

¾ teaspoon cinnamon
12 ounces bittersweet (not unsweetened) or semisweet chocolate, finely chopped
1½ cups finely chopped husked toasted hazelnuts (about 6 ounces)

3 egg whites
1 tablespoon sugar
Additional finely chopped husked toasted hazelnuts

For pastry: Combine 3 cups flour, yeast and baking soda in medium bowl. Cut in butter until mixture resembles coarse meal. Mix buttermilk, yolks, sugar and salt in small bowl. Add to dry ingredients and mix until dough gathers into ball. Turn dough out onto lightly floured surface and knead until smooth, adding flour if dough is sticky, about 1 minute. Divide dough into 3 pieces. Flatten each piece into disc. Wrap in plastic; chill overnight.

For filling: Preheat oven to 350°F. Line heavy large baking sheets with parchment. Melt apricot preserves in heavy small saucepan over medium heat, stirring constantly. Mix in cinnamon. Roll 1 piece of dough between layers of waxed paper or parchment into 12-inch round. Peel off top sheet of paper. Turn dough over onto lightly floured surface. Peel off other sheet of paper. Brush ⅓ of preserves over dough. Sprinkle with ⅓ of chocolate and ½ cup nuts. Cut dough into 16 wedges using pizza cutter or heavy large knife. Roll up each wedge from wide end to pointed end. Transfer to baking sheet, spacing 2 inches apart. Curve ends, forming crescents. Repeat with remaining dough, preserves, chocolate and 1 cup nuts.

Mix whites and 1 tablespoon sugar in small bowl. Brush mixture over crescents. Sprinkle with finely chopped nuts. Bake until crescents are golden brown, about 25 minutes. Transfer to rack and cool slightly. *(Can be prepared 1 month ahead. Cool completely. Freeze in airtight container. Thaw, then rewarm in 350°F oven until heated through.)* Serve warm or at room temperature.

Pecan Waffles with Banana Brandy Ice Cream and Hot Buttered Brandy Sauce

6 to 8 servings

Ice Cream
- 1 quart rich vanilla ice cream, softened
- 4 medium very ripe bananas, mashed until chunky
- 6 tablespoons Hot Buttered Brandy Sauce,* cooled

Waffles
- 2 cups sifted cake flour
- ¼ cup sugar
- 1 tablespoon baking powder
- ½ teaspoon salt
- 1½ cups milk
- ¼ cup (½ stick) butter, melted
- 3 egg yolks
- 4 egg whites, room temperature
- ½ cup chopped pecans
- Melted butter or vegetable oil

Hot Buttered Brandy Sauce*

For ice cream: Place ice cream in bowl. Stir in mashed bananas. Fold in brandy sauce just to incorporate; ice cream should be streaked. Cover and freeze. *(Can be prepared 1 day ahead.)* If frozen solid, soften ice cream slightly in refrigerator before serving.

For waffles: Preheat oven to 150°F. Preheat waffle iron. Sift first four ingredients into large bowl. Make well in center. Add milk, ¼ cup butter and yolks to well and whisk until frothy. Stir in flour with fork just until flour is incorporated. Using electric mixer, beat whites to soft peaks. Gently fold whites, then pecans into batter; do not overmix. Brush waffle iron with melted butter. Spoon enough batter onto iron to fill ⅔ of bottom (1 cup will make one 4-piece waffle). Close iron and cook 1 to 2 minutes after steam subsides. Transfer waffle to oven rack to keep warm. Repeat with remaining waffle batter.

To serve: Set 1 or 2 waffle sections on each plate. Top with ice cream. Drizzle with Hot Buttered Brandy Sauce.

*Hot Buttered Brandy Sauce

Makes about 2⅓ cups

- 1 cup brandy
- ½ cup (1 stick) butter
- 2 cups firmly packed dark brown sugar
- 2 cups water
- ¼ cup light corn syrup
- Pinch of salt

Boil ½ cup brandy in heavy 2½- to 3-quart saucepan until reduced to 3 tablespoons. Reduce heat to medium. Add butter and stir until melted. Add brown sugar, water, corn syrup and salt and boil until thickened and reduced by ⅓; mixture should coat spoon. Blend in remaining ½ cup brandy. *(Can be prepared 1 day ahead. Cool completely, cover and refrigerate. Whisk over medium-high heat to rewarm.)*

 *Cakes*

Bird's Nest Apple Butter Crumb Cake

In this Pennsylvania Dutch recipe, the whole apples nestled inside the cake are reminiscent of eggs in a bird's nest.

12 servings

Crumb Topping
½ cup sugar
¾ cup all purpose flour
¼ teaspoon cinnamon
6 tablespoons (¾ stick) chilled unsalted butter

Cake
6 5-ounce pippin or Granny Smith apples
1 tablespoon fresh lemon juice
½ cup plus 1 tablespoon apple butter
½ cup all purpose flour
Pinch of salt
4 large eggs, separated, room temperature
8 tablespoons sugar
½ teaspoon vanilla extract
¼ cup apricot nectar
⅛ teaspoon cream of tartar

For topping: Mix first 3 ingredients in small bowl. Add butter and cut in until mixture resembles coarse meal.

For cake: Preheat oven to 350°F. Butter 9½-inch springform pan. Butter 12 × 4½-inch foil strip. Cut 1-inch-deep 1½-inch-diameter circle around top of core of 1 apple. Using small sharp knife, cut out core without cutting through base of apple. Peel apple and place in large bowl of water with lemon juice. Repeat with remaining apples. Drain apples thoroughly; pat dry. Fill centers with apple butter.

Sift flour with salt into small bowl. Using electric mixer, beat yolks with 6 tablespoons sugar and vanilla in large bowl until slowly dissolving ribbon forms when beaters are lifted. Fold flour mixture and apricot nectar alternately into yolks. Using clean dry beaters, beat egg whites with cream of tartar in another bowl until soft peaks form. Gradually add remaining 2 tablespoons sugar and beat until stiff but not dry. Fold ⅓ of whites into batter to lighten, then gently fold in remaining whites.

Pour ⅔ of batter into prepared pan. Place 1 apple right side up in center. Arrange remaining apples right side up around center apple, spacing evenly apart (apples should not touch one another or sides of pan). Spoon remaining batter around apples, covering each with thin film of batter. Sprinkle crumb topping over batter. Tie foil strip, buttered side in, around sides of pan, extending 2 inches above rim. Bake until top of cake is deep golden brown and tester inserted in center comes out clean, about 1 hour. Cool cake in pan for 2 hours.

Remove foil collar. Run small sharp knife around pan sides to loosen cake if necessary. Release pan sides. Transfer cake to platter and serve.

Blueberry-Carrot Picnic Cake

This cake is easy to take along on a picnic and ideal for eating out of hand. For a plated presentation, garnish it with a dollop of unsweetened whipped cream and fresh berries.

8 to 10 servings

2 cups unbleached all purpose flour
2 teaspoons baking powder
2 teaspoons cinnamon
1 teaspoon baking soda
1 teaspoon salt
1 cup sugar
½ cup firmly packed golden brown sugar

4 large eggs
1 cup corn oil
4 medium carrots, peeled and coarsely grated
2 cups fresh blueberries or frozen, unthawed
1 cup coarsely chopped walnuts (about 4 ounces)

Preheat oven to 350°F. Butter and flour 10-cup bundt pan (preferably nonstick). Mix first 5 ingredients in medium bowl. Combine both sugars in large bowl. Add eggs 1 at a time, whisking until smooth. Whisk in oil. Stir in carrots, blueberries and walnuts. Add dry ingredients and fold just until blended; do not overmix (batter will be thick). Spoon batter into prepared pan. Bake until cake begins to pull away from sides of pan and tester inserted in center comes out clean, approximately 1 hour.

Cool cake in pan on rack 20 minutes. Invert onto plate. Cool completely. *(Can be prepared 1 day ahead. Wrap in plastic. Store at room temperature.)*

Blueberry-Lime Shortcakes

This reworking of a summer tradition is sure to become a favorite. Much of the work is do-ahead, leaving the cook only a bit of last-minute assembling.

6 servings

Lime Curd
3 large eggs
4 large egg yolks
⅓ cup sugar
⅓ cup fresh lime juice
1 tablespoon minced lime peel
6 tablespoons (¾ stick) chilled unsalted butter, cut into small pieces

Sauce
3 cups fresh blueberries or frozen, thawed
¼ cup sugar
¼ cup crème de cassis
2 tablespoons fresh lime juice

1 tablespoon arrowroot

Biscuits
1½ cups unbleached all purpose flour
3 tablespoons sugar
1 tablespoon grated lime peel
2 teaspoons baking powder
⅛ teaspoon salt
6 tablespoons (¾ stick) chilled unsalted butter, cut into pieces
½ cup chilled whipping cream

Additional fresh blueberries (optional)
Powdered sugar
Peel from 1 lime, cut julienne

For lime curd: Whisk eggs and yolks in heavy small nonaluminum saucepan until foamy. Whisk in sugar, then lime juice. Mix in peel. Stir over low heat until mixture thickens to consistency of heavy custard, about 6 minutes; do not boil. Remove from heat. Immediately whisk in butter. Cool. Cover and refrigerate; mixture will thicken. *(Can be prepared 1 day ahead.)*

For sauce: Stir first 4 ingredients in heavy small nonaluminum saucepan over medium heat until berries burst and mixture is juicy, about 7 minutes. Remove pan from heat. Stir in arrowroot. Cool to room temperature.

Puree sauce in processor until smooth. Pour into bowl. Chill. *(Blueberry sauce can be prepared 1 day ahead.)*

For biscuits: Position rack in center of oven and preheat to 400°F. Mix first 5 ingredients in large bowl. Add butter and cut in until mixture resembles coarse meal. Add cream and stir until dough comes together. Turn dough out onto lightly floured surface and knead until smooth. Pat dough into ½-inch-thick round. Cut out rounds using 2½-inch plain or scalloped cookie cutter. Gather scraps and reshape into ½-inch-thick round. Cut out additional rounds. Transfer rounds to heavy large ungreased baking sheet. Bake until biscuits are puffed and golden brown, about 20 minutes. Transfer biscuits to rack and cool slightly. *(Can be prepared 2 hours ahead. Rewarm biscuits in 350°F oven until heated through, about 5 minutes.)*

Split biscuits in half. Place 1 bottom half on each plate. Spoon 3 tablespoons lime curd over each (reserve remaining curd for another use). Cover with biscuit tops. Spoon blueberry sauce around shortcakes. Sprinkle with blueberries if desired. Sift powdered sugar over. Garnish with peel.

Georgia Peach Cake

This old-fashioned sour cream cake has a subtly spiced filling and buttery crumb topping.

Makes one 8-inch cake

Fruit
- ⅓ cup sugar
- 1 tablespoon quick-cooking tapioca
- ¼ teaspoon freshly grated nutmeg
- 6 ripe unpeeled peaches, pitted and cut into ½-inch-thick slices
- 2 tablespoons fresh lemon juice

Topping
- ½ cup unbleached all purpose flour
- 6 tablespoons firmly packed golden brown sugar
- ¼ cup (½ stick) chilled unsalted butter, cut into tablespoon-size pieces
- ¼ teaspoon cinnamon

Cake
- 6 tablespoons sour cream
- ¼ teaspoon baking soda

- ⅓ cup sugar
- ¼ cup (½ stick) unsalted butter, room temperature
- 1 large egg
- 1½ teaspoons vanilla extract
- ¾ cup unbleached all purpose flour
- ½ teaspoon baking powder
- ¼ teaspoon salt

Peach or vanilla ice cream

Position rack in center of oven and then preheat to 375°F.

For fruit: Combine sugar, tapioca and nutmeg in heavy medium saucepan. Mix in peaches and lemon juice. Cook over high heat until mixture begins to bubble, stirring frequently, about 4 minutes. Spread in 8-inch square glass baking dish. (**Or to microwave:** Combine all ingredients in 8-inch microwave-safe square dish. Cook on High until bubbling, stirring once, 4 to 6 minutes.) Tent with foil to keep warm.

For topping: Blend flour, brown sugar, butter and cinnamon in processor until butter is size of small peas. Remove from work bowl; do not clean work bowl. Cover tightly and refrigerate while preparing cake.

For cake: Stir sour cream and baking soda in medium bowl. Let stand while preparing remaining ingredients.

Mix sugar, butter, egg and vanilla in processor until light and fluffy, about 2 minutes. Add sour cream mixture and blend 10 seconds. Add flour, baking powder and salt and blend until just combined using 3 to 4 on/off turns.

Spoon batter over warm peaches, spreading evenly (batter may not cover peaches completely). Sprinkle topping over. Bake until tester inserted in center of cake comes out clean, 20 to 30 minutes. *(Can be prepared 1 day ahead. Cover and refrigerate. To reheat in oven, place in cold oven. Turn oven to 375°F and warm 10 minutes. To reheat in microwave, cook uncovered on Medium 50 to 60 seconds per serving; 4 to 5 minutes for whole cake.)* Serve warm with ice cream.

Blackberry Corn Muffin Cake

A dense, moist cake with a muffinlike tenderness. Without the glaze it's perfect for breakfast or brunch. It is equally delicious when made with firm raspberries or blueberries.

8 to 10 servings

Cake
2 cups unbleached all purpose flour
1 cup yellow cornmeal
2 teaspoons baking powder
¼ teaspoon salt
¾ cup (1½ sticks) unsalted butter, room temperature
1½ cups sugar
2 tablespoons minced orange peel
3 large eggs, room temperature
1½ cups buttermilk

3 cups fresh blackberries or frozen unsweetened, unthawed

Glaze
⅓ cup orange marmalade
3 tablespoons unsalted butter
3 tablespoons sugar
1½ tablespoons whipping cream

Additional fresh blackberries (optional)

For cake: Preheat oven to 375°F. Butter and flour 12-cup nonstick ring or bundt pan. Mix first 4 ingredients in medium bowl. Using electric mixer, cream butter with sugar and orange peel in large bowl until light and fluffy. Blend in eggs 1 at a time. Fold in half of dry ingredients. Stir in buttermilk and blackberries. Gently fold in remaining dry ingredients.

Spoon batter into prepared pan. Bake until cake begins to pull away from sides of pan and tester inserted in center comes out clean, about 50 minutes. Cool cake in pan on rack 15 minutes. Invert cake onto plate. Cool completely. *(Can be prepared 1 day ahead. Wrap tightly in plastic wrap.)*

For glaze: Stir in first 4 ingredients in heavy small saucepan over low heat until sugar dissolves and butter melts. Increase heat and bring to boil. Reduce heat and simmer until thick and bubbling, stirring frequently, about 5 minutes. Cool completely.

Spoon glaze over cake, allowing excess to run down sides. Garnish cake with additional berries if desired.

Double Dip Cottage Cake

The pair of maple-flavored sauces, one clear and one creamy, were known as "dips" because a spoon was dipped into them for serving atop this cake.

9 servings

Creamy Dipping Sauce
1 tablespoon cornstarch
¾ cup milk
¼ cup pure maple syrup
1 tablespoon whipping cream
¼ teaspoon maple extract
¼ teaspoon vanilla extract
1 tablespoon unsalted butter

Clear Dipping Sauce
1 tablespoon cornstarch
¾ cup water
¼ cup pure maple syrup
½ teaspoon maple extract

¼ teaspoon vanilla extract
1 tablespoon unsalted butter

Cottage Cake
2 cups all purpose flour
4 teaspoons baking powder
½ teaspoon salt
1 cup milk
1 cup sugar
¼ cup (½ stick) unsalted butter, room temperature
2 large eggs, room temperature
1½ teaspoons maple extract
¹⁄₁₆ teaspoon freshly grated nutmeg

For creamy dip: Place cornstarch in heavy small saucepan. Gradually whisk in milk. Blend in syrup, cream, maple extract and vanilla. Boil until thickened, stirring constantly, about 2 minutes. Blend in butter. *(Can be prepared 6 hours ahead. Let creamy dip stand at room temperature in saucepan.)*

For clear dip: Place cornstarch in another heavy small saucepan. Gradually whisk in water. Blend in syrup, maple extract and vanilla. Boil until slightly thickened, stirring constantly, about 2 minutes. Blend in butter. *(Can be prepared 6 hours ahead. Let stand in pan.)*

For cake: Preheat oven to 350°F. Butter and flour 9-inch square baking pan. Sift first 3 ingredients into large bowl. Add remaining ingredients and beat until smooth. Pour batter into prepared pan; smooth top. Bake until cake pulls away from sides of pan and top is deep golden brown, about 40 minutes. Cool slightly in pan on rack.

Rewarm dips over low heat, stirring until heated through. Cut warm cake into 3-inch squares. Place 1 square in each bowl. Spoon some of each dipping sauce over half of each, allowing sauces to flow over sides of cake.

Coffee Toffee Chocolate Cake

Makes one 8-inch cake

Cake

- 7 ounces bittersweet (not unsweetened) or semisweet chocolate, coarsely chopped
- ¼ cup Kahlúa or other coffee liqueur
- 1 tablespoon instant espresso powder
- 10 tablespoons (1¼ sticks) unsalted butter, cut into 10 pieces
- ½ cup firmly packed golden brown sugar
- ⅔ cup unbleached all purpose flour
- 4 large eggs, separated, room temperature

  Pinch of salt
  Pinch of cream of tartar
- ¼ cup firmly packed golden brown sugar

- 3 1³⁄₁₆-ounce packages chocolate-covered English toffee (such as Heath bars), coarsely chopped

Chocolate Glaze

- ¼ cup whipping cream
- 2 tablespoons Kahlúa or other coffee liqueur
- 1½ teaspoons instant espresso powder
- 6 ounces bittersweet (not unsweetened) or semisweet chocolate, coarsely chopped

- 1 1³⁄₁₆-ounce package chocolate-covered English toffee (such as Heath bar), coarsely chopped

For cake: Preheat oven to 350°F. Butter 8-inch-diameter cake pan with 2-inch-high sides. Line bottom with parchment; butter parchment. Dust pan with flour. Melt chocolate with Kahlúa and espresso powder in heavy 2-quart saucepan over low heat, stirring constantly. Add butter 1 piece at a time, stirring until melted. Mix in ½ cup sugar. Remove from heat and mix in flour. Mix in egg yolks 1 at a time. Cool chocolate mixture slightly.

Beat whites, salt and cream of tartar in large bowl until soft peaks form. Add ¼ cup sugar 1 tablespoon at a time, beating until almost stiff but not dry. Whisk chocolate mixture to loosen. Gently fold in whites in 4 additions. Gently fold in toffee. Transfer batter to prepared pan. Bake until center of cake feels just firm and only a few crumbs stick to tester inserted into center, about 45 minutes. Cool in pan 15 minutes (center will fall). Invert onto rack and remove paper. Invert onto another rack and cool completely.

For glaze: Scald cream with Kahlúa in heavy small saucepan over medium heat. Add espresso powder and mix until powder dissolves. Add chocolate and stir 1 minute. Remove from heat and stir until chocolate melts and mixture is smooth. Cool until almost room temperature, stirring occasionally.

Invert cake flat side up onto platter. Slide strips of waxed paper under edges of cake. Pour glaze over cake. Smooth with long metal spatula, allowing some glaze to run down sides of cake. Smooth sides with spatula. Sprinkle toffee around top of cake around edge. Remove waxed paper. *(Can be prepared 4 hours ahead. Let stand at room temperature.)* Serve at room temperature.

Black Bottom Devil's Food Cake

The cheesecake topping is a terrific variation on the traditional recipe.

12 to 16 servings

Cake
2 cups firmly packed dark brown sugar
1¾ cups all purpose flour
¾ cup unsweetened cocoa powder (preferably Dutch process), sifted
2 teaspoons baking soda
1 teaspoon baking powder
¼ teaspoon cinnamon
¼ teaspoon salt
1 cup buttermilk
1 cup strong coffee, room temperature
½ cup vegetable oil
2 eggs, beaten to blend

Cheese Topping
4 ounces cream cheese, room temperature
2 tablespoons sugar
1 egg
1 tablespoon all purpose flour
½ cup mini semisweet chocolate chips

Icing
1¼ cups evaporated milk
2 12-ounce packages semisweet chocolate chips
10 ounces cream cheese, room temperature

For cake: Preheat oven to 350°F. Lightly grease two 9-inch-diameter cake pans with 2-inch-high sides. Line bottoms with parchment. Mix first 7 ingredients in large bowl. Add remaining ingredients and whisk until smooth. Divide batter between pans. Set aside while making topping.

For topping: Mix cream cheese and sugar in small bowl. Blend in egg, then flour, mixing until just combined. Pour topping over batter in 1 pan (topping will not cover batter completely). Sprinkle chocolate chips over topping. Bake cakes until tester inserted in center of plain cake comes out clean, about 30 minutes, and topping-covered cake springs back when lightly touched in center, about 5 minutes more. Cool cakes in pans on racks. Freeze cakes for 3 hours.

For icing: Bring evaporated milk to boil in heavy medium saucepan. Reduce heat to low. Add chocolate and stir until melted and smooth, about 2 minutes. Cool completely.

Using electric mixer, beat cream cheese until fluffy. Gradually blend in chocolate mixture. Run small sharp knife between cakes and pan sides. Turn cakes out onto work surface. Peel off parchment. Using serrated knife, halve each cake horizontally. Set 1 plain cake layer on platter. Spread with ⅔ cup icing. Top with second plain cake layer. Spread with ⅔ cup icing. Top with third cake layer. Spread with ⅔ cup icing. Top with cake layer with topping. Ice top and sides of cake with 1⅔ cups icing. Spoon remaining icing into pastry bag fitted with star tip. Pipe icing in rosettes atop cake. Refrigerate until cake is slightly chilled, about 30 minutes. *(Can be prepared 1 day ahead. Let cake stand 2 hours at room temperature before serving.)*

Grand Marnier Cheesecake with Strawberries and Candied Orange Peel

10 servings

Crust
1¼ cups graham cracker crumbs
1 cup toasted husked hazelnuts (about 5 ounces), ground
5 tablespoons unsalted butter, melted
2 tablespoons firmly packed golden brown sugar
2 teaspoons grated orange peel

Filling
4 8-ounce packages cream cheese, room temperature
1 cup firmly packed golden brown sugar
¼ cup Grand Marnier or other orange liqueur
¼ cup whipping cream
2 teaspoons vanilla extract
3 large eggs, room temperature, beaten to blend
2 large egg yolks

Topping
2 cups sour cream
¼ cup firmly packed golden brown sugar
4 teaspoons Grand Marnier or other orange liqueur
1 teaspoon vanilla extract

4 cups fresh strawberries, hulled
¼ cup red currant jelly
5½ teaspoons Grand Marnier or other orange liqueur

½ cup chilled whipping cream
2 teaspoons powdered sugar
Candied Orange Peel*
Fresh mint leaves (optional)

For crust: Position rack in center of oven and preheat to 350°F. Butter 9½-inch round springform pan. Mix all ingredients in bowl. Press mixture firmly onto bottom and up sides of pan to within ½ inch of top edge. Bake 10 minutes. Maintain oven temperature. Transfer crust to rack and cool completely. Set aside.

For filling: Using electric mixer, beat cream cheese in large bowl until very smooth. Beat in sugar, Grand Marnier, cream and vanilla. Add eggs and yolks and beat just until blended. Pour filling into prepared pan. Bake until top puffs and is golden brown, about 50 minutes. Transfer to rack and cool 15 minutes (cake will fall as it cools). Maintain oven temperature.

Meanwhile, prepare topping: Blend first 4 ingredients in small bowl. Pour over cooled filling, spreading with back of spoon. Bake 5 minutes. Transfer to rack and cool completely. Cover and refrigerate overnight.

Run small sharp knife around edge of pan. Release pan sides. Set cheesecake on platter. Arrange strawberries, pointed ends up, atop cheesecake, leaving 1-inch border around outer edge. Stir jelly in heavy small saucepan over low heat until just melted. Mix in 4 teaspoons liqueur; brush over berries.

Using electric mixer, beat cream in medium bowl until soft peaks form. Add powdered sugar and remaining 1½ teaspoons Grand Marnier and beat to firm peaks. Spoon cream into pastry bag fitted with large star tip. Pipe cream decoratively around outside of strawberry border. Arrange orange peel decoratively atop whipped cream. Garnish platter with mint leaves if desired. *(Can be prepared 2 hours ahead and refrigerated.)*

*Candied Orange Peel

Enough for 1 cheesecake

1 large thick-skinned orange

½ cup cold water
2 tablespoons sugar

Using vegetable peeler, cut peel from orange in 1-inch-wide strips. Cut away any white pith from peel. Cut peel into 3-inch-long ⅛-inch-wide julienne. Blanch peel in small saucepan of boiling water 1 minute. Drain; rinse peel under cold water. Repeat blanching and rinsing of orange peel twice.

Cook ½ cup water and sugar in heavy small saucepan over low heat, swirling pan occasionally, until sugar dissolves. Increase heat and bring to simmer. Add peel and cook until glaze forms and almost all liquid evaporates, swirling pan occasionally, about 10 minutes. Transfer peel to waxed paper–lined plate, separating each piece to prevent sticking. Cool completely. *(Can be prepared 2 days ahead. Cover and let stand at room temperature.)*

Ginger-Crisp Pumpkin Cheesecake

Beyond pies, a scrumptious new use for pumpkin. This recipe makes enough cookies to top the cake itself, plus extras to enjoy later.

10 servings

Cookies
½ cup dark molasses
½ cup firmly packed dark brown sugar
2 tablespoons solid vegetable shortening
2 tablespoons (¼ stick) unsalted butter
1½ teaspoons grated orange peel
1½ teaspoons ground ginger
1½ teaspoons cinnamon
1½ teaspoons ground allspice
1½ teaspoons ground cloves
1½ teaspoons freshly grated nutmeg
¾ teaspoon baking soda dissolved in ½ teaspoon water
Pinch of salt

1½ cups all purpose flour

Filling
5 8-ounce packages cream cheese, room temperature
1¼ cups firmly packed golden brown sugar
5 large eggs, room temperature
2 large egg yolks, room temperature
2 cups solid pack pumpkin
⅓ cup evaporated milk
¼ cup all purpose flour
2 teaspoons vanilla extract
1½ teaspoons minced peeled fresh ginger
1 teaspoon cinnamon
1 teaspoon ground cloves
1 teaspoon ground ginger
Pinch of freshly grated nutmeg
Pinch of ground allspice

Topping
1 cup whipping cream
2 tablespoons powdered sugar
1 teaspoon vanilla extract
¼ teaspoon cinnamon

For cookies: Stir first 4 ingredients in heavy large saucepan over low heat until melted. Mix in next 8 ingredients. Pour into large bowl. Cool.

Stir flour into spice mixture. Cover and refrigerate overnight.

Preheat oven to 350°F. Line 2 heavy large baking sheets with parchment. Roll ⅔ of dough out between sheets of floured wax paper to ¼-inch-thick round. Peel off top sheet of paper. Using base of 10-inch springform pan as guide, cut dough into 10-inch round. Invert round onto 1 prepared baking sheet. Peel off top sheet of paper. Cut round into 10 wedges. Gather scraps and reroll with remaining ⅓ of dough between sheets of waxed paper to thickness of ¼ inch. Peel off top sheet of paper. Cut dough into assorted cookie shapes using floured cookie cutters. Transfer to other prepared sheet, spacing 1 inch apart. Bake wedges and cookies until puffed and brown, about 12 minutes (wedges will bake together). Transfer wedges and cookies to rack and cool 10 minutes. Recut wedges. Cool completely. *(Can be prepared 2 days ahead. Store airtight.)*

For filling: Preheat oven to 425°F. Butter bottom of 10-inch springform pan. Line with parchment. Using electric mixer, beat cream cheese with sugar in large bowl until smooth. Blend in eggs and yolks 1 at a time. Beat in remaining ingredients, stopping occasionally to scrape down sides of bowl.

Pour filling into prepared pan. Bake 15 minutes. Reduce temperature to 225°F. Continue baking until cheesecake is firm in center, about 1 hour 25 minutes. Transfer to rack and cool completely. Refrigerate overnight. *(Can be prepared 2 days ahead.)*

For topping: Using electric mixer, whip cream with sugar, vanilla and cinnamon until stiff peaks form. Spoon into pastry bag fitted with medium star tip.

Run sharp knife around sides of cheesecake. Release pan sides. Transfer cheesecake to platter. Press 10 cookie wedges gently atop cake. Pipe cream in lines between cookies and around cheesecake border. *(Can be prepared 2 hours ahead and refrigerated.)*

White Chocolate Fruitcake

Bourbon-soaked dried pears, apples, figs and currants are among the goodies featured in this sophisticated fruitcake. Bake at least eight days before serving it to allow the flavors to mellow.

10 servings

1 cup finely diced dried figs (about 4 ounces)
¾ cup finely diced dried apples (about 2 ounces)
¾ cup finely diced dried apricots (about 4 ounces)
¾ cup bourbon
½ cup finely diced dried pears (about 2 ounces)
½ cup dried currants (about 2 ounces)
½ cup chopped dried bananas (about 2 ounces)

½ cup (1 stick) unsalted butter, room temperature
½ cup plus 1 tablespoon firmly packed golden brown sugar

1 teaspoon vanilla extract
½ teaspoon cinnamon
¼ teaspoon ground cloves
¼ teaspoon freshly grated nutmeg
4 large eggs, separated, room temperature
8 ounces white chocolate (preferably imported), melted, lukewarm
1 cup sifted all purpose flour
1¼ cups salted toasted pecans (about 4 ounces)
3 tablespoons all purpose flour

2 ounces white chocolate, melted

Mix first 7 ingredients in small bowl. Cover and let stand at least 24 hours at room temperature, stirring once.

Preheat oven to 300°F. Butter 9×5×3-inch loaf pan. Line bottom with waxed paper. Dust pan with flour. Using electric mixer, cream ½ cup butter with sugar in large bowl until light and fluffy. Add vanilla, cinnamon, cloves and nutmeg. Add egg yolks 1 at a time, beating well after each addition. Beat in 8 ounces chocolate, then 1 cup flour. Mix pecans and 3 tablespoons flour into dried-fruit mixture. Stir into batter. Using clean dry beaters, beat whites in medium bowl until soft peaks form. Mix ⅓ of whites into batter to lighten, then gently fold in remaining whites.

Pour batter into prepared pan. Cover pan with buttered aluminum foil. Place pan in baking dish. Add enough hot water to dish to come halfway up sides of loaf pan. Bake until metal skewer inserted in center of cake comes out clean, about 2½ hours. Remove loaf pan from water. Cool cake completely in pan on rack. Unmold cake. Wrap in plastic, then foil. Let stand at least 8 days at room temperature. *(Can be prepared 3 weeks ahead.)*

Dip fork into 2 ounces melted chocolate. Drizzle chocolate decoratively over top of cake (chocolate can also be piped through parchment cone). Let stand until cool. Cut into slices and serve.

🍎 *Cookies*

Brown Sugar Almond Crisps

Serve the cookies with small clusters of green or red grapes that have been rinsed and then frozen for about an hour for a refreshing light dessert.

Makes about 5 dozen

⅓ cup sliced almonds
1 cup all purpose flour
½ cup firmly packed dark brown sugar
¼ cup sugar
½ teaspoon baking powder
⅛ teaspoon salt
6 tablespoons (¾ stick) chilled unsalted butter, cut into pieces
1 large egg
½ teaspoon vanilla extract

Finely chop almonds in processor using on/off turns. Add flour, both sugars, baking powder and salt and blend until no lumps of sugar remain. Add butter and cut in using on/off turns until size of peas. Whisk egg with vanilla in small bowl. With machine running, add egg mixture and blend just until dough gathers together. Turn dough out onto large sheet of plastic wrap. Shape into 1¾-inch-diameter smooth cylinder, using plastic as aid. Wrap dough tightly and refrigerate until very firm, reshaping into cylinder if necessary, at least 1 hour. *(Can be prepared 1 day ahead.)*

Preheat oven to 400°F. Lightly grease heavy large baking sheets. Cut dough crosswise in half; refrigerate one half. Remove plastic from other half and cut into ⅛-inch-thick rounds. Arrange on prepared sheets, spacing 1 inch apart. Repeat with remaining half of dough. Bake cookies until edges are light golden brown, about 7 minutes. Immediately transfer cookies to racks and cool. *(Can be prepared 3 days ahead. Store in airtight container.)*

Lemon Cooler Cookies

Makes about 3½ dozen

1 cup (2 sticks) unsalted butter, room temperature
½ cup sugar
1½ tablespoons grated lemon peel
1 egg yolk
1 teaspoon lemon extract
¼ teaspoon salt
2¼ cups all purpose flour

Sugar
Powdered sugar

Preheat oven to 375°F. Using electric mixer, cream butter in medium bowl until light. Gradually add ½ cup sugar and beat until fluffy, stopping occasionally to scrape down sides of bowl. Beat in lemon peel, yolk, extract and salt. Add flour and beat just until blended (if dough is very stiff, beat with wooden spoon).

Roll dough by tablespoonfuls into balls. Set dough balls on ungreased heavy baking sheets, spacing 3 inches apart. Dip bottom of 2½-inch-round glass into sugar. Press down onto 1 dough ball, flattening into ¼-inch-thick round. Repeat with remaining dough balls. Bake until cookie edges begin to brown, about 10 minutes. Transfer cookies to racks and cool. Sift powdered sugar over tops. *(Can be prepared 3 days ahead. Store at room temperature in airtight container.)*

Raspberry Thumbprint Cookies

Makes about 3 dozen

1 cup (2 sticks) unsalted butter, room temperature
½ cup sugar
2 cups all purpose flour

2 egg yolks
2 teaspoons grated lemon peel

¼ cup (about) raspberry jam

Preheat oven to 325°F. Using electric mixer, cream butter with sugar until light and fluffy. Add flour, yolks and lemon peel and beat just until light. Form dough into 1¼-inch rounds.

Arrange rounds 2 inches apart on ungreased baking sheets. Butter large pieces of waxed paper. Set buttered side down atop rounds. Using palm of hand, flatten rounds to ¼-inch thickness. Remove waxed paper. Re-form ragged edges. Using thumb, make imprint in center of each round. Fill with about ¼ teaspoon jam. Bake cookies until firm, about 13 minutes; do not brown. Cool on rack. Store airtight. *(Can be prepared 2 days ahead.)*

Red Wine–Pine Nut Rusks

Try dipping these cookies into a glass of red wine, as the Italians do.

Makes about 5½ dozen

½ cup dried currants
¼ cup dry red wine

1¾ cups all purpose flour
½ teaspoon baking soda
½ teaspoon baking powder
⅛ teaspoon salt
½ cup (1 stick) unsalted butter, room temperature

1 cup sugar
2 eggs, room temperature
1 tablespoon grated lemon peel
1½ teaspoons vanilla extract
½ teaspoon almond extract
1½ cups pine nuts, lightly toasted
2 teaspoons aniseed, crushed

Combine dried currants and red wine in glass jar. Cover and let soak 24 hours, shaking jar occasionally.

Sift flour, baking soda, baking powder and salt into small bowl. Using electric mixer, cream butter in medium bowl until light. Gradually add sugar and beat until fluffy, stopping occasionally to scrape down sides of bowl. Add eggs 1 at a time, blending well after each addition. Blend in lemon peel, vanilla and almond extract. Mix in pine nuts and aniseed. Drain currants; mix currants into butter mixture. Add dry ingredients and mix just until blended. Cover dough; chill well, about 2 hours.

Preheat oven to 350°F. Butter and flour 2 heavy baking sheets. Divide dough into 4 pieces. Using lightly floured hands, roll each piece into 1½-inch-wide log on lightly floured surface; dough will be sticky. Arrange 2 logs on each prepared sheet, spacing 5 inches apart. Bake until tops are lightly browned, about 18 minutes. Cool slightly on baking sheets. Maintain oven temperature.

Carefully transfer all logs to cutting board. Cut crosswise into ½-inch-wide slices. Arrange cookies cut side down on baking sheets. Bake until golden brown, about 10 minutes. Transfer cookies to rack and cool completely. *(Can be prepared 1 month ahead. Store in airtight container.)*

Peanut Butter Chocolate Chip Cookies with Glazed Peanuts

Makes about 3 dozen

1 cup (2 sticks) unsalted butter, room temperature
1 cup firmly packed dark brown sugar
½ cup sugar
1½ cups chunky peanut butter (do not use old-fashioned style or freshly ground)

1 egg
2 teaspoons vanilla extract
Pinch of salt
1½ cups sifted unbleached all purpose flour
2 cups (12 ounces) semisweet chocolate chips
Glazed Peanuts*

Preheat oven to 350°F. Lightly grease large baking sheet. Using electric mixer, cream butter until light. Gradually beat in sugars and continue beating until fluffy. Add peanut butter and beat until blended. Add egg, vanilla and salt and beat until fluffy. Using rubber spatula, quickly fold in flour, then chocolate chips and peanuts; dough will be stiff. For each cookie, mound 3 tablespoons dough onto prepared sheet, then flatten to 4-inch round. (Space cookies 1 inch apart.) Bake until golden brown, about 17 minutes. Transfer to rack and cool. Store in airtight container. *(Can be prepared 2 days ahead.)*

*Glazed Peanuts

Makes 2 cups

½ cup sugar
¼ cup water
1 tablespoon light corn syrup

1 tablespoon butter
1 teaspoon vanilla extract
1 cup salted peanuts

Line baking sheet with foil; brush lightly with oil. Cook first 3 ingredients in heavy medium saucepan over medium-low heat until sugar dissolves, swirling pan occasionally. Increase heat to high and boil until amber, brushing down sides of pan with moistened brush to prevent crystals from forming. Immediately stir in butter, vanilla, then peanuts. Spread mixture in single layer on prepared sheet. Let cool until hardened, about 30 minutes. Coarsely chop glazed peanuts; do not use processor. *(Can be prepared 4 days ahead. Store in airtight container.)*

Chocolate Chip Date-Nut Squares

Makes about 40

1¼ cups chopped pitted dates
1 cup boiling water
1 teaspoon baking soda

1¾ cups sifted all purpose flour
2 tablespoons unsweetened cocoa powder
½ teaspoon salt
½ cup (1 stick) unsalted butter, room temperature

½ cup solid vegetable shortening
1 cup sugar
2 eggs
1¼ teaspoons vanilla extract

1 cup chopped walnuts (4 ounces)
¾ cup semisweet chocolate chips

Place dates in bowl. Combine boiling water and baking soda and pour over. Let stand at room temperature until cool.

Position rack in center of oven and preheat to 350°F. Grease and flour

15½ × 10½-inch jelly roll pan. Sift 1¾ cups flour, cocoa and salt together. Using electric mixer, cream butter and shortening with sugar in large bowl until light and fluffy. Beat in eggs 1 at a time, then vanilla. Mix in dry ingredients and date mixture alternately in 3 batches, beginning with dry ingredients.

Spread batter evenly in prepared pan. Sprinkle walnuts and chocolate chips over top. Bake until tester inserted in center comes out clean and cake pulls away from sides of pan, about 35 minutes. Cool completely. Cut into 2-inch squares.

White Chocolate Brownies

Makes 16

Unsalted butter
½ cup (1 stick) unsalted butter
8 ounces white chocolate chips or coarsely chopped white chocolate

2 large eggs
Pinch of salt

½ cup sugar
½ teaspoon vanilla extract
½ teaspoon salt
1 cup all purpose flour
8 ounces semisweet chocolate chips

Preheat oven to 350°F. Lightly butter 8-inch square pan. Line bottom with foil or parchment. Lightly butter foil. Melt ½ cup butter in heavy small saucepan over low heat. Remove pan from heat. Add half of white chocolate; do not stir.

Using electric mixer, beat eggs with pinch of salt in large bowl until frothy. Gradually add sugar and beat until pale yellow and slowly dissolving ribbon forms when beaters are lifted. Add butter–white chocolate mixture, vanilla and ½ teaspoon salt, then flour, and mix until just combined. Stir in semisweet chips and remaining white chocolate chips. Spoon mixture into prepared pan; smooth top with spatula. Bake until tester inserted in center comes out almost clean, covering top with foil if browning too quickly, about 30 minutes.

Cool brownies in pan on rack. Cut into 16 squares. *(Can be prepared 1 day ahead. Store in airtight container.)*

Candies

Raspberry Creams

Each delicate candy is filled with a whole fresh raspberry surrounded with a cream fondant.

Makes 18

1 cup sugar
¾ cup whipping cream
1 tablespoon light corn syrup
1 tablespoon unsalted butter

1 tablespoon framboise (raspberry eau-de-vie)

36 fresh raspberries

Powdered sugar

12 ounces bittersweet (not unsweetened) or semisweet chocolate, finely chopped

18 paper candy cups

Generously butter small metal bowl. Stir 1 cup sugar, cream and corn syrup in heavy 2-quart saucepan over medium heat until sugar dissolves. Increase heat to medium-high and stir until candy thermometer registers 234°F, about 10 minutes. Pour mixture into prepared bowl; do not scrape pan. Add butter to bowl; do not stir. Set bowl over larger bowl filled with ice and water. Let stand 5 minutes. Fold firm outside edges of mixture into center; do not stir. Cool to lukewarm, about 15 minutes.

Transfer mixture to processor. Add framboise and blend until mixture is creamy and no longer glossy, 3 to 5 minutes. Freeze until firm enough to shape, about 30 minutes.

Line 2 baking sheets with waxed paper. Spoon cream mixture by teaspoons onto 1 prepared sheet, forming 18 mounds. Set 1 raspberry atop each. Cover each with another teaspoon of cream mixture. Using fingers, seal raspberries completely with cream mixture. Freeze until almost firm, about 20 minutes.

Gently roll each mound into ball, using hands dusted with powdered sugar to prevent sticking. Return to same sheet. Freeze until firm, about 4 hours.

Melt chocolate in top of double boiler over barely simmering water, stirring frequently, until candy thermometer registers 115°F. Remove from over water. Working quickly, submerge 1 cream ball into chocolate, tilting pan if necessary. Scoop out ball with dinner fork. Tap bottom of fork on sides of pan, allowing excess chocolate to drip back into pan. Using small sharp knife, slide ball off fork onto second prepared sheet. Top with 1 raspberry. Repeat with remaining cream balls, setting double boiler over hot water occasionally to rewarm chocolate if necessary. Refrigerate until chocolate is set. Set candies in paper cups. (Can be prepared 2 days ahead. Refrigerate in airtight container.) Serve Raspberry Creams at room temperature.

Peanut Butter Dreams

Peanut butter and white chocolate balls are rolled in a peanut praline for these delicious sweets.

Makes about 18

¾ cup powdered sugar
⅓ cup super chunky peanut butter (do not use old-fashioned style or freshly ground)
2 ounces cream cheese, room temperature
2 ounces imported white chocolate, melted and cooled

2 tablespoons (¼ stick) unsalted butter, room temperature

Powdered sugar

¾ pound milk chocolate, finely chopped

Peanut Praline*
18 (about) paper candy cups

Blend first 5 ingredients in medium bowl. Freeze until firm enough to shape, about 20 minutes.

Line 2 baking sheets with waxed paper. Roll 1 tablespoon peanut butter mixture into ball, using hands dusted with powdered sugar. Set on 1 prepared sheet. Repeat with remaining mixture. Freeze until very firm, about 3 hours.

Melt milk chocolate in top of double boiler over barely simmering water, stirring frequently until smooth. Remove from over water. Working quickly, submerge 1 peanut butter ball into chocolate, tilting pan if necessary. Scoop out candy using dinner fork. Tap bottom of fork on sides of pan, allowing excess chocolate to drip back into pan. Using small knife, slide candy off fork and onto second waxed paper–lined sheet. Repeat with remaining balls, setting double boiler over hot water occasionally to rewarm chocolate if necessary. Freeze candies until chocolate is set. (Reserve remaining chocolate in top of double boiler.)

Line another baking sheet with waxed paper. Rewarm remaining chocolate over barely simmering water. Remove from over water. Place praline in large shallow dish. Dip half of 1 candy into chocolate. Roll around in palm to coat candy lightly with chocolate. Set in praline and roll gently, covering completely. Transfer to prepared sheet. Repeat with remaining candies. Refrigerate until firm. Set candies in paper cups. *(Can be prepared 1 week ahead. Refrigerate in airtight container.)* Bring to room temperature before serving.

*Peanut Praline

Makes about 2 cups

1 cup sugar
¼ cup water

1 cup skinned roasted unsalted peanuts

Butter baking sheet. Cook sugar and water in heavy small saucepan over low heat, stirring until sugar dissolves. Increase heat to medium and boil without stirring until syrup turns deep golden brown. Mix in peanuts. Immediately pour mixture onto prepared sheet. Cool completely. Break into 2-inch pieces. Finely grind in processor using on/off turns. *(Can be prepared 2 months ahead. Cover and refrigerate in airtight container.)*

Ginger-Orange Macadamia Bark

Marbled bittersweet and white chocolate make for a very elegant candy that's surprisingly quick.

Makes about 1¼ pounds

6 quarter-size pieces crystallized ginger

10 ounces imported white chocolate, finely chopped

8 ounces bittersweet (not unsweetened) or semisweet chocolate, finely chopped

1½ cups halved toasted unsalted macadamia nuts

2 tablespoons minced orange peel (orange part only)

Add ginger to small saucepan of boiling water and stir until sugar crystals on surface dissolve, about 1 minute. Drain ginger; pat dry and mince.

Line baking sheet with waxed paper. Place white chocolate in small bowl and set over saucepan of barely simmering water. Place bittersweet chocolate in another bowl and set over another saucepan of barely simmering water. Heat both chocolates, stirring frequently, until candy thermometer registers 115°F.

Stir 1 tablespoon ginger, ½ cup nuts and 1 tablespoon orange peel into white chocolate. Pour down length of prepared sheet in three 2-inch-wide 12- to 14-inch long strips, spacing 2 inches apart. Add 1 tablespoon ginger, ½ cup nuts and remaining 1 tablespoon orange peel to bittersweet chocolate. Pour down length of pan between white chocolate lines. Draw tip of knife through both chocolates, forming swirl pattern. Lift sheet and tilt to swirl chocolates together. Sprinkle top with remaining ½ cup nuts. Refrigerate until firm. Break bark into large pieces. *(Can be prepared 1 week ahead. Refrigerate in airtight container.)* Bring to room temperature before serving.

Buttery Hazelnut Toffee

Brown sugar and a touch of honey add extra richness to this crunchy favorite.

Makes about 1½ pounds

Unsalted butter
1¼ cups (2½ sticks) unsalted butter
1 cup sugar
¼ cup firmly packed golden brown sugar
¼ cup water
1 tablespoon honey

1 cup very coarsely chopped husked toasted hazelnuts (about 5 ounces)

6 ounces bittersweet (not unsweetened) or semisweet chocolate, finely chopped
½ cup finely chopped husked toasted hazelnuts (about 2½ ounces)

Butter small baking sheet. Melt 1¼ cups butter in heavy 2½-quart saucepan over low heat. Add both sugars, water and honey and stir until sugar dissolves. Increase heat to medium and cook until candy thermometer registers 290°F, stirring slowly but constantly and scraping bottom of pan with wooden spatula, about 15 minutes.

Remove pan from heat. Mix in 1 cup coarsely chopped nuts. Immediately pour mixture onto prepared sheet; do not scrape pan. Let stand 1 minute. Sprinkle toffee with chocolate. Let stand 1 minute to soften. Spread chocolate with back of spoon over toffee until melted. Sprinkle with finely chopped nuts. Refrigerate until firm. Break into 3-inch pieces. *(Can be prepared 4 days ahead. Refrigerate in airtight container.)* Serve at room temperature.

Double-Decker Mint Patties

Mint-enhanced white and dark chocolate are layered—then dipped in more chocolate—in this after-dinner candy.

Makes about 16

¼ cup plus 2 tablespoons whipping cream
2 tablespoons (¼ stick) unsalted butter
6 ounces bittersweet (not unsweetened) or semisweet chocolate, finely chopped
7 drops of peppermint oil*

6 ounces imported white chocolate, finely chopped
2 teaspoons sour cream

1 pound bittersweet (not unsweetened) or semisweet chocolate, finely chopped

16 (about) paper candy cups

Line 9½ × 5½-inch loaf pan with foil. Bring ¼ cup cream and butter to boil in heavy small saucepan. Reduce heat to low. Add 6 ounces bittersweet chocolate and stir until melted and smooth. Mix in 4 drops of peppermint oil. Pour into prepared pan. Freeze until firm.

Bring remaining 2 tablespoons cream to boil in heavy small saucepan. Reduce heat to low. Add white chocolate and stir until melted and smooth. Remove from heat and stir in sour cream and remaining 3 drops of peppermint oil. Cool to lukewarm. Pour over dark chocolate layer. Smooth with back of spoon. Tap pan on counter to even. Freeze until firm, about 1 hour.

Line baking sheet with waxed paper. Lift chocolate from pan using foil sides as aid. Cut candy into 1¼-inch rounds, using cookie cutter dipped into hot water and wiped clean between cuts. Set rounds on prepared sheet. Freeze until very firm, about 1 hour.

Melt 1 pound bittersweet chocolate in top of double boiler over barely simmering water, stirring frequently until candy thermometer registers 115°F. Remove from over water. Working quickly, submerge 1 patty into chocolate, white chocolate side up. Scoop out using long dinner fork. Tap fork sharply and quickly on sides of pan, allowing excess chocolate to drip back into pan. Using small knife, slide patty off fork and onto prepared sheet. Lightly press back side of fork atop patty and lift off, forming decorative pattern. Repeat with remaining patties, setting double boiler over hot water occasionally if necessary to rewarm chocolate. Refrigerate until firm.

Set candies in paper candy cups. *(Can be prepared 1 week ahead. Refrigerate airtight.)* Let stand at room temperature 10 minutes before serving.

*Available at cake decorating and candy supply stores, some specialty foods stores and pharmacies.

Rocky Road Fudge

For those who prefer a simple old-fashioned milk chocolate fudge, omit the marshmallows and chocolate drizzle.

Makes about 28 pieces

1½ cups sugar
¾ cup whipping cream
¾ cup half and half
1 tablespoon light corn syrup
5 ounces milk chocolate (preferably imported), finely chopped
1½ ounces unsweetened chocolate, finely chopped

⅔ cup coarsely chopped toasted walnuts
⅓ cup miniature marshmallows

2 ounces bittersweet (not unsweetened) or semisweet chocolate

28 (about) paper candy cups

Generously butter small bowl. Line 9½ × 5½-inch loaf pan with foil. Stir sugar, cream, half and half and corn syrup in heavy medium saucepan over medium heat until sugar dissolves. Add milk chocolate and unsweetened chocolate. Stir constantly but slowly, occasionally washing down sides of pan with wet pastry brush, until candy thermometer registers 228°F, about 20 minutes. (Tiny flecks of chocolate may still remain.) Pour into prepared bowl; do not scrape pan. Set bowl over larger bowl filled with ice and water. Cool 20 minutes. Fold firm outside edges of mixture into center; do not stir. Let cool to lukewarm (110°F).

Transfer chocolate mixture to processor. Blend until uniformly thick and creamy, about 5 minutes. (Mixture will resemble thick, sticky caramel and then gradually relax into smooth, barely liquid mass.) Scrape mixture into bowl. Beat with wooden spoon until almost cool and thickened, about 2 minutes. Mix in ⅓ cup nuts and marshmallows. Spoon into prepared pan. Smooth with back of spoon. Sprinkle top with remaining nuts; press in gently.

Melt bittersweet chocolate in top of double boiler set over barely simmering water, stirring until smooth. Remove from over water. Immediately drizzle in random lines over fudge. Refrigerate until firm enough to cut, about 1 hour.

Lift fudge from pan, using foil sides as aid. Fold down foil sides. Cut into 1 × 1¼-inch pieces. Transfer to paper candy cups. *(Can be prepared 4 days ahead. Refrigerate in airtight container.)* Serve at room temperature.

 *Index*

News '88

The Year of Food and Entertaining in Review

Trends & New Products

Foods & Info by Mail

Books

Restaurants & People

Getaways

For the Kitchen & Table

Diet News

Trends & New Products

It's chocolate. It's creamy. And it's instant. This dream dessert, called Mousse Eclat, goes from store to table in a snap. Dark and white chocolate flavors come in eight-ounce pressurized cans (like whipped cream). Cans are about $8 each at specialty foods stores. For important occasions, dress it up with a dollop of whipped cream, chocolate shavings and fresh berries. For information, contact Gourmet International Foods Inc., 399 W. Fullerton Parkway, Suite 15W, Chicago, IL 60614; (312) 880-5572.

Steuben Foods's new cheeses—Castleborg and Ste. Rochelle—are made in New York State, using traditional European methods under quality-controlled conditions. Ste. Rochelle, a semisoft cheese with a buttery texture, is best served with fruit and wine. Castleborg has a slightly sweet, nutty flavor and is also a good table cheese. Watch for these two delicious newcomers in specialty foods stores.

Be a home bread baker the easiest way, with a bag of mix and a bottle of beer. Based on a classic European formula, Dassant Beer Bread Mix produces a 27-ounce crusty loaf—all you do is stir a 12-ounce bottle of beer into the mix and turn the dough into a greased loaf pan. No kneading, no measuring, no rising time. Just bake and enjoy. Available nationwide in classic, whole wheat and garlic Provençal flavors, bags cost about $3.50 each. For a source in your area, contact Northwest Specialty Bakers, Ltd., P.O. Box 25240, Portland, OR 97225; or telephone (503) 228-1727.

For those who haven't quite mastered the art of barbecuing and for those who want shortcuts to success, pre-cooked ribs from Chicago's Sparrer Sausage Company, Inc., are at the ready. The vacuum-packed baby back ribs and St. Louis cut spareribs are available plain or with barbecue sauce in about two-pound packages. Just heat and serve. Since these ribs are as fresh as possible, prices vary according to market conditions. Watch for these in your local deli or supermarket, or call (312) 762-3334.

Finger foods from the Orient are showing up in your favorite supermarket. Dim sum, the little stuffed dumplings that are perfect for snacking or for hors d'oeuvres, are now available in six varieties for steaming or frying or microwaving. Produced by Eastern Foods Corporation, 3235 East Hennepin Ave., Minneapolis, MN 55413.

The always inventive Alan Zeman, chef of the Tucson Country Club, adds another feather to his toque by bringing forth a line of seasonings and condiments called Southwestern Originals. The first venture was his zippy Sonoran Seasoning, a blend that includes garlic, paprika, black tea and orange peel.

The newest product from Chef Zeman's cornucopia is the Prickly Pear Barbecue Glaze. Watch for it at specialty foods stores and in food sections of department stores nationwide. For more information, contact Chef Alan Zeman Southwestern Originals, P.O. Box 31283, Tucson, AZ 85712; or telephone (602) 296-0398.

America's favorite white button mushroom may soon have to move over for the Japanese *shiitake,* with its beefy flavor, woodsy aroma and larger size. Once rarely available fresh, it can now be found in many specialty greengroceries at about $6.50 per pound. DelfTree, the most popular shiitake brand, is grown in Massachusetts and used by many of the finest chefs.

Sharon fruit is the persimmon without the pucker that originated in Israel. This shiny orange fruit can be eaten when it is very ripe or as hard as an apple. It's terrific for sauces and chutneys, and easily made into sherbets or eaten out of hand.

Tea lovers notice: If you like yours straight up, unblended, unscented, unherbed, etc., then look to the loose Darjeeling from Barrows Tea Company, which also offers American breakfast tea and Japanese green tea (both loose). Available at specialty foods stores nationwide.

Samuel Adams Boston Lightship lager, named for the eighteenth-century rebel who also owned a brewery in Boston, was voted best beer in America over more than 120 entries at the Great American Beer Festival held last year.

James Koch—a fifth-generation brewmaster—uses his great-great-grandfather's recipe to create Boston lager, which happens to be the first and only American beer sold in the beer drinker's paradise of West Germany. Sales are concentrated in the Northeast, with new areas opening soon.

The late Andy Warhol has left his mark on a wine bottle. His pop art label for the magnum of Cuvaison's 1984 Napa Valley Merlot has a hand-torn top edge, a scattering of red and purple grapes on a white surface, and a fuchsia and blue background. And—as if the label weren't a collector's delight enough—the wine it graces is outstanding. Only 84 bottles were produced, and one brought $3,200 in Idaho at the Sun Valley Wine Auction. The Warhol magic lives on.

Wine labels from California vintners have become something of a new art form. Now several small companies are using labels for notepaper and greeting cards. Lee Davis Selections hand-mounts over 60 different authentic labels on color-coordinated notecards with matching envelopes. There are inserts of ivory writing paper and each card is packaged in a clear protective cover. They come eight per box for $12 from Lee Davis Selections, P.O. Box 1492, Healdsburg, CA 95448. Include $2 with each order for shipping.

Another company, Vintage Greetings, features over 150 original California wine labels, also hand-mounted on fine-quality coordinated colored cards with gold cord-tied inserts of cream-colored notepaper. These are available in boxes of five cards and envelopes at $9.95, postage included. For information, write Vintage Greetings, P.O. Box 164, Shaver Lake, CA 93664.

Fans of traditional Yankee dishes can get the recipes for such treats as Maine blueberry waffles, New England crab cakes, lobster stew and Boston baked beans just by mailing a postcard. A pretty packet of ten recipe cards, charmingly illustrated, is $6, plus 75¢ handling, by mail from Timid Moon Designs, P.O. Box 1113, Camden, ME 04843; (207) 236-2466. These are also sold throughout New England at selected kitchen shops and bookstores.

A series of 35 reproductions of posters issued by the venerable seed firm of Vilmorin-Andrieux & Cie in Paris between 1850 and 1884 is available from J. Pocker, one of Manhattan's best framers. In full-color offset reproduction on heavy stock, each unframed poster is 19¼x25 inches and can be ordered for $18 plus $4 postage from J. Pocker & Son, Inc., (212) 838-5488. These prints are beautifully reproduced from the original Album Vilmorin catalog, which is quite rare today.

Not a peck, but 17 red and green peppers parade across a white pure cotton Hanes Beefy-T shirt in a nicely silk-screened array. A good bet for those with a passion for the hottest of foods and flavors, the shirts come in small, medium, large and X-large for $14.95 plus postage from Peppers. Call to order 602/990-8347.

🌱 Foods & Info by Mail

Fannie Farmer is once more offering a lifetime membership in its Candy-of-the-Month Club—for $1,989 that is. If you give this to a 30-year-old chocophile who lives to be 70, at a pound a month that's 480 pounds of chocolate, or 1,600,000 calories. A one-year membership for $150 is also available. To enroll, call (800) 225-1363 (ext. 415).

True-love tokens for Valentine's Day could be a golden box of hearts and teddy bear-decorated, chocolate-covered Oreo cookies or a batch of chocolate and caramel lollipops with pink and red hearts. Both are from the firm of Karl Bissinger and can be ordered by calling toll-free (800) 325-8881. Cookies are $16.75 plus $4.75 for shipping per box of 12; lollipops are $13.75 plus $3.75 per box of 10.

Toffee and brittle are the specialties of Buckley's Candies, made fresh for every order and vacuum-packed in tins to keep the buttery flavor preserved. Created in 1957 in Mr. M.S. Buckley's family kitchen and sold at a local church bazaar, these crunchy candies are still made the same way by his daughter, Beverly Buckley Stern. Buckley's Original English Toffee and Pecan Butter Brittle are available at department and specialty foods stores for about $8 for one pound. Or call toll-free to order: (800) 445-3957.

Look like a professional pastry chef, courtesy of The Famous Pacific Dessert Company, when you serve their Chocolate Decadence cake with raspberry puree. This simply devastating dense dessert serves six for $13.75; a 15-ounce jar of the puree is $7.25. (Add $2.75 shipping for each item plus $1.50 handling charge per order.) Look for them in specialty foods stores, or for a source in your area,

contact The Famous Pacific Dessert Company, 420 East Denny Way, Seattle, WA 98122; (206) 328-1950, or call toll-free (800) 666-1950.

It's rich, smooth, moist, delicious and—chocolate. It's also five pounds and four layers, and it can be yours in 48 hours. For any occasion you can think of, you can't beat this nine-inch cake, which will serve 15 to 20 guests for just $34.95. Carefully packed, the cake is guaranteed to arrive in perfect condition with your personal message enclosed, or your money will be refunded. To order, call Send A Cake at (800) 338-7840.

The "New York, Texas, Cheesecake" is a New York-style cheesecake made in New York, Texas. Confused? Its ingredients are much simpler than its name: fresh eggs, pure cream cheese—and no preservatives. It can be yours (or a friend's) for $23.50 for a 2-pound cake or $34 for a 4-pound cake, plus $8.50 refrigerated shipping for each. Contact Neiman-Marcus Mail Order, P.O. Box 2968, Dallas, TX 75221; or call toll-free (800) 634-6267.

Believe it. Courtesy of Carolyn Collins Caviar Company, those fancy fish eggs have gone southwestern. Eminently successful with whitefish, trout and salmon caviars, Ms. Collins now offers Caviar Peppar. This whitefish caviar, flavored with jalapeño and serrano chilies and Absolut Peppar vodka, is terrific with tortilla chips, sour cream and avocados. It is available in 2-ounce jars for $14.50, 4-ounce jars for $24, 8-ounce jars for $34.50 and 16-ounce jars for $48 in specialty foods stores. To order by mail, include $8 for overnight shipping and contact Carolyn Collins Caviar Company, P.O. Box 662, Crystal Lake, IL 60014; or telephone (312) 939-7567.

Planning to take that special someone on a romantic picnic? Les Trois Petits Cochons Pâtés can provide the nourishment. Their "petit" pâtés, each weighing one pound, are gift-packed in three assortments: The Classic includes truffle mousse, wild mushroom pâté, country pâté and a 12-ounce jar of French cornichons ($67.75); The Huntsman features the cornichons, a duck liver mousse, rabbit pâté with Armagnac and a venison pâté ($69.75); and The Gastronomic has duck pâté with orange, country pâté, goose liver mousse, wild mushroom pâté and green peppercorn pâté ($85.75). Prices include next-day delivery. Shipping is through Nationwide Gift Liquor Services; to order, call (800) CHEER-UP.

An American Beekeeping Federation award winner, Christmas Ridge honey earned high marks for aroma, flavor, clarity, brightness, moisture content and purity. Color-classified as white or extra white, this clover honey's blue-ribbon-winning properties are a result of brief heating at lower temperatures than commercially produced honeys. It is also hand-strained. This sweet stuff is available by mail in packages of three 17.5-ounce jars for $12 plus $2.50 shipping: Christmas Ridge Handcrafts, 322 Crab Orchard Road, Lancaster, KY 40446.

Baseball, picnics, barbecues. When summer rolls around, a good mustard should be at the ready. Story's, made on the banks of the Mississippi River, comes in original recipe, natural honey and extra hot and spicy. Made without any additives, all three are packed in 5-ounce jars in a handmade wooden crate for $9.00 plus $2.50 shipping. Also available separately in 7½-ounce jars for $3.00 plus $1 shipping. Contact Story's Gourmet Foods, Inc., P.O. Box 13, Wolf Island, MO 63881; call toll-free (800) 345-8479 or, in Missouri, (314) 649-5621.

Blanchard & Blanchard's Country Gift Cottage could be a nifty present for a weekend host. Housed in an attractive package—which could be some tot's dollhouse later—are bottles of lemon pepper vinaigrette, honey mustard salad dressing with tarragon, and chunky catsup, minijars of hot and sweet and horseradish mustards and others of fudge and caramel sauces. All products hail from the Vermont kitchens of the Blanchards and are made only with natural ingredients. A 21-page collection of country-style recipes comes with the sampler, which is $19.95 plus postage. To order, call toll-free (800) 334-0268, or (802) 649-1327 in Vermont.

Solly's Choice, a purveyor of garden seeds for herbs, vegetables and edible flowers, makes charmingly packaged window herb gardens. These nice self-contained planters come complete with soil, three different seed varieties and directions, and are available for about $11.50 at kitchen and garden shops or by mail. Contact Solly's Choice, 3814 4th Ave. South, Seattle, WA 98134; (800) 678-SEED.

A basket of fruit can be sensational if it's one of Frieda's Finest's exotic collections. Depending on the season, cherimoyas, Asian pears, kiwanos, baby pineapples, crab apples, passion fruit or feijoas might be part of the package. Also included are recipes and information about the individual items. The baskets are available in two sizes: the premier basket holds 15 pounds and costs $85. The exotic basket has 8 pounds of fruit and costs $45. Contact Frieda's By Mail, P.O. Box 58488, Los Angeles, CA 90058; call toll-free (800) 421-9477 or, in California, (213) 627-2981.

Handmade pasta with a homemade flavor is what Rossi Pasta is all about. It's made with the freshest of ingredients: eggs from free-range chickens, extra-virgin olive oil, ripe olives, fresh pimientos, herbs and hard, unbleached, high-gluten spring wheat flour. This delicate pasta is available in a pastel rainbow of colors and flavors. You will find four prepacked boxes with selections of pastas (each weighing 12 ounces). One of them, the five-selection box, contains spinach-basil-garlic fettuccini, Italian spices linguine, *capelli d'angelo,* tomato-garlic fettuccini and black olive linguine (number 205, $25.95). Another is the Rossi Pasta Sampler of four short pastas, their choice (number S4, $13.95). For more information and to order, call (800) 22R-OSSI.

It just might be the chewiest, the nuttiest, the crust-crunchiest sourdough bread in all of California. And, San Luis Sourdough in San Luis Obispo makes these handmade-to-order loaves available to you, wherever you are. There is basic sourdough in rounds or sticks, and some new variations on the same, including cracked wheat and cracked wheat raisin. For information about mail order, call (805) 543-6142.

Atlanta's Texas State Line Bar-B-Que serves ribs so meaty that one is enough to make a meal. Now you can try these at home, wherever you are, along with their chili beans, coleslaw and jalapeño corn bread. Just call and ask about next-day delivery: (404) 255-4510.

Calves at Summerfield Farm are raised on whole milk directly from the cow and roam unconfined on the grassy slopes of the Blue Ridge Mountains. The resultant veal is pinker and more flavorful than the usual supermarket variety. Want to try some? This excellent meat is available from Summerfield Farm, SR 4 Box 195A, Brightwood, VA 22715; (703) 948-3100.

Longer than most newsletters, *World of Cookbooks* offers an insider's view of the cookbook world—16 to 24 bimonthly pages on authors, critics and food writers from all over the globe. A one-year subscription costs $30. Contact Grace Kirschenbaum at World of Cookbooks, 1645 S. Vineyard Ave., Los Angeles, CA 90019; or telephone (213) 933-1645.

Roundly applauded by food writers, "The Art of Eating" is a quarterly letter written and published by Edward Behr, a man who delights his readers with recipes and food facts as well as his own thoughts on food and eating. Get it for $20 a year by sending a check to The Art of Eating, HCR 30, Box 3, Peacham, VT 05862.

Fashions in pasta? You bet. Mueller's has updated its line of 64 pastas with a trio of regular, spinach and tomato *fusilli* called Spring Trio. Two more trendy shapes—Frills and Swirls—make dishes even more fun. A free folder, "Endless Pastabilities," offers recipes. You can contact Mueller's Endless Pastabilities, Dept. EP-C, Box 307, Coventry, CT 06238.

The brown mushroom, once the most common variety of *Agaricus bisporus,* grown in the U.S., is back in the marketplace, thanks to Campbell's Fresh. In conjunction, they have released a new leaflet filled with microwave recipes that use this new-old mushroom. It's yours free by writing to: "Campbell's Fresh Presents the Microwavable Mushroom," P.O. Box 4236, Monticello, MN 55365.

Whiskering its way into haute cuisine territory, *Ictalurus punctatus,* commonly known as catfish, is getting high marks for its sweetness, versatility and nutritive value. In other words, catfish doesn't always have to be battered and deep fried. For new ways to prepare this Mississippi farm-raised delicacy, send $2 for *Fishing for Compliments* to: The Catfish Institute, Box 327, Department P, Belzoni, MS 39038.

Two spirited new booklets are available for the asking: Kahlúa's 30-page recipe book with everything from desserts to cookout cuisine. Contact Kahlúa, Dept. RB, P.O. Box 230, Los Angeles, CA 90078. The second, from Heaven Hill Distilleries, called *Cooking with Bourbon,* also offers recipes for sweet and savory temptations. Write Heaven Hill Distilleries, c/o FS&M PR, P.O. Box 1031, Louisville, KY 40201.

🍒 *Books*

The most-beautiful-book-of-the-year award will undoubtedly go to *Pacific Flavors* (Stewart, Tabori & Chang, 1988) by chef Hugh Carpenter and his wife, photographer Teri Sandison. This work of art has more than 150 recipes and 86 color photographs.

Food writer Diane Rossen Worthington makes warm-weather entertaining easy with *The Taste of Summer* (Bantam Books, 1988), a lovely collection of simple recipes for casual entertaining.

Two new books of note are *The Fish Book* (Harper & Row, 1988) by Kelly McCune and *365 Ways to Cook Pasta* (Harper & Row, 1988) by *Bon Appétit* columnist Marie Simmons. The former, with stunning photographs by Victor Budnik, provides 25 complete seafood menus and an extensive glossary of 50 kinds of fish and shellfish. The latter offers recipes ranging from lasagnes and seafood pastas to unusual noodle desserts.

One of the year's most satisfying books on *la cucina italiana* comes from that savvy team of food, wine and travel writers Tom Maresca and his wife, Diane Darrow. *La Tavola Italiana* (William Morrow, $22.95) is a joyous paean to the classic cuisines of Italy in some 235 recipes. We are taken through northern, central and southern Italian cookery with menus for each course—*antipasti, primi, secondi, contorni* and *dolci*. Here are the much-loved dishes, the home cooking, the real *cucina casalinga* (home cooking) and the carefully selected wines that properly marry with each menu. Basic techniques of making breads, sausage, pasta and more are also included. This is an affectionate journey into the heart of Italian cooking.

Looking for some entertaining reading? The following books might be just the ticket. Michael Roberts, chef and co-owner of Los Angeles's celebrated Trumps restaurant, has written *Secret Ingredients* (Bantam Books, 1988), a thought-provoking book with tips and tricks of his trade. Abbie Zabar's nicely written and illustrated *The Potted Herb* (Stewart, Tabori & Chang, 1988) shows us how topiary turns simple gardening into an art.

Two more on food lore and history are *Much Depends on Dinner* (Grove Press, 1988) and *The Best of De Gustibus* (Simon and Schuster, 1988). The former, the result of intensive research by author Margaret Visser, is a critical and social history of our daily bread, in the guise of one seemingly ordinary meal. The latter, by *New York Times* food columnist Marian Burros, is a collection of her piquant essays on such topics as food faddists and guests who insist on helping.

Perfect Presents is a series of short stories from Redpath Press. Two for food buffs: *Taste* by Roald Dahl is a one-upmanship tale of a wine expert and his dinner host's amusing attempts to impress him; and *The Three Fat Women of Antibes* by W. Somerset Maugham, which will strike responsive chords in dieters. Available for $3.95 each in card and gift shops, or call (800) 722-4443 or in the state of Minnesota, (612) 332-1278 collect.

Bon Appétit wine editor, Anthony Dias Blue, has produced one of the most valuable handbooks in the wine world—a paperback titled *Buyer's Guide to American Wine* (Perennial Library, Harper & Row Publishers, 1988). It is a down-to-earth list with ratings of more than five thousand wines. This will help us all to find America's best at the best prices.

Restaurants & People

Remi means "oars" in Italian; it is also the name of a popular Venetian restaurant on New York's Upper East Side. The stylish eatery is done in glossy white wainscoting with real gondola oars crossed on the white canvas ceiling. Chef/co-owner Francesco Antonucci (formerly of Alo Alo) has some irresistible specialties. (Remi, 323 East 79th Street; 212/744-4272.)

Huberts restaurant, famed for its terrific food, has finally found a new Manhattan location equal to its cuisine—63rd Street off Park Avenue. The interior was designed by Adam Tihany, who did Remi, Bice and Alo Alo. The waiters' uniforms were designed by Geoffrey Beene.

Manhattan's China Grill is packing in patrons curious about its "crossover cooking." The popular fare is described by owner Jeffrey Chodorow as "nouvelle French with the taste sensation of the Orient, while it is also oriental food with a French sensibility." As you study the reasonably priced menu, bask in the luminous dining room, which is lit beautifully through white fabric shades overhead. (China Grill, 52 West 53rd St., New York, NY 10019; 212/333-7788.)

Restaurants in the nation's capital and its environs can be casual and comfortable, elegant and exclusive—or anywhere in between.

For good old-fashioned food in a relaxed atmosphere, Gunning's Crab House serves up spiced crabs steamed over beer, vinegar and pickle juice; fried soft-shell crab sandwiches and deep-fried pepper rings dusted with powdered sugar. The newly renovated Occidental restaurant offers a more stately experience, with grilled and roasted entrées served in a handsome dining room. Or, if you are feeling on the trendy side, you can order pasta or pizza from the wood-burning oven at Primi Piatti Ristorante, a new Italian art deco trattoria with an enthusiastic following. (Gunning's Crab House, 3901 South Hanover Street, Baltimore MD 21225, 301/354-0085; Occidental, 1475 Pennsylvania Avenue, NW, Washington, DC 20004, 202/783-1475; Primi Piatti Ristorante, 2013 I Street, NW, Washington, DC 20006, 202/223-3600.)

A giant tomato marks the entrance to the latest Windy City success story from restaurateur Richard Melman, the man with the culinary Midas touch. Although this state-of-the-moment spot called Scoozi! seats four hundred, you'll feel cozy enough as you snuggle into one of the big leather booths in the smartly decorated room. The menu offers a creative cross section of classic and contemporary Italian—at remarkably reasonable prices. On the hit parade of entrées is a glorious risotto made fresh on the half hour from 6 P.M. to 10 P.M. (Scoozi!, 410 West Huron Street, Chicago, IL 60610; 312/943-5900.)

Located on the fortieth floor of a new skyscraper, The Everest Room in Chicago gives you a breathtaking panorama of the city and serves food equal to such heights. The talented man responsible for the innovative light cuisine is French chef Jean Joho. Look for such specialties as squab and pheasant with black truffle sauce, gateau of French prawns on leek *confit,* Alsatian cheesecake and a composition of chocolate desserts. (The Everest Room, The LaSalle Club, 440 South LaSalle, Chicago, IL 60605; 312/663-8920.)

In Providence, where the reputation of Al Forno restaurant grew almost overnight, owners Johanne Killeen and George Germon have opened a second winner. Lucky's, bright with innovative French country cooking, is at 577 South Main Street; (401) 272-7980.

Indianapolis visitors would do well to head for the two-in-one restaurant called Fletcher's American Grill & Cafe. The street-level grill is breezy and comfortable, with a well-dressed crowd that enjoys making dinner the evening's main event. The most popular dish on chef Tad DeLay's menu is creamy Canadian crab soup. There are imaginative grilled entrées, too, like salmon with apple-basil vinaigrette.

Downstairs, both the dining room and the menu are more formal. Owner Fletcher Boyd calls the cuisine "contemporary Hoosier eclectic"—familiar recipes with unusual twists. Choose loin of veal served over a bed of romaine lettuce with prosciutto and shallots in a Madeira sauce, or lamb stuffed with garlic, vegetables and snails, in a garlic and mint brown sauce. (Fletcher's American Grill & Cafe, 107 South Pennsylvania Street, Indianapolis, IN 46204; 317/632-2500.)

Longwood Gardens, a 350-acre tree park created in 1700, is a lovely place for any weary traveler to relax. This quiet piece of land in Pennsylvania, ten miles north of Wilmington, Delaware, embraces vast conservatories, fountains, an open-air theater, topiary—and just the right cafe for a world of trees and flowers.

The Terrace Restaurant stands between lawn and woodland, an intimate room with full-length windows and surrounding decks for dining alfresco in late spring and summer. Baskets of ivy swing from the skylight, gardenias from the walls. Specialties are Atlantic coast fish and seafood. Wines are mostly Californian, but local vineyards are also represented. (The Terrace Restaurant at Longwood Gardens, Kennett Square, PA 19348; 215/388-6771. For information call 215/388-6741.)

When executive chef Patrick Healy left Colette in Beverly Hills to open his own restaurant, Champagne, on Los Angeles's Westside, Christopher Blobaum took over and the transition couldn't have been smoother. In the intimate Parisian-style dining room, he offers light and sophisticated California-American dishes, scarcely skipping a beat with Colette's clientele.

Meanwhile, over at Champagne, Healy is still dazzling the crowd. His delicious French fare is served in a charming and unpretentious dining room, which is run like clockwork by his wife, Sophie.

The menu is divided into six sections: contemporary, classic, rustic, spa, gastronomic and nightly specials. What seems complicated is not; it's a brilliant way for Healy to share his multifaceted talent with us. (Colette, The Beverly Pavillion Hotel, 9360 Wilshire Boulevard, Beverly Hills, CA 90212, 213/273-1151; Champagne, 10506 Little Santa Monica, Los Angeles, CA 90025, 213/470-8446.)

It's fast, it's cheap and it's fun—it's Chopstix, a new dim sum cafe and takeout that's the latest to join the lineup on L.A.'s hip Melrose Avenue. Chinese cooking expert Hugh Carpenter shows his talents as executive chef, and the fare is simple, straight-forward and light—Chinese food with a California consciousness.

Nothing on the varied menu is more than $4.25, with most dishes hovering in the $2.95 to $3.50 range. The portions are just right for two people to share, or take a group and sample a lot. Recommended dim sum include sea bass surprise—fish- and mushroom-stuffed dumplings accented with a garlic, sesame seed and chive dressing—and Szechwan firecrackers, chicken dumplings tossed with green onion and cilantro. Other possibilities include *mu shu* and stir-fry dishes, meats, seafood and "New Wave Noodles and Risqué Rice." You might even wind things up with a couple of chocolate coconut almond cookies. There are the usual soft drinks, iced tea, beer, wine or—for the Hollywood aerobics crowd—fruit smoothies to go with it all. (Chopstix, 7229 Melrose Avenue, Los Angeles, CA 90046; telephone 213/6-CHPSTX.)

Dim sum devotee Ken Hom reports that if it's impossible to get to Hong Kong for these terrific treats, the next best stop is the spectacular Harbor Village in San Francisco's Embarcadero Center. Elegant ambience is complemented by extremely good food in this modern Chinese setting.

Traditional dim sum items, selected from the passing carts, are executed with a light touch and are beautifully presented. Be sure to try the soup dumpling—shark's-fin soup encased in dough. The cold-platter cart carries such delicacies as tender jellyfish and sliced boneless pork shank, as well as an array of Chinese barbecue foods. Other possibilities include stir-fried rice noodles and shredded chicken with panfried noodles, both very popular in Hong Kong. Come here with a crowd of friends so you can sample a bit of everything. (Harbor Village, Four Embarcadero Center, San Francisco, CA 94111; 415/781-8833.)

Cafe Terra Cotta is an exciting find on the Tucson dining scene. The restaurant's open interior is airy and sophisticated, with pastel furnishings and a sleek copper-topped bar perfect for lingering over cocktails. Large windows look out onto the pretty courtyard of St. Philip's Plaza.

It's an appropriate setting for some imaginative takes on the new southwestern cooking, offered here by talented chef Donna Nordin.

For example, try pizza from a wood-burning oven, topped with anything from herbed mozzarella, prawns and artichoke bottoms to pesto and fresh tomatoes; grilled salmon with sour cream and tomato, garlic and mint salsa; or lamb chops with lime, tequila and honey. Or, choose an updated classic, such as the black bean chili with sirloin and Asiago cheese.

Donna studied with master pastry chef Gaston Lenôtre—an experience that is reflected in her desserts, including mocha framboise layer cake and the Queen of California—minced brandied apricots in a rich chocolate cake. (Cafe Terra Cotta, 4310 N. Campbell Avenue, Tucson, AZ 85718; 602/577-8100.)

Raymond Blanc, the French proprietor of Le Manoir aux Quat'Saisons (a bucolic retreat in Great Milton, England), is considered by many to be England's finest chef. Now he has opened a less formal place, Le Petit Blanc, in nearby Oxford. Housed in an eighteenth-century glass conservatory, the domed dining room replicates an English garden with tables surrounding towering ficus trees, beneath a bower of hanging plants. The fine French menu is the work of resident chef Bruno Loubet, who calls his cuisine "old traditional dishes made contemporary. The food here," he says, "is less complex than at the Manoir." (Le Petit Blanc, 61a Banbury Road, Oxford, England OX2 6PE; 0865/53540.58346.)

The Beaver Club restaurant, titled after the group of the same name founded in 1785 by 19 Northwest explorers, is one of Montreal's favorite spots. Located in The Queen Elizabeth Hotel, the warm dining room is decorated in hunter style. Game is the menu's highlight: Chef Edward Mérard offers such dishes as deer with glazed chestnuts in pepper sauce and partridge with sweetbreads and morels. The wine list—French, of course—is superb. (The Beaver Club, The Queen Elizabeth Hotel, 900 René Lévesque Boulevard West, Montreal, Quebec H3B 4A5; 514/861-3511.)

In Hong Kong, where hotels are commonly superbly luxurious, the best is generally voted to be the Mandarin Oriental. And in a city of more than eight thousand restaurants, one of the finest may be the Man Wah in that hotel. Sumptuous and opulent in its decoration, Man Wah offers Cantonese cuisine at its most glorious, served against a backdrop of padded royal blue silk walls and a black and gold sixteenth-century screen from the Ming imperial court. Guests dine lavishly here: Banquets of staggering variety appear on gold service with ivory and gold chopsticks. Be prepared for such delicacies as crab coral, tiger shrimp, pigeon eggs and shredded turtle meat. (Mandarin Oriental, 5 Connaught Road, Central, GPO Box 2623, Hong Kong; telephone 5/220111.)

🍂 *Getaways*

April is daffodil time in Nantucket with more than one million of the nodding posies joining in the island's annual spring festival. Among other events, a formal dinner and dance and flower exhibits are held at the Harbor House, a genial hotel with cottages. During your stay, you might also try the handsome and historic 21 Federal restaurant where dinner is a treat. (Harbor House, P.O. Box 1048, Nantucket, MA 02554, 617/228-1500; 21 Federal, 21 Federal Street, Nantucket, MA 02554, 617/228-2121.)

Sprawled on the gentle curve of Pleasant Bay in Chatham, Massachusetts, where sailboats dot the harbor in picturesque profusion, the Wequassett Inn offers all the quiet pleasures of Cape Cod. The 19 cottages, each with two or more rooms, feature interiors charmingly decorated with early American memorabilia and cozy pine furniture. Dinner in the main building is a special treat where the chef works wonders with a bounty of Atlantic seafood. This romantic spot with bicycle and walking trails offers sailboats for rent, tennis, golf nearby and deep-sea fishing trips. (Wequassett Inn, Pleasant Bay, Chatham, MA 02633; 800/225-7125 or, in Massachusetts, telephone 508/432-5400.)

With a view of the Mississippi, St. Anthony Falls and century-old Stone Arch Bridge, the luxurious Whitney Hotel offers Minneapolis visitors a refuge from city bustle. Located in the old milling district, which is designated for the National Register of Historic Places, the hotel boasts 97 rooms and suites richly appointed with brass chandeliers, marble baths, four-posters and mahogany and cherry furniture. Free parking and a limousine service to and from town are provided. Should you chose to dine in, there is the Whitney Grille, which serves fine American cuisine. (Whitney Hotel, 150 Portland Avenue, Minneapolis, MN 55401; 612/339-9300.)

In Boston, The Ritz-Carlton continues its International Cultural Festival featuring 13 visiting chefs. Food and fashion, music and art are all part of the festivities, which are combined in a weekend getaway plan, for a modest $75 per person, to include accommodations based on double occupancy and a gift certificate booklet for shopping on famous Newbury Street. Call (800) 241-3333 for details.

Stay there, dine there, have tea by the fire or a drink in the Marble Bar. The Heathman, restored, revitalized and redecorated, is the boast of Portland, Oregon. What's more, it is listed in the National Register of Historic Places. The hotel is handsome and, more important, comfortable, with a staff that hoteliers dream about—attentive, warmly cordial and ever helpful. And in its snappy new dining room, with a parade of Andy Warhol's *Endangered Species* animal art, hearty breakfasts, lunches and dinners are masterminded by the chefs, Greg Higgins and George Tate, who have a fierce pride in fish and seafood. No tricks, no manipulation of food, nothing ostentatious—just simple, hands-off dishes.

The 152-room hotel is in the center of town, next to the Performing Arts Center and within walking distance of all of Portland's major shopping areas as well as many art galleries and museums. (The Heathman, SW Broadway at Salmon, Portland, OR 97205; 503/241-4100.)

Not yet two years old, the Guanahani resort on St. Bart's in the Caribbean remains relatively undiscovered, as it nestles in a cove on the island's calm north coast. Just a few steps from the sea, many of the beachfront cottages also have their own swimming pools.

For dinner, there's Bartolomeo, a comfortable and luxurious semi-open-air dining room. Under the consulting eye of Dominique Nahmias of Restaurant l'Olympe in Paris, chef Philippe de

Bize turns out a very French menu with local lobster oven-roasted to sweetness or duck breast with a tangy shallot and vinegar sauce. (For reservations and information, contact Crown International; 800/628-8929 or, in New York, 201/265-5151.)

Cromlix House is a great stop-off when you tour the Scottish Lowlands and Highlands. Here, on a five-thousand-acre estate owned by the same family for over four centuries, you can catch fish and game—everything from wild duck and grouse to brown and rainbow trout—and then have the kitchen prepare them for you. If it's Scotland's renowned beef and lamb you'd rather have, head chef Mark Salter and staff serve them up in puddles of savory wine gravies, with no nonsense about the portions. Fine food here. Fine wines. And fine lodgings with large bedrooms and sitting rooms with antique furnishings.

In addition to hunting and fishing, riding, tennis and croquet are offered. Or you can play golf on the nearby course. The estate features country living at its best, but for a little city life, Edinburgh and Glasgow are each just an hour away. (Cromlix House, Kinbuck, Dunblane, Perthshire, FK 15 9JT Scotland; 0786/822125.)

Directed by American Gregory Usher, the Ecole de Gastronomie Française Ritz-Escoffier at the Ritz in Paris is a formidable school, designed to challenge Le Cordon Bleu and La Varenne. Usher is a disciple of nouvelle cuisine chef Michel Guérard. For details, contact the school at 38 rue Cambon, Paris, 75001; 42.60.38.30.

A one-of-a-kind, 15-day gastronomic tour to Spain and France is offered by The Annemarie Victory Organization. This grand trip, which leaves on September 15, begins in Madrid at the Ritz and finishes at Paris's Hôtel Le Bristol. For details, contact the organization at 136 E. 64th St., New York, NY 10021; (212) 486-0353.

What's the ultimate way to celebrate New Year's? How about dinner in the *belle époque* restaurant Le Louis XV, of Monaco's Hôtel de Paris? Luring *becs fins* to this posh watering hole is chef Alain Ducasse, who worked with master chefs Guérard, Vergé, Chapel and Lenôtre before guiding the dining room of Hôtel Juana in Juan-les-Pins to two stars in the Michelin Guide. He combines classic French, northern Italian and Provençal specialties for a startlingly unique cuisine. Selected vintages from the hotel's prodigious caves of some 200,000 bottles make up the restaurant's stellar wine list. (Le Louis XV, Hôtel de Paris, place du Casino, Monte-Carlo; 93.50.80.80.)

Visiting Italy sometime soon? Head for Tamburini, the Balducci's of Bologna. A mainstay of smart shoppers and eaters since the Tamburini family took it over 60 years ago, this fabulous emporium has the tins, jars and baskets of ingredients basic to every kitchen.

To sample Italy's best wines, knowledgeable tourists go to Siena's Enoteca Italica Permanente. Located in a beautiful brick exposition hall, this "library" of close to six hundred wines selected from all over Italy for their excellence may be sampled by glass or bottle. The staggering collection is an education in itself.

High in the hills above Budapest, a small restaurant called Vadrózsa (meaning wild rose) nestles in a garden, presenting a variety of Hungarian specialties. The charming country house attracts cinema celebrities (you just might rub elbows with Marcello Mastroianni) and the artistic community of Budapest. Manager and co-owner Margó Vetter offers a menu with such treats as fresh foie gras, pheasant, saddle of venison with fruit, and a Morello cherry strudel, for which guests are said to travel far and wide to enjoy. (Vadrózsa, 1025 Budapest 2. ker., Pentelei Molnár ut 15, Hungary; 351-118.)

For the Kitchen & Table

Tosca, the first new stemware pattern to be released by Lalique in ten years, is not really new. Rather, it is a revived and refined design, one of René Lalique's first, originally called Hagueneau. Formerly made of glass instead of crystal (as it is today), this elegant stemware graced the banquet table at the Sèvres Pavilion at Paris's celebrated 1925 Exposition Internationale des Arts Décoratifs, from which the art deco movement acquired its name and fame. Prices range from $115 to $155 for stemware; the decanter and pitcher cost $385 each. Available in fine department stores nationwide.

The traditional harbinger of spring— the bunny—goes elegant in crystal by designer Olle Alberius for Orrefors. A compact 3x4½ inches, this little treasure is available in fine china and crystal departments and at gift shops throughout the country for about $75.

In 1933, Alvar Aalto, a renowned architect of the time, participated in a glass design competition sponsored by Riihimäki Glass Factory. Afterward, his entry, a series of stackable bowls and bar glasses, went unreproduced— until a picture of the glasses was found recently in the Aalto family archives. The glasses are now being made by iittala glassworks in Finland. Their simple and functional lines evoke the era's design style, and they are perfect for the bar. In sets of two: old-fashioned, about $30; tall, about $30; large cordial, about $25; small cordial, about $20. From The Museum Store, The Museum of Modern Art, 11 West 53rd St., New York, NY 10019; (212) 708-9888.

All is not lost. That missing heirloom Waterford glass, that discontinued Lenox plate that was broken—either or both may be in stock at Replacements, Ltd., in Greensboro, North Carolina.

Located in a warehouse of more than a million china, crystal and earthenware items, Replacements is the world's largest retail supplier of discontinued patterns. Call (919) 668-2064.

Full-blown, old-fashioned pink roses circle the Vista Alegre porcelain pattern appropriately called Romance Rose. The delicate design evokes Victorian summers with luncheons in wicker-furnished gazebos, and may inspire some equally elegant parties. A five-piece place setting is about $47.50 at fine department stores and china shops. Imported from Portugal by The Zrike Company, 225 Fifth Ave., New York, NY 10010.

Charmingly graced with whimsical cows, Woody Jackson's porcelain tableware is perfect for serving up rustic country fare. A five-piece place setting costs $60 at fine department stores nationwide. For information, contact Holy Cow Inc., Box 906, Middlebury, VT 05753; (800) 543-COWS or, in Vermont, (802) 388-6737.

For those ultra-elegant dinner parties, Tiffany & Co. offers formal invitations engraved and made up to match the borders on your best china. That is, if your best china is one of Tiffany's lovely private stock designs: Black Shoulder, Bigouden or Coeur Fleur. Invitations are $45 per dozen.

A seashell-topped tureen from the elegant ceramists of Italy takes to fish and shellfish chowders perfectly. Its hand-painted, marine blue base looks like marble. Made exclusively for Thaxton & Company (780 Madison Avenue, New York, NY 10021), it is $185. Other pieces in the line include soup bowls ($38 each), salad plates ($33), dinner plates ($60) and a magnificent platter ($98). They have the *faux* marble border with a shell design painted in the center. The tureen and dinnerware all come in black as well.

China's dragon kiln pottery cookware, produced in a thousand-year-old kiln using an ancient firing method, is now available in the United States. Among the hand-painted servers and bakeware is our favorite—a charming pickling jar. A 1½-quart pot-bellied affair, the jar is designed to hold the makings for the spicy, crispy pickles so great for munching at mealtime or for snacks. It comes with directions and recipes. Send check or money order for $15 to International Sources, P.O. Box 77066, San Francisco, CA 94103.

Whistling "Tea for Two" (well, the first 25 notes of the 1924 tune), Metrokane's new teakettle is as musical as it is handsome. Called what else but T42, it begins its happy tune when the water starts to boil—thanks to a little steam engine under the lid. Of heavy hand-polished stainless steel, with handle, cover and steam elements of high-temperature thermoplastics, it costs about $130. Designed by aeronautical engineer Charles Hutter, T42 is available at fine department stores.

Looking for the perfectly grilled steak? The Steak Button miniature meat thermometer gives you specially calibrated readings on rare, medium and well, and, as they say, you'll never again ruin a piece of meat. This stainless steel gadget costs $4.50 and is available at most cookware stores. For a store near you, contact Charcoal Companion, 1150 6th Street, Berkeley, CA 94710; telephone (415) 525-3800, outside California (800) 521-0505.

A new lever-model cork puller and foil cutter from Screwpull combine to make volume cork pulling a breeze. A twist of the patented foil cutter neatly removes the foil, and a swing of the lever handle operates the Teflon-coated corkscrew, which smoothly extracts the cork—all in seconds. This foolproof tool set is available at wine shops and major department stores throughout the country for about $100. A separate foil cutter is $5.50. For more information, contact the Hallen Company, P.O. Box 1392, Houston, TX 77251; (713) 683-8111.

Oster's new toasters are the talk of the kitchen. With a slot that adjusts automatically to fit everything from thinly sliced bread to small baguettes to thick bagels, the toaster stays cool on the outside while toasting on the inside. It has six heat settings and is available in white, red or black for about $46 at fine department stores.

Serve up extra-moist barbecued meats with the Swedish-designed Vertikal Grill, a portable unit that cooks meats vertically, allowing the juices to flow through the length and not just the thickness of the meat. Smoke is eliminated too, since drippings go directly to the pan below and do not touch the hot coals racked up in the center. Featuring 170 square inches of cooking surface, the unit packs away neatly into a 17¼x16¾x4½-inch carrying case and costs about $50. It's perfect for small patios, on the table, on a boat or at the beach. For a store in your area, contact Posh Products, 1815 W. 213th Street, Suite 207, Torrance, CA 90501; (800) 782-2547.

Pyromid offers America's Freedom Grill, a state-of-the-art, portable outdoor cooking system that is truly compact and convenient. Folded down, it is 12x12x¾ inches and can be stored in a hamper, a briefcase, on a bike or under a car seat. Made of rustproof stainless steel, it opens to form a pyramid with heat-reflective sides and uses only 8 to 10 charcoal briquettes to cook four medium-size steaks. With a soft carrying case it is about $60, and with a hard case, $70. Call (800) 824-4288 or, in Oregon, (503) 548-1041.

🎗 *Diet News*

The American Health Foundation offers a free pocket-size book called *Health Passport,* in which you may record five years of results from your annual health exams. Also included are tidy charts of calories burned during various aerobic and anaerobic activities, a food guide, health glossary and a table of common sources of cholesterol and fat. Write the American Health Foundation, Attention: Health Passport, 320 East 43rd St., New York, NY 10017. Include 50¢ for postage and handling.

Another valuable freebie is the recipe booklet for diabetics from former baseball pitcher Jim ("Catfish") Hunter. A 20-page booklet with Hunter's own recipes (including his Pitcher's Mound Pie) is available by writing to *Cooking with "Catfish" Hunter,* P.O. Box 307, Coventry, CT 06238.

Along with good food there's now mood food. Pasta releases serotonin, the "feel good" chemical, which enhances relaxation. And since the latest statistics show that Americans ate about three billion pounds of pasta—or 14 pounds per person—last year, we should all be in better spirits. Nearly fat-free, low sodium, low calorie and high in carbohydrates, pasta may be the perfect food.

Paul's Peanuts are presumably unique. They are air-squeezed to press out the oil, thereby getting rid of unnecessary fats, grease, weight—and half the calories. Available lightly salted or salt-free, "Paul's ½ Calorie Peanuts" are vacuum-packed in 7-ounce cans and contain a total of 1,000 calories per can. Mail order from Paul's Peanuts, Inc., P.O. Box 2061, Great Neck, NY 11022; (516) 466-0011.

Looking for something interesting to spread on your morning toast? Try Stonehill Farm's fat-free fruit butters in five flavors: apple, peach, pear, plum and sweet tomato. Peach and plum are also available sugar free. For information, write Stonehill Farm, P.O. Box 158, Schwenksville, PA 19473.

Tamari is the original Japanese soy sauce, developed a thousand years before the processed soy sauce we use today. Full of protein, it is distinguished for its wheat-free properties, yet is full flavored. San-J Tamari, once sold largely in natural foods stores, is making its way into supermarkets now.

Sea vegetables are high in vitamins and minerals. Dulse, kelp, nori and alaria from Maine's coastal waters are now available sun dried. Look for them in natural foods stores, or contact Maine Coast Sea Vegetables, (207) 565-2907.

According to researchers at the Massachusetts Institute of Technology, among the best sources of heart-protecting omega-3 fatty acids in fish are salmon, sardines and now canned solid white (albacore) tuna. The water-packed variety is best: It has about the same omega-3 content and less than half the calories of oil-packed.

❦ *Credits and Acknowledgments*

The following people contributed the recipes included in this book:

Jeffrey Alford
Susan Auler
Elga Balodis
Melanie Barnard
Nancy Verde Barr
Lois Baru
Kreis Beall
Beau Nash, Hotel Crescent Court,
    Dallas, Texas
Susan Brener
Cardini, Los Angeles Hilton, Los Angeles,
    California
Thomas Catherall
Myrna Christopherson
Sanford D'Amato
Gary Darling
Rita DeNitti
Brooke Dojny
Roberto Donna
Kate Dowling
Vicki Finson
Anne and Eric Flescher
Janet Fletcher

Marcy Goldman-Posluns
Joyce Goldstein
Laura Halloran
Honey Bear Bakery, Seattle, Washington
Jamboree Cafe, The Newporter Resort,
    Newport Beach, California
Bonnie Joseph
Jane Helsel Joseph
Karen Kaplan
Lynne Rossetto Kasper
Kristine Kidd
Robert Kinkead
Faye Levy
Judy Litwin
Sylvia Lovegren
Madeleine Low
Abby Mandel
Kathy Martin
Ardis Matthews
Nancie McDermott
Terry McGrew
Michael McLaughlin
Jefferson and Jinx Morgan

Pamela Morgan
Selma Morrow
Tamilyn Munson
Beatrice Ojakangas
Jane Porzio
Steven Raichlen
Carol Robertson
Betty Rosbottom
Julie Sahni
Richard Sax
Gary Selden
Harold Seymour
The Sign of the Dove, New York,
    New York
Marie Simmons
Frank Stitt
Sarah Tenaglia
Anthony Terlato
Suneeta Vaswani
Chip Wickett
Faye Wieselman
Roy Yamaguchi
Bret Young

"News '88" text was supplied by:
    Zack Hanle

Editorial Staff:
    William J. Garry
    Barbara Fairchild
    Nancy D. Roberts
    MaryJane Bescoby

Graphics Staff:
    Bernard Rotondo
    Gloriane Harris

Rights and Permissions:
    Karen Legier

Indexer:
    Rose Grant

The Knapp Press
is a wholly owned subsidiary of
KNAPP COMMUNICATIONS CORPORATION

Composition by American Typesetting, Inc., Reseda, California

This book is set in Sabon, a face designed by Jan Teischold in 1967
and based on early fonts engraved by Garamond and Granjon.